STUDY GUIDE

MARY NISBET
UNIVERSITY OF CALIFORNIA, SANTA BARBARA

FINANCIAL ACCOUNTING
THE IMPACT ON DECISION MAKERS

SECOND EDITION

GARY A. PORTER
Loyola University Chicago

CURTIS L. NORTON
Northern Illinois University

The Dryden Press
Harcourt Brace College Publishers
Fort Worth Philadelphia San Diego New York Orlando Austin San Antonio
Toronto Montreal London Sydney Tokyo

ISBN: 0-03-020519-0

Address for orders:
The Dryden Press
6277 Sea Harbor Drive
Orlando, FL 32887-6777
1-800-782-4479

Address for editorial correspondence:
The Dryden Press
301 Commerce Street, Suite 3700
Fort Worth, TX 76102

Web site address:
http://www.hbcollege.com

Printed in the United States of America

8 9 0 1 2 3 4 5 6 7 202 9 8 7 6 5 4 3 2 1

The Dryden Press
Harcourt Brace College Publishers

Contents

Preface

This Study Guide is designed as a self-study aid for use with Gary Porter and Curtis Norton's text "Financial Accounting - The Impact on Decision Makers". The Study Guide will help you master the material in the text, since it expands the explanation and illustration of text material, and provides practice test questions and problems that you can use to test your understanding. For each chapter in the text, there is a corresponding chapter in the Study Guide containing each of the following components.

- An **introduction** identifies the chapter's main focus, states the learning objectives of the chapter and highlights key text book exhibits.
- A **review of key concepts** provides a comprehensive outline, keyed to learning objectives, of the material covered in the text chapter. As well as highlighting important material, the Study Guide illustrates particularly complex concepts with additional examples and exhibits. An innovation is the use of "Test Your Understanding!" boxes where you are encouraged to interpret and apply the preceding concepts.
- A **review of key terms** gives a complete listing of new terms introduced in each chapter. Each term is defined and keyed to the relevant learning objective.
- **Practice test questions and problems**, which are also keyed to learning objective, include 15 fill in the blanks questions, 15 true/false questions, 15 multiple choice questions and an average of four problems. Each chapter contains one problem that is identified as emphasizing critical thinking, and that encourages you to apply what you have learned to a particular decision making situation.
- The **solutions** to test questions and problems provide answers to all questions, explanations for all true/false questions and solutions to all problems.

The way you use the Study Guide will depend on your personal study habits and preferences. However, one possible approach is to first read the Study Guide's introduction. Then read each section of the text chapter followed by the corresponding section of the Study Guide's review of key concepts. The Study Guide will provide both a summary of what you have read in the text and additional explanatory problems and exhibits. You can reinforce your understanding of new words by using the review of key terms. The practice test questions and problems could then be tackled, using the answers and solutions provided to correct any mistakes and misunderstanding.

The Study Guide adopts the innovative approach of the Porter and Norton text by providing a conceptual introduction to financial accounting, while covering essential procedural material. This approach ensures that the needs of both accounting majors and non-majors are satisfied, since both a user focus and an adequate preparation for intermediate accounting are provided. Published financial statements are used throughout the Study Guide, particularly in problems highlighting decision making.

I must thank the following reviewers for their constructive, helpful and careful reviews.

Mary Houser, Western Michigan University
Sarah Brown, University of North Alabama
Steven Wong, San Jose City College
Richard Silkoff, Quinnipac College

I must also thank Karen Misler of O'Donnell Associates for her outstanding support in this project. Her constant encouragement, advice and good humor have been a major determinant in the completion of the Study Guide.

The litmus test of any Study Guide is whether or not students find it useful. I have therefore included a Student Comment Form on the next page and I encourage you to complete the form and send it to me with any comments, corrections and suggestions.

Mary Nisbet
Santa Barbara
October 1997

Student Comment Form

Send to: Mary Nisbet
Department of Economics
University of California, Santa Barbara
Santa Barbara
California 93106

From: ______________________________

____

____

____

Date: ______________________________

I like the following about the study guide:

I dislike the following about the study guide:

I think the following would improve the study guide:

Chapter 1

Accounting as a Form of Communication

Accounting provides organizations with one of the most important ways of collecting, processing, and communicating financial information. This chapter begins the study of accounting by looking at the different forms that organizations can take, the activities they engage in, and the importance of accounting in organizational decision making. Your overall objective in this chapter is to understand the role that accounting plays in communicating financial information about various forms of enterprise.

Learning Objectives

LO 1 Explain why financial information is important in making decisions.
LO 2 Distinguish among the forms of organization.
LO 3 Describe the various types of business activity.
LO 4 Identify the primary users of accounting information and their needs.
LO 5 Explain the purpose of each of the financial statements and the relationships among them, and prepare a set of simple statements.
LO 6 Identify and explain the primary assumptions made in preparing financial statements.
LO 7 Describe the process of setting standards in financial accounting and the groups involved in the process.
LO 8 Describe the various roles played by accountants in organizations.

Key Textbook Exhibits

Exhibit 1-1 illustrates the various types of organization that exist in our economy. Note that the principal division is between those that are organized to earn a profit (business entities) and those that are not (nonbusiness entities).

Exhibit 1-3 summarizes the key activities of a business. Note that the three activities are interrelated and all are necessary for the success of the business.

Exhibits 1-4, 1-5, 1-6, and 1-7 give Ben & Jerry's principal financial statements. Review these carefully and make sure that you understand the function of each statement and the type of information that is presented in it.

Exhibit 1-8 identifies the links between the four principal financial statements. You should understand both the purpose of each of the four statements identified and the relationships between them.

Review of Key Concepts

LO 1 The financial implications of many decisions are critical. Both personal decisions (such as which school to attend, which job to accept, which apartment to rent) and business decisions (which products to sell, how and when to borrow money, whether to build a new factory) require financial information.

LO 2 Business entities are organized to make a profit. There are three main types:

- **Sole proprietorships** have a single owner, who often both owns and operates the business. The owner is ultimately responsible for any unpaid debts that the business incurs. Consequently, the business and its owner are not regarded as separate legal entities. However, financial statements are prepared for the business separate from its owner. The owner and the business are therefore separate accounting entities, but not legal entities.
- **Partnerships** are businesses owned by at least two people. The agreement between the partners is a statement of their financial rights in, and obligations to, the partnership. Again the partnership and the partners are separate accounting, but not legal, entities.
- **Corporations** are organizations that are distinctive because they are separate legal as well as accounting entities. A **share of stock** is a certificate that provides evidence of part ownership of the corporation. A **bond** is a certificate that provides evidence of a loan to the company. The advantages of corporations include the ability to raise large amounts of capital; easy transfer of ownership, since many stocks are traded on stock exchanges; and the limited liability of the stockholder.

Test Your Understanding!

Question: Of the three types of business entity, which one provides the owner(s) with the greatest financial protection?

Answer: The corporation. Although the business is a separate accounting entity for all three types, in both partnerships and sole proprietorships the owners can be held responsible for the business's debts and therefore could lose their personal assets. Stockholders in a corporation are normally liable only for the amount they have contributed to the corporation, so their personal assets are protected.

LO 2 **Nonbusiness entities** are organized for purposes other than to make a profit and do not normally have clearly defined owners. A special type of accounting called *fund accounting* is used for this type of entity.

LO 3 Business activities can be classified into three main types:

- **Financing activities** relate to raising the money (or capital) needed to start and operate a business. The principal financing activities of corporations relate to selling bonds and issuing stock. Bonds represent a liability of the company and are therefore a temporary form of financing; stock represents part ownership in the company and is therefore a permanent source of financing for the company.
- **Investing activities** are concerned with acquiring (and sometimes disposing of) the **assets** needed for the business. These assets can be long-term (for example, property, plant, and equipment) or short term (for example, inventory and cash).
- **Operating activities** are the activities that are necessary to achieve the purpose of the business. These could include manufacturing products, selling inventory, employing staff, and using utilities such as water and gas.

LO 4 Users of financial information are traditionally split into two groups: internal users and external users. **Internal users** are the management of the company and they can obtain any information they need in a form that meets their needs. **Management accounting** is the branch of accounting concerned with providing information to internal users for planning and controlling a business.

External users include groups with very diverse motivations and interests. Stockholders, bondholders, other creditors, and government agencies all have an interest in the financial information provided by the company. External users do not have day-to-day access to the financial information of the company and must therefore use information presented to them by the company management. **Financial accounting** is the branch of accounting concerned with providing financial information to external users.

LO 5 The fundamental equation underlying the entire accounting system is as follows:

Assets = Liabilities + Owners' Equity

The left-hand side of the equation identifies the resources controlled by the company, and the right-hand side identifies the parties having claims against these resources. When the financial statements relate to a corporation, the owners' equity is called **stockholders' equity.** Stockholders' equity usually consists of the amount contributed by the stockholders when the stock was first purchased **(capital stock)** and **retained earnings,** which are defined as the accumulated earnings of a business minus any dividends paid to stockholders.

LO 5 The four principal financial statements prepared for external users are the income statement, the balance sheet, the statement of retained earnings, and the cash flow statement. The four statements are inextricably linked, and changes in one will impact one or more of the other three. Exhibit 1-8 identifies the links between the four principal financial statements.

- The **balance sheet** summarizes the assets, liabilities, and owners' equity of the business at a specific point in time. Both sides of the balance sheet must be equal.
- The **income statement** summarizes the revenues and expenses of the business over a period of time and shows whether the business made a profit or loss over the period. Note that the income statement is prepared on an **accrual basis,** which means that revenue and expenses appear on the income statement during the period they are earned or incurred, even though the related cash is not received or paid during that period.
- The **statement of retained earnings** summarizes the changes in retained earnings over a time period. These changes derive from profits or losses for the period (summarized in the income statement) minus dividends paid to stockholders.
- The **statement of cash flows** summarizes the cash effect of the company's operating, financing, and investing activities during the period.

Test Your Understanding!

Question: What are the two principal differences between the statement of cash flows and the income statement?

Answer: The statement of cash flows reports on **all** activities of the period (investing, financing and operating) while the income statement reports only on the operations of the company. The statement of cash flows summarizes only the cash transactions of the period, while the income statement is prepared on an accrual basis and so is concerned with when the benefit or cost is realized rather than when cash is received or paid.

LO 6 The conceptual framework of accounting provides accountants with a set of principles, standards, and assumptions that guide the preparation of financial statements.

- The **economic entity concept** is based on the premise that business entities are separate economic units from their owners and must have separate and distinct accounting records.
- The **cost principle** requires that assets are recorded and carried on the balance sheet at their original (historic) cost.
- The **going concern assumption** states that the business entity will continue to exist indefinitely.
- The **time period assumption** states that measurement of financial condition and operations can be made at relatively short intervals, such as one year.
- The **monetary unit** that is used to prepare financial statements is assumed to have a constant value.
- **Generally accepted accounting principles (or GAAP)** refer to the set of methods, rules, practices, and procedures that have evolved over time and regulate the preparation of financial statements.

LO 7 Several bodies are jointly responsible for determining GAAP:

- The **Securities and Exchange Commission** (SEC) was set up in 1934 by an act of Congress and has the ultimate authority to determine how and when financial statements are to be prepared and reported. The SEC, however, has delegated authority for setting accounting principles to the **Financial Accounting Standards Board** (FASB).
- FASB is an independent group of seven individuals who have the authority to set accounting standards. Currently, the board has issued more than one hundred standards dealing with a variety of financial reporting issues.
- The **American Institute of Certified Public Accountants** (AICPA) is the professional organization of certified public accountants. It has an advisory role in setting GAAP but is responsible for setting auditing standards.
- The **International Accounting Standards Committee** (IASC) is the body that is attempting to develop worldwide accounting standards. A major constraint on its effectiveness is that compliance with its standards is voluntary, and it therefore does not have the authority that FASB has in the United States.

LO 8 Accountants fulfill many different roles in many different organizations. In business entities, accountants can work in three related areas. The **controller** has the responsibility for the overall operations of the accounting system. The **treasurer** ensures the safekeeping and efficient use of the company's cash (liquid resources). The **internal audit function** is responsible for the review and appraisal of the company's accounting and administrative controls. In nonbusiness entities, accountants have a major role to play in reporting on the assets, liabilities, and operations of the entity. Public accounting firms provide both auditing and tax services to clients. In addition, many public accounting firms also provide management consulting services to their clients. Education is another major area in which accountants are employed. The **American Accounting Association** is a professional organization of accounting educators and has a major influence on both accounting education and academic research.

Review of Key Terms

Accounting	The process of identifying, measuring, and communicating economic information to various users.
American Accounting Association (AAA)	The professional organization for accounting educators.
American Institute of Certified Public Accountants (AICPA)	The professional organization for certified public accountants.
Asset	A future economic benefit.
Auditing	The process of examining the financial statements and the underlying records of an entity in order to render an opinion as to whether the statements are fairly presented.
Balance sheet	A statement that summarizes the assets, liabilities, and owners' equity at a point in time.
Bond	A certificate issued by corporations representing the promise to repay a certain amount of money and interest in the future.
Capital stock	The amounts contributed to a corporation by the stockholders.
Certified Public Accountant (CPA)	The professional designation for public accountants.
Controller	The chief accounting officer of a company.
Corporation	A form of entity that is legally separate from its owners; ownership is evidenced by shares of stock.
Cost principle	Assets recorded at the cost of acquiring them.
Creditor	Someone to whom the entity owes a debt.
Dividends	A distribution of the net income of a corporation to its owners.
Economic entity concept	The assumption that requires that an enterprise be accounted for separately from its owners.
Expense	An outflow of assets resulting from the sale of goods or services.
Financial accounting	The branch of accounting concerned with the preparation of general-purpose financial statements for both internal and external users.
Financial Accounting Standards Board (FASB)	The group in the private sector with authority to set accounting standards.
Generally accepted accounting principles (GAAP)	The methods, rules, and practices that regulate the preparation of financial statements.
Going concern	The assumption that an entity has an infinite life.
Income statement	A statement that summarizes revenues and expenses.
Internal audit	The department in a company responsible for the review and appraisal of the company's accounting and administrative controls.
International Accounting Standards Committee (IASC)	The organization formed to develop worldwide accounting standards.

Liability	An obligation of an entity.
Management accounting	The branch of accounting concerned with providing management of entities with information to help in planning and controlling the enterprise.
Monetary unit	The measurement unit used in financial statements: the dollar in the United States.
Nonbusiness entity	An organization operated for some reason other than to earn a profit.
Owners' equity	The owners' claim on the assets of the entity.
Partnership	A business owned by two or more people.
Retained earnings	The part of owners' equity that represents the income earned less dividends paid over the life of the entity.
Revenue	An inflow of assets resulting from the sale of goods or services.
Securities and Exchange Commission (SEC)	The federal agency with ultimate authority over the preparation of financial statements by publicly held corporations.
Sole proprietorship	Form of organization with a single owner.
Statement of cash flows	A statement that summarizes the cash effects of the operating, investing, and financing activities of the entity over a period of time.
Statement of retained earnings	A statement that summarizes the changes in retained earnings over the accounting period.
Stockholder	One of the owners of a corporation.
Stockholders' equity	The owners' equity in a corporation.
Time period	The segment on the calendar for which financial statements are prepared.
Treasurer	The financial officer responsible for safeguarding and efficient use of the company's liquid resources.

Practice Test
Questions and Problems

Complete each of the following statements:

LO 4 1. ____________________ is the branch of accounting concerned with the preparation of financial statements for both external and internal users.

LO 2 2. Businesses owned by at least two people are known as ____________________.

LO 2 3. Entities that are organized for reasons other than to make a profit are called ____________________.

LO 5 4. If an entity has net earnings for a year of $10,000, and pays no dividend to stockholders during that year, the effect on its retained earnings balance is $____________________.

LO 3 5. Issuing stock and selling bonds are examples of the ____________________ activities of a business.

LO 5 6. Revenues and expenses are reported on an entity's ____________________.

LO 7 7. The ____________________ is a government body that has the ultimate authority over how publicly held corporations present their financial statements.

LO 5 8. The amount in the balance sheet of a corporation that represents both the amount contributed by the stockholders and retained earnings is ____________________.

LO 6 9. The assumption that business entities are separate and distinct from their owners is known as the ____________________ concept.

LO 8 10. The financial officer responsible for safeguarding, and the efficient use of, the company's liquid resources is called the ____________________.

LO 5 11. The financial statement that summarizes the resources of the enterprise and the claims against those resources by both creditors and owners is the ____________________.

LO 5 12. The income statement, unlike the statement of cash flows, reports only on the ____________________ activities of the business.

LO 7 13. The methods, rules, and practices that regulate the preparation of financial statements are called ____________________.

LO 5 14. The three types of activity reported on an entity's cash flow statement are ____________________, ____________________, and ____________________.

LO 5 15. On a company's balance sheet, total assets are reported as $5,000, total liabilities are $2,000, and stockholders' equity is ____________________.

Indicate whether each of the following statements is true or false:

LO 2 16. The form of organization that provides the greatest financial protection to its owners is the sole proprietorship.

LO 3 17. Investing activities include both the sale and purchase of long-term assets.

LO 4 18. Because stockholders can gain unlimited access to the company's records, they are mostly concerned with management accounting concepts.

LO 4 19. Creditors, bondholders, labor unions, and government agencies are all external users of accounting information.

LO 5 20. An alternative title for the balance sheet is the statement of financial position.

LO 5 21. The statement of retained earnings summarizes the cash effect of the company's operations over the period.

LO 6 22. The time period assumption states that one should take into account the fact that the company may discontinue operations in the near future.

LO 6 23. The monetary unit in that accounts are prepared is assumed to have a constant value over time.

LO 8 24. Public accounting firms provide only audit services for their clients.

LO 8 25. Changes in a company's assets over a period can be found by comparing the income statements at the beginning and end of the period.

LO 7 26. The International Standards Committee has the same authority in the world as the Financial Accounting Standards Committee has in the USA.

LO 5 27. If the income statement shows a company has made a loss in a year and the company pays no dividend in that year, the balance on retained earnings will reduce from the beginning to the end of the year.

LO 6 28. The cost principle ensures that even if a company's land has increased in value since it was purchased, the amount the land is reported at in the balance sheet is the original cost.

LO 4 29. Internal users of accounting information include both management and stockholders.

LO 5 30. The information in the cash flow statement is independent of the information in the balance sheet.

For each of the following questions, circle the alternative that best answers the question:

LO 2 31. Which of the following is a feature of a sole proprietorship?

a) An ability to raise large amounts of capital
b) Easy transfer of ownership
c) Limited liability of owners
d) Management of the company normally carried out by owners

LO 2 32. Which certificate provides evidence of a long-term loan to the company?

a) A bond
b) A share of stock
c) An invoice
d) An account

LO 7 33. Which of the following organizations is responsible for the setting of accounting standards?

a) The Financial Accounting Standards Board
b) The American Accounting Association
c) The Securities and Exchange Commission
d) The American Institute of Certified Public Accountants

LO 7 34. Which of the following organizations has the ultimate authority to determine how and when accounts of public companies are to be prepared and reported?

a) The Financial Accounting Standards Board
b) The American Accounting Association
c) The Securities and Exchange Commission
d) The American Institute of Certified Public Accountants

LO 5 35. Which of the following types of information would you expect to see reported on a balance sheet?

a) Stockholders' equity, bonds, plant and equipment, inventory
b) Revenues, depreciation expense, tax expense, cost of goods sold
c) Cash used in investing activities, cash provided by operations, cash provided by financing activities
d) Earnings for current year, dividends, retained earnings brought forward from previous periods

LO 5 36. Which of the following types of information would you expect to see reported on an income statement?

a) Stockholders' equity, bonds, plant and equipment, inventory
b) Revenues, depreciation expense, tax expense, cost of goods sold
c) Cash used in investing activities, cash provided by operations, cash provided by financing activities
d) Earnings for current year, dividends, retained earnings brought forward from previous periods

LO 5 37. Which of the following types of information would you expect to see reported on a statement of cash flow?

a) Stockholders' equity, bonds, plant and equipment, inventory
b) Revenues, depreciation expense, tax expense, cost of goods sold
c) Cash used in investing activities, cash provided by operations, cash provided by financing activities
d) Earnings for current year, dividends, retained earnings brought forward from previous periods

LO 5 38. Which of the following types of information would you expect to see reported on a statement of retained earnings?

a) Stockholders' equity, bonds, plant and equipment, inventory
b) Revenues, depreciation expense, tax expense, cost of goods sold
c) Cash used in investing activities, cash provided by operations, cash provided by financing activities
d) Earnings for current year, dividends, retained earnings brought forward from previous periods

LO 3 39. Which of the following groups of activities would be classified as operating activities?

a) Issue of stock, redemption of bonds, payment of dividends
b) Sale of goods, purchase of inventory, payment of wages
c) Purchase of plant, purchase of stock, sale of land

LO 3 40. Which of the following groups of activities would be classified as financing activities?

a) Issue of stock, redemption of bonds, payment of dividends
b) Sale of goods, purchase of inventory, payment of wages
c) Purchase of plant, purchase of stock, sale of land

Use the following information to answer questions 41 through 45:
Terra Corporation's financial statements for the year ended July 31, 1997, are as follows:

Terra Corporation
Income statement for the year to July 31, 1997

Revenues		$12,000
Cost of sales		?
Gross margin		3,500
Selling and administrative expenses	?	
Net earnings		$ 1,300

Terra Corporation
Balance sheet on July 31, 1997

Assets		
Cash	$?	
Inventories	1,500	
Total current assets		$ 4,800
Land and buildings	1,500	
Total long-term assets		1,500
Total assets		$?
Liabilities and stockholders' equity		
Long-term liabilities		$ 1,800
Stockholders' equity		
Capital stock	$?	
Retained earnings	4,300	
Total stockholders' equity		4,500
Total liabilities and stockholders' equity		$?

LO 5 41. Gross margin is defined as the difference between revenues and cost of sales. Terra Corporation's cost of sales for the year ended July 31, 1997, was

a) $12,000
b) $8,500
c) $15,500
d) $3,500

LO 5 42. Net income is found by deducting selling and administrative expenses from gross margin. Terra Corporation's selling and administrative expenses for the year ended July 31, 1997, were

a) $3,500
b) $1,300
c) $4,800
d) $2,200

LO 5 43. Terra Corporation's cash balance on July 31, 1997, was
a) $3,300
b) $6,300
c) $4,800
d) $1,500

LO 5 44. Terra Corporation's total assets on July 31, 1997, were
a) $6,300
b) $1,500
c) $4,800
d) $3,300

LO 5 45. Terra Corporation's capital stock on July 31, 1997, was
a) $4,300
b) $200
c) $4,800
d) $9,100

Answer each of the following problems:

LO 4 46. Alpha Corporation is a large manufacturing firm, producing steel rods for the fastener industry. Their primary manufacturing is carried out in California and Illinois, and they are currently considering expanding their manufacturing capacity by building a new factory in Texas. The new factory will require that the company raise more capital, probably by issuing bonds. Which of the following items from the company's most recent financial statements would stockholders be interested in to help them assess the advisability of bond issue? Code each line in the stockholders' column to
A. Need to know
B. Helpful to know
C. Not necessary to know

	INFORMATION	STOCKHOLDERS
1.	Ten-year record of sales	
2.	Ten-year record of earnings	
3.	Interest expense	
4.	Long-term debt	
5.	Cash on hand	
6.	Wages expense	
7.	Dividends paid	
8.	Property, plant and equipment	
9.	Stockholders' equity	
10.	Accounts payable	

LO 2 47. For each of the entities listed below, recommend the type of organization that suits it best and list at least three items, other than cash, that are likely to appear in the entities' financial statements.

1. A law firm is owned and operated by two lawyers, who are all equally active in the practice.

2. A hot dog stand is owned and operated by a student during the summer.

3. A shipbuilding business, owned by a large group of people none of whom is actively involved in the day-to-day running of the business, employs managers to run the business on their behalf.

4. A dental building is owned jointly by seven dentists, and they rent space for their individual practices from the building.

5. An organization owns and operates a large number of fast food restaurants, including franchises. It was originally owned and operated by one man but is now a large multinational organization with the ownership and day-to-day management separated.

LO 5 48. The following items appear in the financial statements of the Dillon Department Stores Company for the year to December 31, 1997. In the table below, indicate whether the item is an asset, liability, owners' equity, revenue, or expense, and whether it appears on the balance sheet or income statement. Then use this information to prepare the income statement and balance sheet for that year. (Hint! Remember that receivables and payables appear on the balance sheet, and that expenses and revenues appear on the income statement.)

ACCOUNT		ASSET, LIABILITY,OWNERS' EQUITY, REVENUE OR EXPENSE	INCOME STATEMENT OR BALANCE SHEET
Accounts payable	$ 700		
Accounts receivable	2,400		
Land and buildings	1,500		
Cash	900		
Capital stock	200		
Furniture	1,887		
Interest expense	300		
Long-term liabilities	3,000		
Inventories	1,500		
Retained earnings	4,300		
Revenues	12,000		
Selling expenses	2,200		
Cost of sales	8,500		

Critical Thinking Problem

LO 5 49. The income statement of the Walt Disney Company for the years ended September 30, 1993, 1992, and 1991 are presented below.

Walt Disney Company
Consolidated Statement Of Income

(In millions, except per-share data)

Year ended September 30	1995	1994	1993
Revenues			
Filmed entertainment	$6,001.50	$4,793.30	$3,673.40
Theme parks and resorts	3,959.80	3,463.60	3,440.70
Consumer products	2,150.80	1,798.20	1,415.10
	12,112.10	10,055.10	8,529.20
Costs and Expenses			
Filmed entertainment	4,927.10	3,937.20	3,051.20
Theme parks and resorts	3,099.00	2,779.50	2,693.80
Consumer products	1,640.30	1,372.70	1,059.70
	9,666.40	8,089.40	6,804.70
Operating Income			
Filmed entertainment	1,074.40	856.1	622.2
Theme parks and resorts	860.8	684.1	746.9
Consumer products	510.5	425.5	355.4
	2,445.70	1,965.70	1,724.50
Corporate Activities			
General and administrative expenses	183.6	162.2	164.2
Interest expense	178.3	119.9	157.7
Investment and interest income	-68	-129.9	-186.1
	293.9	152.2	135.8
Loss from Investment in Euro Disney	-35.1	-110.4	-514.7
Income before income taxes and cumulative effect of accounting changes	2,116.70	1,703.10	1,074.00
Income taxes	736.6	592.7	402.7
Income before cumulative effect of accounting changes	1,380.10	1,110.40	671.3
Cumulative effect of accounting changes			
Preopening costs	--	--	-271.2
Postretirement benefits	--	--	-130.3
Income taxes	--	--	30
Net income	$1,380.10	$1,110.40	$299.80
Amounts per common share			
Earnings per share	$2.60	$2.04	$0.55

Required

1. Over the three years, which of the three main activities in the income statement (theme parks and resorts, filmed entertainment, and consumer products) provided Disney with the largest sales volume? Which activity generated the largest total operating income? Which activity generated the largest operating income relative to its sales? Can you use this analysis to advise Disney on which, if any, of its activities it should expand?

2. Why do you suppose that Disney reported the loss on Eurodisney separately from its other activities? If Disney had not made the large loss on Eurodisney, what would its income before income taxes and accounting changes have been for the year to September 30, 1993?

3. If they are reporting a large loss in any year, some companies take the opportunity to report other losses too so that they report all the bad news in one year. (It's often called "taking a bath"!) Why do you think companies may choose to do this? Is there any evidence that Disney "took a bath" in 1993?

Solutions

Fill in the Blanks

1. financial accounting
2. partnerships
3. nonbusiness entities
4. $10,000 increase
5. Financing
6. income statement
7. Securities and Exchange Commission
8. stockholders' equity
9. entity
10. treasurer
11. balance sheet
12. operating
13. generally accepted accounting principles
14. operating, financing, investing
15. $3,000

True/False

		COMMENT/EXPLANATION
16.	False	Because stockholders have limited liability, the corporation provides the greatest protection to owners.
17.	True	
18.	False	Only the corporation's management can gain unlimited access to the records, and they are the group mostly concerned with management accounting.
19.	True	
20.	True	
21.	False	The statement of retained earnings summarizes changes in the retained earnings balance on the balance sheet over the accounting period.
22.	False	The time period assumption states that accounts should be drawn up for a specific period of time.
23.	True	
24.	False	Public accounting firms provide audit, tax, and business consulting services for their clients.
25.	False	The income statement summarizes operating activities over the period and ignores changes in assets and liabilities due to financing and investing activities.
26.	False	The IASC is advisory only and has no legal authority over its members.
27.	True	
28.	True	
29.	False	Stockholders are external users of accounting information, since they are remote from the day-to-day operations of the enterprise.
30.	False	The statement of cash flows explains the change in the cash balances that appear on the balance sheets at the beginning and end of the period.

Multiple Choice

31. d
32. a
33. a
34. c
35. a
36. b
37. c
38. d
39. b
40. c
41. b
42. d
43. a
44. a
45. b

Problem 46

One set of answers to this problem appears below. However, your answers may differ from these and still be correct since the questions are open to interpretation. The main purpose of this question is to encourage you to realize that different users have different needs.

	INFORMATION	STOCKHOLDERS
1.	Ten-year record of sales	C
2.	Ten-year record of earnings	B
3.	Interest expense	A
4.	Long-term debt	A
5.	Cash on hand	B
6.	Wages expense	C
7.	Dividends paid	A
8.	Property, plant and equipment	C
9.	Stockholders' equity	A
10.	Accounts payable	C

Problem 47

1. Partnership; fee revenue, professional subscriptions, office expenses.
2. Sole proprietorship; cash sales, cost of sales, asset (hamburger stand).
3. Corporation; ships in progress, wages expense, inventory (steel, etc.).
4. Partnership; rental income, building maintenance expense, utilities expense.
5. Corporation; income from foreign operations, franchise fees, advertising.

Problem 48

ACCOUNT		ASSET, LIABILITY, OWNERS' EQUITY, REVENUE OR EXPENSE	INCOME STATEMENT OR BALANCE SHEET
Accounts payable	$ 700	Liability	Balance sheet
Accounts receivable	2,400	Asset	Balance sheet
Land and buildings	1,500	Asset	Balance sheet
Cash	900	Asset	Balance sheet
Capital stock	200	Stockholders' equity	Balance sheet
Furniture	1,887	Asset	Balance sheet
Interest expense	300	Expense	Income statement
Long-term liabilities	3,000	Liability	Balance sheet
Inventories	1,500	Asset	Balance sheet
Retained earnings	4,300	Stockholders' equity	Balance sheet
Revenues	12,000	Revenue	Income statement
Selling expenses	2,200	Expense	Income statement
Cost of sales	8,500	Expense	Income statement

Maxwell Department Stores Company
Income statement for the year to December 31, 1997

Revenues	$ 12,000
Cost of sales	(8,500)
Gross margin	3,500
Selling expenses	(2200)
Interest expense	(300)
Net earnings	$1,000

Maxwell Department Stores Company
Balance sheet on December 31, 1994

Assets		
Cash	$ 900	
Accounts receivable	2,400	
Inventories	1,500	
Total current assets		$ 4,800
Furniture	1,900	
Land and buildings	1,500	
Total long-term assets		3,400
Total assets		$ 8,200
Liabilities and Stockholders' Equity		
Accounts payable		$ 700
Long-term liabilities		3,000
Total liabilities		3,700
Stockholders' equity		
Capital stock	200	
Retained earnings	4,300	
Total stockholders' equity		4,500
Total liabilities and stockholders' equity		$ 8,200

Critical Thinking Problem 49

1. The following table summarizes the performance of the three business segments of the Walt Disney Company for 1991, 1992, and 1993:

THEME PARKS AND RESORTS	1995	1994	1993
Revenues	$3,959.80	$3,463.60	$3,440.70
Percentage increase from previous year	14%	1%	
Operating income	860.8	684.1	746.9
Percentage increase from previous year	26%	-8%	
Operating income as a percentage of revenues	22%	20%	22%

FILMED ENTERTAINMENT	1995	1994	1993
Revenues	$6,001.50	$4,793.30	$3,673.40
Percentage increase from previous year	25%	30%	
Operating income	1,074.40	856.1	622.2
Percentage increase from previous year	25%	38%	
Operating income as a percentage of revenues	18%	18%	17%

CONSUMER PRODUCTS	1995	1994	1993
Revenues	2,150.80	1,798.20	1,415.10
Percentage increase from previous year	20%	27%	
Operating income	510.5	425.5	355.4
Percentage increase from previous year	20%	20%	
Operating income as a percentage of revenues	24%	24%	25%

Filmed entertainment provided the largest revenues in all three years. Although in all three years, consumer products generated the smallest revenues, it also had the largest operating income as a percentage of revenues each year and had strong revenue growth.

Given both the large increase in revenues over the three years and the high profitability in consumer products, it would appear that Disney should continue to expand its consumer products segments. Before making that recommendation, however, we would need to know other information, such as how large the potential market is, who Disney's competitors are in this market, and what impact the consumer products segment has on the other segments of Disney's operations.

2. The loss on Eurodisney was probably reported separately so that it would not distort the results of Disney's other operations. For example, including the loss in the operating income for theme parks would have resulted in a drop from $746.9 million to $232.2 million. Excluding the Eurodisney loss would have resulted in an income before taxes and accounting changes of $1,588.7 million. Reporting the Eurodisney loss separately allowed users of the financial statements to assess the performance of both Eurodisney and the other activities of the Disney Company.

3. Companies often "take a bath" in the hope that the negative impact on investors of all the bad news together will be less than if each item of bad news were reported separately. In addition, many management incentive schemes depend on *increases* in reported earnings, and a really bad year followed by a good year will generate higher bonuses in this type of scheme. The year that Disney reported the huge loss on Eurodisney, the company appears to be "taking a bath", since it chose that year to report a further $401.5 million loss due to accounting changes.

Chapter 2

Financial Statements and the Annual Report

The success of financial reporting is measured by whether or not it meets the needs of decision makers. This chapter discusses the objective of financial reporting and how the various financial reports help to achieve that objective. Your overall aim in this chapter is to understand the form, content, and purpose of the annual report and of the various financial statements contained in it.

Learning Objectives

LO 1 Describe the objectives of financial reporting.

LO 2 Describe the qualitative characteristics of accounting information.

LO 3 Explain the concept and purpose of a classified balance sheet and prepare the statement.

LO 4 Use a classified balance sheet to analyze a company's financial position.

LO 5 Explain the difference between a single-step and a multiple step income statement and prepare each type of income statement.

LO 6 Use a multiple step income statement to analyze a company's operations.

LO 7 Identify the components of the statement of retained earnings and the statement of stockholders' equity and prepare each statement.

LO 8 Identify the components of the statement of cash flows and prepare the statement.

LO 9 Describe the various elements in the annual report of a publicly held company.

Key Textbook Exhibits

Exhibit 2-5 shows Starbucks' comparative balance sheets. Note how the assets, liabilities, and stockholders' equity of the company are classified and presented. Also make sure that you can calculate the measures of liquidity (working capital and current ratio) and solvency (debt-to-equity ratio) for this firm.

Exhibit 2-8 shows Starbucks' Comparative Income Statements. Make sure that you understand how the statement is presented and how to use the statement to calculate the various profitability measures (gross profit, profit margin, earnings per share, and return on stockholders' equity).

Review of Key Concepts

LO 1 The primary objective of financial reporting is to assist users of the reports in making informed decisions. General-purpose financial statements provide both internal and external users with information about the activities of the company. The type of information needed by users includes

- **Likely future cash receipts to investors and creditors**. These could include future interest and dividend payments made by the company as well as estimates of the future price at which the company's stocks could be sold.
- **Likely future cash flows to the company.** These are useful since there is a relationship between the cash flow the company receives and the cash flow it can generate for its investors and creditors.
- **Resources and claims on resources.** Users wish to know both the resource base of the company and the claims against it.

LO 2 The qualitative characteristics that make accounting information useful are these:

- **Understandability** - The information must be comprehensible to the reasonably informed user.
- **Relevance** - The information should be able to make a difference in a decision.
- **Reliability** - Users should be able to depend on the information. In order to fulfill this requirement, information should be verifiable, it should faithfully represent the underlying economic conditions, and it should not be slanted to portray the company in any particular light, either good or bad.
- **Comparability and consistency** - Users should be able to compare the accounts of different companies within the same time period and accounts of the same company over time. Note that comparability does not require all companies to use exactly the same accounting principles and methods, but rather that companies provide enough information about their accounting methods for users to be able to make meaningful comparisons.
- **Materiality** - Information is material if a user's judgment is affected by the omission or misstatement of the information. Note that what constitutes material information will vary according to the type and size of the organization.
- **Conservatism** – In a choice between alternative but equally likely ways of presenting information, the method that provides the lowest asset valuation or the least amount of income should be chosen.

LO 3 The **classified balance sheet** is constructed by distinguishing long-term from short-term items.

- **Current assets** are those assets that are expected to be sold, or realized in cash, either within the normal operating cycle of the business or within one year if the operating cycle is shorter than one year. Examples of current assets are cash, inventory, accounts receivable, prepaid expenses, and marketable securities.
- **Noncurrent assets** are all assets that do not fall within the category of current assets. Examples are investments in other companies and property, plant, and equipment. Another group of noncurrent assets are **intangible assets** that, unlike other noncurrent assets, lack physical substance. The process of spreading the cost of a long-term asset over its useful life is called **depreciation**.
- **Current liabilities** are obligations of the business that must be satisfied within one year. If, however, the operating cycle is greater than one year, current liabilities are those liabilities that mature within the operating cycle. Examples of current liabilities are accounts payable and wages payable.
- **Long-term liabilities**, as the name suggests, are liabilities of the company that mature in more than one year. If, however, the operating cycle is greater than one year, long-term liabilities are defined as liabilities that do not mature within the operating

cycle. Bonds issued by the company are the most common form of long-term liability, but obligations under certain types of leasing arrangements and notes payable are also classified as long-term liabilities.

- **Stockholders' equity** represents owners' claims on the business and is composed of two parts: money or other assets that have been paid into the company by the stockholders - **capital stock,** and earnings that the company has made since its inception less any dividends it has paid - **retained earnings**. Note that capital stock can also be split into two parts: **par value** and **paid-in capital in excess of par value**.

Test Your Understanding!

Question: At what amount should intangible assets be shown on the balance sheet and what principle is being applied?

Answer: Intangibles should be shown at the cost of acquiring them. This is an application of the cost principle. If the intangible asset has not been acquired through a formal transaction, it will not have a cost assigned to it and will not appear on the balance sheet. For example, the Coca Cola Company's most valuable asset is its trademark and, because it was not formally acquired through a purchase, it does not appear as an asset on the Coca Cola Company's balance sheet.

LO 4 The classified balance sheet can be used to analyze a company's financial position.

Liquidity measures the company's ability to pay its debts. Two possible measures of liquidity are these:

$$\text{Working capital} = \text{Current Assets} - \text{Current Liabilities}$$

$$\text{Current ratio} = \frac{\text{Current Assets}}{\text{Current Liabilities}}$$

Test Your Understanding!

Question: Which of the two measures of liquidity is better for making comparisons both across time for the same company and across companies?

Answer: The current ratio. Because it is a ratio, you can compare companies of different size and changes in a single company over time. Working capital is a dollar amount, which may or may not be useful for comparisons.

Solvency measures the ability of the company to stay in business over the long run. The company's capital structure, or proportion of debt to equity, is a major determinant in its solvency since a large burden of debt could generate large interest charges, which the company might not be able to meet. Two measures of capital structure that we use to indicate solvency are these:

$$\text{Debt-to-equity ratio} = \frac{\text{Total Liabilities}}{\text{Stockholders' Equity}}$$

$$\text{Debt-to-total-assets ratio} = \frac{\text{Total Liabilities}}{\text{Total Assets}}$$

LO 5 The **income statement** is used to summarize the results of the entity's operations over a period, by reporting the revenues, the expenses, and the difference between them. If revenues exceed expenses, the company reports a profit or earnings; if expenses exceed revenues, the company reports a loss. In a **single-step income statement**, all expenses are added together and the total is deducted from the total revenues to arrive at net income. In a **multiple-step income statement**, expenses are subdivided to provide more information for the user.

LO 6 Multiple-step income statements can be used to analyze the company's **profitability**. Both the gross profit ratio and the profit margin give insights into how much margin the company is generating from each dollar of sales - in the case of gross profit ratio, how much is left after paying for the goods that have been sold; in the case of net profit ratio, how much is left after all expenses have been paid. Insights into the return available to stockholders can be found by calculating earnings per share and return on stockholders' equity.

$$\text{Gross profit ratio} = \frac{\text{Gross Profit}}{\text{Sales}}$$

$$\text{Profit margin} = \frac{\text{Net Income}}{\text{Sales}}$$

$$\text{Earnings per share} = \frac{\text{Net Income}}{\text{Average No. of Common Shares Outstanding}}$$

$$\text{Return on stockholders' equity} = \frac{\text{Net Income}}{\text{Average Stockholders' Equity}}$$

LO 7 **A statement of stockholders' equity** explains the changes in stockholders' equity, both in capital stock and retained earnings, over the accounting period. If there are no changes to capital stock, **a statement of retained earnings** can be presented instead, which explains the changes in retained earnings between the beginning and end of the period.

LO 8 Recall from Chapter 1 that the **statement of cash flows** summarizes the cash effects of the company's operating, investing, and financing activities for the period.

LO 9 Annual reports are prepared by the company to provide information for stockholders' about the company's activities during the financial period. They contain the following information in addition to the financial statements discussed above.

- In the **management discussion and analysis**, the company management discusses and explains certain aspects of the company's performance.
- The **report of management,** on the other hand, sets out the responsibilities of the company's management. In particular, the report points out that the responsibility for the information in the annual report rests with the management of the company.
- The **report of the independent auditors** expresses the opinion of the independent auditor on the fairness of the financial statements. Note that the independent auditors do not certify the accuracy of the financial statements; rather, they express an opinion as to whether or not there is material misstatement in the financial reports.
- The **footnotes** to the accounts provide essential details about how the accounting numbers were calculated. They are an essential part of the financial reports and you will find as you progress in your study of accounting that they are an invaluable aid to analyzing financial reports.

Review of Key Terms

Comparability	The quality of accounting information that allows a user to meaningfully compare two or more companies.
Conservatism	The practice of using the least optimistic estimate when two or more possible estimates are equally likely.
Consistency	The quality of accounting information that allows a reader to compare two or more accounting periods for a single company.
Current asset	An asset that is expected to be realized in cash, sold, or consumed within the operating cycle, or within one year if the cycle is shorter than one year.
Current liability	An obligation that will be satisfied within the operating cycle, or within one year if the cycle is shorter than one year.
Current ratio	Current assets divided by current liabilities.
Debt-to-equity ratio	Total liabilities divided by total stockholders' equity.
Debt-to-total-assets ratio	Total liabilities divided by total assets.
Earnings per share	Net income divided by the number of common shares outstanding.
Gross profit	The difference between revenues and cost of goods sold.
Gross profit ratio	Gross profit divided by sales
Liquidity	The ability of a company to pay its debts.
Materiality	The magnitude of an omission or misstatement in accounting information that will affect the judgment of someone relying on the information.
Multiple-step income statement	An income statement that provides classification of revenues and expenses as well as subtotals.
Profit margin	Net income divided by sales.
Relevance	The ability of information to make a difference in a decision.
Reliability	The quality of accounting information that makes it dependable in reporting what it purports to represent.
Return on stockholders' equity	Net income divided by average stockholders' equity.
Single-step income statement	An income statement in which all expenses are added together and subtracted from total revenues.
Solvency	The ability of the company to survive in the long run.
Understandibility	The quality of accounting information that makes it comprehensible to readers willing to spend the necessary time.
Working capital	The difference between current assets and current liabilities.

Practice Test
Questions and Problems

Complete each of the following statements:

LO 2 1. ________________ is a method of allocating the cost of a long-term asset over its life that results in more cost being allocated in the earlier years.

LO 5 2. ________________ is the difference between sales and cost of goods sold; selling expenses and general and administrative expenses are deducted to find ________________.

LO 4 3. A company's current assets are $5,000 and its current liabilities are $2,000. Its working capital is ________________ and its current ratio is ________________.

LO 4 4. A company has a debt-to-equity ratio of 0.5 to 1 and has accounts payable on its balance sheet. Its debt-to-total-assets ratio will be ________________ than 0.5 to 1.

LO 4 5. Company A's current ratio is 2:1, and Company B's current ratio is 1:1. On this evidence, Company A is more ________________ than Company B.

LO 6 6. Company Z has sales of $10,000, gross profit of $3,000, and net income of $1,000. Its gross profit ratio is ________________, and its profit margin is ________________.

LO 6 7. If a company's gross profit is $8,000 and its cost of goods sold is $4,000, its revenue is ________________.

LO 7 8. Stockholders' equity consists of two main components: ________________ and ________________.

LO 9 9. The ________________ gives management's interpretation of the financial statements and provides stockholders with explanations for various items in the reports.

LO 9 10. The ________________ provides an independent opinion on the fairness of the financial statements.

LO 4 11. The ________________ ratio, which gives a measure of the enterprise's liquidity, is calculated by dividing current ________________ by current ________________.

LO 4 12. The ability of a company to stay in business in the long run is known as its ________________.

LO 2 13. The capacity of information to make a difference in a decision is called ________________.

LO 2 14. The quality of accounting information that makes it dependable in reporting what it purports to represent is called _______________.

LO 6 15. The ratio of market price per share divided by earnings per share is closely watched by many investors and is known as _______________.

Indicate whether each of the following statements is true or false:

LO 3 16. If you wish to find the amount of cash that a firm invested in property, plant and equipment during the accounting period, you should look in the balance sheet.

LO 3 17. Purchase of equipment on credit increases long-term assets and increases retained earnings.

LO 4 18. The debt-to-equity ratio is a measure of the company's ability to pay its debts as they come due.

LO 8 19. If a company shows a cash flow from operations of $55 million in its cash flow statement, its net income must also be $55 million in its income statement.

LO 8 20. If a firm has retained earnings of $3,000, then it must have cash available to pay dividends of at least $3,000.

LO 3 21. Accounts payable are current liabilities resulting from a firm buying inventory but not yet having paid the supplier.

LO 3 22. Retained earnings is a measure of the total earnings of the business since its inception.

LO 5 23. Investors and other users of financial statements are primarily concerned with the cash a company can generate, so there is no need to provide any statement other than the statement of cash flows.

LO 5 24. A single-step income statement is simpler and easier to read than a multiple-step income statement, but since it provides less information, it may not be as useful to investors and other users.

LO 2 25. Consistency refers to the feature of accounting that ensures that every company conforms to the same set of accounting standards.

LO 4 26. If a company's working capital increases, its current ratio must also increase.

LO 6 27. If a company's gross profit ratio increases, its profit margin must also increase.

LO 4 28. If a company's total liabilities are $8,000 and its stockholders' equity is $2,000, its debt-to-equity ratio is 0.8 to 1, and its debt-to-total-assets ratio is 4 to 1.

LO 3 29. Land is the only tangible fixed asset that is not depreciated.

LO 9 30. The responsibility for the information in the annual report rests with the company's independent auditors.

For each of the following questions, circle the alternative that best answers the question:

LO 3 31. Which of the following economic events does NOT result in a corporation incurring a liability?

a) The corporation buys merchandise on credit.
b) The corporation declares a dividend to be paid in two months.
c) The corporation announces a pay increase for the following year for its hourly paid workers.
d) The corporation sells bonds.

LO 2 32. Which of the following statements best describes the principle of consistency?

a) When uncertainty exists, understating assets, overstating liabilities, accelerating recognition of losses, and delaying recognition of gains is preferred.
b) Similar events are measured using identical accounting procedures from period to period.
c) Different firms use identical accounting measurement methods for similar events.
d) The measurement of an event is verifiable and reliable.

LO 2 33. Which of the following accounting principles is being applied when a firm delays recognition of a sale made to a customer who has declared bankruptcy until cash is received from the customer?

a) Matching
b) Objectivity
c) Going concern
d) Conservatism

LO 3 34. Which of the following best describes the amount that appears on the balance sheet as liabilities?

a) What the company owes and must pay in the future
b) Cash that stockholders have contributed
c) The shareholders' claim on the assets of the firm
d) The total past earnings minus the amount distributed in dividends

LO 3 35. Which of the following best describes the amount that appears on the balance sheet as capital stock?

a) What the company owes and must pay in the future
b) Cash or other assets that stockholders have contributed to the company in exchange for shares
c) The shareholders' claim on the assets of the firm
d) The total past earnings minus the amount distributed in dividends

LO 9 36. A statement that "in our opinion the financial statements present fairly, in all material respects, the financial position of X Corporation " would most likely be found in

a) the management letter.
b) the auditor's report.
c) the management's discussion and analysis.
d) the president's letter to the stockholders.

LO 3 37. Which of the following is NOT a creditor of Beta Corporation?

a) A supplier of inventory to Beta Corp. who will collect payment for merchandise next month
b) A bank that lends money to Beta Corp.
c) The IRS, who are owed taxes by Beta Corp.
d) A person who buys stock in Beta Corp.

LO 3 38. Which of the following contains only assets?

a) Accounts payable, retained earnings, notes payable
b) Supplies expense, cost of goods sold, interest expenses
c) Sales revenue, dividends, net income
d) Plant and equipment, inventory, cash

LO 3 39. Which of the following best describes the amount that appears on the balance sheet as retained earnings?

a) What the company owes and must pay in the future
b) Cash that stockholders have contributed
c) The shareholders' claim on the assets of the firm
d) The total past earnings minus the amount distributed in dividends

LO 4 40. Liquidity

a) is the amount of cash that the company has available.
b) deals with the ability of the company to pay its debts as they come due.
c) is current assets minus current liabilities.
d) is the cash flow from operations minus cash flow used in investment activities.

Use the following information to answer questions 41, 42, and 43:
The following items appear in the balance sheet of Company A at the end of Year 2 and Year 3:

	Year 3	Year 2
Current assets	$ 6,000	$ 3,000
Long-term assets	7,000	4,000
Current liabilities	2,000	3,000
Long-term liabilities	7,000	0
Stockholders' equity	4,000	4,000

LO 4 41. Between Year 2 and Year 3,

a) Company A's working capital and current ratio both increased.
b) Company A's working capital and current ratio both decreased.
c) Company A's working capital increased and its current ratio decreased.
d) Company A's working capital decreased and its current ratio increased.

LO 4 42. Between Year 2 and Year 3,

a) Company A's debt-to-equity ratio and debt-to-total assets ratio both increased.
b) Company A's debt-to-equity ratio and debt-to-total assets ratio both decreased.
c) Company A's debt-to-equity ratio increased and its debt-to-total assets ratio decreased.
d) Company A's debt-to-equity ratio decreased and its debt-to-total assets ratio increased.

LO 4 43. Between Year 2 and Year 3,

a) Company A's liquidity and solvency both increased.
b) Company A's liquidity and solvency both decreased.
c) Company A's liquidity increased and its solvency decreased.
d) Company A's liquidity decreased and its solvency increased.

Use the following information to answer questions 44 and 45:
The following items appear in the income statement of Company B for the years ending December 31, Year 2 and Year 3:

	Year 3	**Year 2**
Sales	$ 30,000	$ 25,000
Cost of goods sold	20,000	15,000
Other expenses	5,000	5,000

LO 6 44. Between Year 2 and Year 3,

a) Company B's gross profit ratio and profit margin ratio both increased.
b) Company B's gross profit ratio and profit margin ratio both decreased.
c) Company B's gross profit ratio increased and its profit margin ratio decreased.
d) Company B's gross profit ratio decreased and its profit margin ratio increased.

LO 6 45. Between Year 2 and Year 3,

a) Company B's revenue and net income as a percentage of sales both increased.
b) Company B's revenue and net income as a percentage of sales both decreased.
c) Company B's revenue increased and its net income as a percentage of sales decreased.
d) Company B's revenue decreased and its net income as a percentage of sales increased.

Answer each of the following problems:

LO 4,5 46. Complete the table below to show the effect of each transaction on assets, liabilities, or stockholders' equity. Use + if the item increases, - if the item decreases, 0 if the event has no effect on the item, and ? if the effect of the event cannot be determined. The first one is done for you.

	EFFECT ON ASSETS	EFFECT ON LIABILITIES	EFFECT ON STOCKHOLDERS' EQUITY
Cash collections from accounts receivable	+ Cash - Accounts receivable		
Purchase of long-term asset for cash			
Purchase of inventory for cash			
Purchase of inventory on credit			
Repayment of long-term loan			
Issue of capital stock for cash			
Cash payment of accounts payable			
Issue of bonds for cash			
Cash payment of taxes payable			

LO 5,6 47. The consolidated statement of earnings for Goleta Corporation for the eleven months ended January 30, 1997, and for the year ended February 1, 1996, include the following amounts:

	January 30, 1997	February 1, 1996
Net sales	$7,169,290	$6,124,209
Costs and expenses:		
Cost of sales	$4,968,555	4,286,639
Selling, advertising, general and administrative	1,342,262	1,153,576
Depreciation and amortization	119,034	100,701
Interest expense	69,134	57,885
Interest and other income	18,719	13,521
Taxes on income	251,500	199,400

Required

1. Prepare in good form a multiple-step income statement for each period, showing gross profit, income from operations, income before taxes, and net income.

2. Restate each item in the multiple-step income statements as a percentage of sales.

3. Calculate the gross profit and profit margin.

4. On the basis of your calculations, compare the company's profitability over the two years and explain why it is more meaningful to use ratios to compare these statements than to directly compare the total numbers in each statement.

LO 5 48. Sandy Mactavish has been in business as a beautician for a year and believes she has found a lucrative niche in providing on-site beautician services to retirement homes. She now wants to expand the business by employing an additional beautician but the new employee would need a new car. She therefore wants you to invest in the business either by lending her money or by becoming a partner. She shows you the following "statement of earnings" for the year, which she has drawn up by summarizing her personal checkbook:

Revenues	$20,000
Expenses	15,000
Net earnings	$5,000

You examine the statement and talk to Sandy who gives you the following additional information:

a) She owes $5,000 to Alma Beauty Supplies for beauty supplies that have already been used but not paid for.

b) She used her own car for the business at a cost of $1,000 for the year.

c) The revenue figure in her income statement does not include cash of $2,000 received from customers that Sandy has used for her own living expenses.

Required

1. Sandy has clearly not provided you with a statement of earnings. What has she given you?

2. Draw up the statement of earnings for the year for Sandy's business.

3. Would you be willing to invest money in Sandy's business? What problems do you see? Would you prefer to lend her money or become a partner? Why?

Critical Thinking Problem

LO 4 49. Exhibit 1 below shows extracts from the consolidated balance sheets of Fly-By-Night Airlines on June 30, 1997 and 1996. The numbers are in millions of dollars.

	1997	1996
Current assets		
Cash	$ 1,180	$ 50
Accounts receivable	1,024	1,090
Inventory	120	250
Prepaid expenses	495	305
Total current assets	$ 2,819	$ 1,695
Current liabilities		
Notes payable	$ 46	$ 821
Accounts payable	2,390	2,204
Taxes payable	533	514
Total current liabilities	$ 2,969	$ 3,539

Required

1. Calculate Fly-By-Night's working capital and current ratio for the two years.

2. By considering both your answer to question 1 and changes in the components of Fly-By-Night's current assets and current liabilities over the year, comment on whether or not you think that Fly-By-Night's liquidity has improved over the period.

Solutions

Fill in the Blanks

1. Accelerated depreciation
2. gross profit, income from operations
3. $3,000, 2.5 to 1
4. greater
5. liquid
6. 30%, 10%
7. $12,000
8. capital stock, retained earnings
9. management's discussion and analysis
10. auditors' report
11. current, assets, liabilities
12. Solvency
13. Relevance
14. Reliability
15. price-earnings ratio

True/False

		COMMENT/EXPLANATION
16.	False	The statement of cash flows shows the amount of cash expended on property, plant, and equipment.
17.	False	Long-term assets and liabilities increase.
18.	False	The debt-to-equity ratio measures the company's capital structure.
19.	False	Cash flows from operations rarely equal net income because of noncash revenues and expenses that occur during the accounting period.
20.	False	The earnings that the company generates may not result in an increase in cash.
21.	True	
22.	False	Retained earnings equals the total earnings, since the company was incorporated minus the dividends the company has paid to its stockholders.
23.	False	Investors are also interested in the assets and liabilities of the company (on the balance sheet) and the company's earnings (the income statement).
24.	True	
25.	False	Consistency refers to the feature of accounting that ensures that users are able to compare the accounts of different companies within the same time period and accounts of the same company over time.
26.	True	
27.	False	Even although the gross margin increases, selling and other expenses can increase by more than the decrease in gross margin, leading to a decrease in profit margin.
28.	False	Its debt-to-equity ratio is 4 to 1, and its debt-to-total-assets ratio is 0.8 to 1.
29.	True	
30.	False	Management is responsible for the information in the annual report. The auditors comment on the fairness of that information.

Multiple Choice

31. c
32. b
33. d
34. a
35. b
36. b
37. d
38. d
39. d
40. b
41. a
42. a
43. a
44. b
45. c

Problem 46

	EFFECT ON ASSETS	EFFECT ON LIABILITIES	EFFECT ON STOCKHOLDERS' EQUITY
Cash collections from accounts receivable	+ Cash - Accounts receivable		
Purchase of long-term asset for cash	+ Long-term assets - Cash		
Purchase of inventory for cash	+ Inventory - Cash		
Purchase of inventory on credit	+ Inventory	+ Accounts payable	
Repayment of long-term loan	- Cash	- Long-term loan	
Issue of capital stock for cash	+ Cash		+ Capital stock
Cash payment of accounts payable	- Cash	- Accounts payable	
Issue of bonds for cash	+ Cash	+ Bonds	
Cash payment of taxes payable	- Cash	- Taxes Payable	

Problem 47

1. & 2.

	January 30, 1997		February 1, 1996	
	$	%	$	%
Net sales	7,169,290	100%	6,124,209	100%
Cost of sales	(4,968,555)	(69%)	(4,286,639)	(70%)
Gross profit	2,200,735	31%	1,837,570	30%
Selling, advertising, general and administrative	(1,342,262)	(19%)	(1,153,576)	(19%)
Depreciation and amortization	(119,034)	(2%)	(100,701)	(2%)
Income from operations	739,439	10%	583,293	9%
Interest expense	(69,134)	(1%)	(57,885)	(1%)
Interest and other income	18,719	0%	13,521	0%
Income before taxes	689,024	10%	538,929	9%
Taxes on income	(251,500)	(4%)	(199,400)	(3%)
Net income	$437,524	6%	$339,529	6%

3.

Gross profit	31%	30%
Profit margin	6%	6%

4. Goleta Corporation has produced good profit figures over the two years and it is interesting to see how stable these results are. Using ratios lets you see the relationship between sales and expense over the two accounting periods, which is particularly helpful in a case where the two accounting periods are not of equal length.

Problem 48

1. Sandy has provided you with a partial summary of cash payments and receipts, which is more like a statement of cash flows than a statement of earnings. However, the statement she has provided you with is not complete, and therefore it cannot even be called a statement of cash flows.

2. **Statement of earnings**

Sales		$22,000
Expenses	15,000	
Supplies expense	5,000	
Car expenses	1,000	
Total expenses		21,000
Net earnings		**$1,000**

Note: Sales equals $20,000, as reported, plus $2,000 taken for Sandy's use.

3. The business is clearly not as profitable as Sandy had claimed, and therefore you would probably be reluctant to invest money in it until you could see some further results. However, of greater concern is the confusion of Sandy's personal accounts with the business accounts. A system of accounting for the business separate from Sandy's personal spending should be established. Until such a system is operational, you cannot put much reliance on the information provided by her. If you were to invest, probably a loan would be preferable, especially if it could be secured on an asset such as her car.

Critical Thinking Problem 49

1.	1997	1996
Working capital ($ millions)	$2,819 - $2,969 = $(150)	$1,695 - $3,539 = $(1,844)
Current ratio	$\frac{\$2,819}{\$2,969}$ = 0.95	$\frac{\$1,695}{\$3,539}$ =0.48

2. The component of Fly-By-Night's current assets that has changed most significantly over the year is the balance of cash, which increased by approximately $1.1 billion dollars. The main changes in current liabilities over the period are the reduction in short-term notes payable, which are used for short-term borrowing. Overall, Fly-By-Night's liquidity has improved over the year, and it appears that its cash position is much healthier than it was. However, Fly-By-Night's current assets are still smaller than its current liabilities, and Fly-By-Night therefore does not have enough current assets to satisfy its current liabilities. In addition, companies in the airline industry require relatively large cash balances, since there is often a delay in receiving cash from their customers (see, for example, Fly-By-Night's large accounts receivable balance). Although it has improved substantially over the year, Fly-By-Night's liquidity is likely to continue to be a matter of concern.

Chapter 3

Processing Accounting Information

Accounting information is the result of a process that begins with an economic event and ends with the production of financial reports. This chapter starts the exploration of that process. Your overall aim is to understand the basic accounting tools and procedures that are needed to record accounting information.

Learning Objectives

LO 1 Explain the difference between an internal and an external event.

LO 2 Explain the role of source documents in an accounting system.

LO 3 Analyze the effects of transactions on the accounting system.

LO 4 Define the concept of a general ledger and the use of the T account as a method for analyzing transactions.

LO 5 Explain the rules of debit and credit.

LO 6 Explain the purpose of a journal and the posting process.

LO 7 Explain the purpose of the trial balance.

Key Textbook Exhibits

Exhibit 3-1 illustrates the impact on the accounting equation of various transactions. Note how each entry maintains the equality of the basic accounting equation

Assets = Liabilities + Owners' Equity

Exhibit 3-5 illustrates how transactions are posted from the journal to the ledger. Make sure you can follow the logic of the posting from the journal to each ledger account.

Review of Key Concepts

We use the following example to illustrate the concepts in this chapter. The Pacioli Corporation, a retailer of accounting software, was incorporated on January 1, 1997. Pacioli's transactions for its first year of operations to December 31, 1997 included the following:

1. Stockholders invested $250,000 cash in exchange for 250,000 common shares with a par value of $1 each.
2. Software inventory was bought over the year totaling $180,000. All purchases were made on credit.
3. Office furniture was bought for $36,000 cash on February 1, 1997. The furniture has a three year life and zero residual value.
4. Pacioli paid its creditors $150,000 in cash.

LO 1 Any event that is recognized in a set of financial statements is called a **transaction.** Transactions are the basic building blocks of any accounting system. Internal events, such as the transfer of material to production or the use of a piece of equipment, occur wholly within the enterprise. External events, such as the purchase of inventory or a stock issue for cash, involve interactions with an outside party or group.

LO 2 **Source documents** are used to identify transactions. For external transactions, source documents may be generated externally (for example, an invoice from a supplier) or internally (for example, a receipt for payment received from a customer). For internal transactions, source documents are generated internally (for example, material requisitions used to transfer goods from inventory to production).

LO 3 One way of analyzing the impact of economic events on the accounts is to use the accounting equation.

Assets = Liabilities + Owners' Equity

Every transaction has a **dual effect** on the accounting equation, i.e., there is always both an increase and a decrease in the terms of the equation. Note that the increase and decrease may both be in the same term of the equation. For example, if inventory is bought for cash, one asset (inventory) increases and another asset (cash) decreases by the same amount.

The accounting equation must always balance after each transaction has been recorded. To illustrate, we analyze the transactions of the Pacioli Corporation.

	Assets				Liabilities		Stockholders' Equity	
	Cash	**Software Inventory**	**Furniture**		**Accounts Payable**		**Capital Stock**	
1.	+250,000						+250,000	Both the assets and stockholders' equity increase.
	250,000			=		+	250,000	Balance
2.		+180,000			+180,000			Both assets and liabilities increase.
	250,000	+180,000		=	180,000	+	250,000	Balance
3.	-36,000		+36,000					One asset (furniture) increases and one asset (cash) decreases. Total assets are unaffected.
	214,000	+180,000	+ 36,000	=	180,000	+	250,000	Balance
4.	-150,000				-150,000			Both cash and accounts payable are reduced.
	64,000	+180,000	+ 36,000	=	30,000	+	250,000	Balance

LO 4,5 It is unwieldy and impractical to use the accounting equation to analyze and record large volumes of transactions. Therefore, in practice two main tools are used: **ledger accounts** and **journal entries**.

- An **account** is used to record the detailed information about changes in each type of asset and liability and in each component of owners' equity. A chart of accounts lists all the accounts that an entity uses. Each entity will have its own unique chart of accounts.
- A **general ledger** is a file, book, disc or magnetic tape that contains the accounts of a business.
- A **debit** is the name given to increasing an asset or expense account and to decreasing a revenue, dividend, liability, or owners' equity account. By convention, debits are recorded on the left side of an entry or account.
- A **credit** is the name given to decreasing an asset or expense account and to increasing a revenue, dividend, liability, or stockholders' equity account. By convention, credits are recorded on the right side of an entry or account.
- A **T account** is a convenient way of symbolizing a general ledger account, but in practice general ledger accounts come in many different forms, including computer files. We illustrate the recording of transactions in T accounts using the Pacioli Corporation example.

CASH	
1. 250,000	

CAPITAL STOCK	
	1. 250,000

Cash is increased and therefore the asset account, cash, is debited. Capital stock also increases and the owners' equity account, capital stock, is credited.

SOFTWARE INVENTORY	
2. 180,000	

ACCOUNTS PAYABLE	
	2. 180,000

Software inventory is increased and the asset account, software inventory, is debited. Liabilities increased and therefore the liability account, accounts payable, is credited.

CASH	
	3. 36,000

OFFICE FURNITURE	
3. 36,000	

Office furniture increased and the asset account, office furniture, is debited. Cash decreased and the asset account, cash, is credited.

CASH	
	4. 150,000

ACCOUNTS PAYABLE	
4. 150,000	

Cash decreases and therefore the asset account, cash, is credited. Accounts payable decreases and the liability account, accounts payable, is debited.

LO 6 The **journal** is the place where transactions are recorded in the order they occur. Transactions are first recorded in the journal, which is therefore called a book of original entry. Once the journal entries are complete, the effects of the transactions are posted to the ledger accounts. Journal entries take the following general form (with xxx representing the dollar sum involved):

		Debit	Credit
Date	[Account(s) to be debited]	xxx	
	[Account(s) to be credited]		xxx
	Explanation of transaction		

For example, the journal entries for the transactions for Pacioli Corporation are as follows:

		Debit	Credit
1.	Cash	250,000	
	Capital stock		250,000
	Receipt of cash in exchange for stock issue.		

		Debit	Credit
2.	Software inventory	180,000	
	Accounts payable		180,000
	Purchase of inventory on credit.		

		Debit	Credit
3.	Office furniture	36,000	
	Cash		36,000
	Purchase of furniture for cash.		

		Debit	Credit
4.	Accounts payable	150,000	
	Cash		150,000
	Capital stock		250,000
	Payment of accounts payable.		

Once the journal entries are complete, the ledger accounts are posted with the effects of the transactions. As this continues throughout the accounting period, each ledger account builds up into a complete record of all transactions relating to that account that have taken place during the period. The ledger accounts can then be used as the basis for preparing the periodic financial statements. To illustrate the posting of transactions to ledger accounts, we show the postings to the cash account of the transactions of the Pacioli Company using a **running balance form of account**:

General Ledger
Cash

Ref.	Explanation	Debit	Credit	Balance
1.	Stock issue	250,000		250,000
3.	Purchase of office furniture		36,000	214,000
4.	Payment of accounts payable		150,000	64,000

Note that in this form of ledger account, the account balance is clearly seen after each transaction is posted, hence the name "running balance".

LO 7 A **trial balance** is a list of account balances at a particular point in time, and is usually drawn up at the end of a period. It is not itself a financial statement, but is simply a convenient device to help in detecting errors. During the journalizing and posting of transactions, total debits should always equal total credits. If, when the trial balance is drawn up, the total of the credit balances does not equal the total debit balances, there must have been a mistake made either in journalizing or in posting the transactions. An imbalance in the trial balance can therefore be used to help detect and correct errors. The trial balance for the Pacioli Corporation on December 31, 1997, is as follows:

Pacioli Corporation

Trial balance on 12/31/97	Debit	Credit
Cash	64,000	
Software inventory	180,000	
Furniture	36,000	
Accounts payable		30,000
Capital stock		250,000
	$280,000	$280,000

Review of Key Terms

Account	The record used to accumulate the monetary amounts for each individual asset, liability, revenue, expense, and component of owners' equity.
Chart of accounts	A list of all the accounts used by a company.
Credit	The name given to decreasing an asset or expense account, and to increasing a revenue, dividend, liability, or owners' equity account. It is recorded on the right side of an account.
Debit	The name given to increasing an asset or expense account, and to decreasing a revenue, dividend, liability, or owners' equity account. It is recorded on the left side of an account.
Double entry system	An accounting system in which every transaction is recorded with equal debits and credits and the accounting equation is kept in balance.
External event	An event involving the interaction between an entity and its environment.
General journal	The journal used in place of a specialized journal.
General ledger	A book, file, magnetic tape or disc containing all of a company's accounts.
Internal event	An event occurring entirely within the business.
Journal	A chronological record of transactions, also known as the book of original record.
Journalizing	The process of recording journal entries.
Posting	The process of transferring the amounts from a journal to the appropriate ledger accounts.
Source document	A piece of paper used as evidence to record a transaction.
Transaction	Any event, internal or external, that is recognized in a set of financial statements.
Trial balance	A worksheet showing the balance in each account.

Practice Test Questions and Problems

Complete each of the following statements:

LO 3 1. The record used to accumulate monetary amounts for each asset, liability, and component of owners' equity is called an ____________________.

LO 3 2. The numerical list of all of the accounts used by an entity is the ____________________.

LO 4 3. A general ledger is often supplemented by ____________________, which contain detailed accounts for a particular class of accounts such as accounts receivable.

LO 1 4. The transfer of raw materials into production, the use of plant and equipment in manufacturing and the movement of finished goods into a company's own retail stores are examples of ____________________ events.

LO 6 5. The ____________________ is where transactions are first recorded in preparation for posting to ledger accounts.

LO 7 6. The ____________________ is a list of all accounts and their balances and is a way of proving the equality of debit and credit account balances.

LO 2 7. Time cards, invoices received from suppliers, and cash register tapes are examples of ____________________ that provide evidence needed to record a transaction.

LO 1 8. The sale of bonds, the payment of wages to employees, and the transfer of finished goods to customers are examples of ____________________ events.

LO 5 9. Increasing an asset or expense and decreasing a liability, owners' equity, or revenue account all require the account to be ____________________.

LO 6 10. In ____________________ journal entries, more than one account is either debited or credited.

LO 4 11. If the cash account is ____________________, cash has been received.

LO 3 12. Every transaction has a ____________________ on the accounting equation. In other words, there is always both an increase and a decrease in the terms of the equation.

LO 4 13. When cash is paid to satisfy an account payable, the cash account is ____________________ and the accounts payable account is ____________________.

LO 5 14. By convention, ____________________ are recorded on the left side of an entry or account, and ____________________ are recorded on the right side of an entry or account.

LO 8 15. When Company A issues bonds for cash, the bookkeeper debits the cash account by $3,000 and credits stockholders' equity with $30,000. All other events are recorded correctly. At the end of the period, the debit balance on the trial balance was ____________________ and the credit balance was $227,000.

Indicate whether each of the following statements is true or false:

LO 4 16. The difference between a manual system and a computerized accounting system is the form in which the accounts are stored.

LO 5 17. Dividends and expense accounts normally have debit balances.

LO 1 18. The only events that require source documents are external events.

LO 1 19. Internal events need not be recorded in journal entries but can be posted straight to ledger accounts.

LO 1 20. Only events that can be measured reliably should be recorded in the accounts.

LO 5 21. In accounting, as in common usage, credits imply something positive has happened to the organization.

LO 6 22. A journal entry is the first formal record of a transaction made in the accounting system.

LO 4 23. A T account is a form of account used to analyze transactions and is so called because it contains the total transactions for each account.

LO 2 24. Time sheets are used as source documents to identify wages payable to employees.

LO 6 25. Specialized journals are used to record repetitive transactions in which the debit or the credit is always to the same account.

LO 3 26. When cash is received to satisfy an account receivable, total assets increase.

LO 3 27. When bonds are issued for cash, stockholders' equity decreases.

LO 3 28. When inventory is bought for cash, the current ratio increases.

LO 3 29. When stock is issued for cash, the debt-to-total-assets ratio increases.

LO 3 30. When accounts payable are paid in cash, the debt-to-equity ratio decreases.

For each of the following questions, circle the alternative that best answers the question:

LO 5 31. Which of the following describes the purchase of $1,000 of supplies on credit?

a) Increase assets and increase owner's equity for $1,000.
b) Decrease owners' equity for $1,000 and decrease assets for $1,000.
c) Increase assets and increase liabilities for $1,000.
d) Decrease liabilities and decrease assets for $1,000.

LO 3 32. The effect on the balance sheet of paying accounts payable with cash is that

a) total assets increase and total liabilities increase.
b) total liabilities decrease.
c) total assets are unaffected.
d) stockholders' equity increases.

LO 4 33. The ledger is

a) the book of the original entry in which debit and credit descriptions of events that change assets, liabilities, and owners' equity are recorded.
b) the place where economic information is accumulated with respect to the accounts affected.
c) a summary of accounts and their balances, which is used to prepare financial statements.
d) a record of all events that affect the company.

LO 3 34. The effect on the balance sheet of issuing bonds for cash is that

a) total assets increase and total liabilities increase.
b) total liabilities decrease.
c) total assets are unaffected.
d) Stockholders' equity increases.

LO 7 35. The trial balance is

a) the book of the original entry in which debit and credit descriptions of events that change assets, liabilities, and owners' equity are recorded.
b) the place where economic information is accumulated with respect to the accounts affected.
c) a summary of accounts and their balances that is used to prepare financial statements.
d) a record of all events that affect the company.

LO 3 36. Which of the following changes describes the receipt of $1,000 from the issue of bonds?

a) Assets and owners' equity increase by $1,000.
b) Assets and owners' equity decrease by $1,000.
c) Assets and liabilities increase by $1,000.
d) Assets and liabilities decrease by $1,000.

LO 5 37. An asset account

a) has a debit balance.
b) is decreased with a credit.
c) is a balance sheet account.
d) All of the above are correct.

LO 3 38. The effect on the balance sheet of buying furniture on credit is that

a) total assets increase and total liabilities increase.
b) total liabilities decrease.
c) total assets are unaffected.
d) stockholders' equity increases.

LO 5 39. When you deposit money in the bank, the teller informs you that your account has been credited. You are now totally confused because in your accounting class you have just learned that a debit increases your assets and therefore the bank should have debited your account. Which statement best clarifies your confusion?

a) The definitions of debits and credits given by your instructor are wrong.
b) The bank is increasing its liability to you by accepting your money and is therefore recording an increase in the bank's liability to you with a credit.
c) This situation is one of life's great mysteries that we will never fully understand.
d) The banks are attempting to change the definition of credit to be consistent with everyday usage, as in "she is a credit to her family".

LO 5,6 40. Which of the following statements is TRUE?

a) The double entry system means that for every debit, there must be a corresponding credit; therefore, the total debits posted to the general ledger must equal the total credits.

b) Accounts that normally have credit balances include capital stock, long-term liabilities, and expenses.

c) The general ledger is the book of original entry.

d) Journal entries must include the accounts to be debited and credited, and may include the relevant dollar amounts.

LO 7 41. Which of the following statements is TRUE?

a) If the total debits equals the total credits in a trial balance, there is an error in the ledger, the journal, or the trial balance, or in the posting from one to the other.

b) The trial balance is a tool used to prove the equality of debits and credits in the general ledger.

c) A trial balance is a supplement to the balance sheet that provides more timely information for investors.

d) Financial statements should be prepared before the trial balance is balanced.

LO 3 42. The effect on the balance sheet of selling inventory for cash at a profit is that

a) total assets decrease and total liabilities increase.

b) total liabilities decrease.

c) total assets are unaffected.

d) Stockholders' equity increases.

LO 6 43. The journal is

a) the book of original entry in which debit and credit descriptions of events that change assets, liabilities and owners' equity are recorded.

b) the place where economic information is accumulated with respect to the accounts affected.

c) a summary of accounts and their balances that is used to prepare financial statements.

d) a record of all events that affect the company.

LO 7 44. Alpha Corporation buys $35,000 worth of computer equipment for cash. All of the following outline journal entries incorrectly record this transaction. Which of them will lead to the debit balance on the trial balance being greater than the credit balance?

	Debit	Credit
a) Computer equipment	$38,000	
Cash		$35,000
b) Cash	$35,000	
Computer equipment		$35,000
c) Computer equipment	$33,000	
Cash		$33,000
d) Computer equipment	$35,000	
Cash		$38,000

LO 3 45. The effect on the balance sheet of receiving cash for accounts receivable is that
a) total assets decrease and total liabilities increase.
b) total liabilities decrease.
c) total assets are unaffected.
d) stockholders' equity increases.

Answer each of the following problems:

LO 5 46. The following economic events took place in the year ended June 30, 1997, for Computit Corporation, a retailer of computer equipment. Match each event with the correct type of accounting entry:

Accounting Entry

A. increase assets and increase liabilities
B. increase assets and increase capital stock
C. increase assets and increase retained earnings
D. decrease liabilities and decrease assets
E. decrease capital stock and decrease assets
F. decrease retained earnings and decrease assets
G. increase one asset and decrease another asset
H. is not communicated by the formal accounting system

ECONOMIC EVENT	ACCOUNTING ENTRY
1. Postage stamps were bought and used to send invoices	
2. The chairman of the company resigned	
3. Received cash for the sale of stock	
4. Received cash for the issue of bonds	
5. Purchased computer equipment on credit	
6. Sold computer equipment for cash	
7. President Clinton was reelected for another four years	
8. Paid interest to the bond holders	
9. Paid dividends to owners of the company	
10. Paid an account payable	

LO 1,2 47. Refer to the transactions in Problem 46.

Required

For the transactions that **are** recorded in the accounts:

1. Identify at least one source document that is generated from the event.
2. Identify which information on the source document is most useful in recording the events in the accounts.

ECONOMIC EVENT	SOURCE DOCUMENTS	INFORMATION
1.		
2.		
3.		
4.		
5.		
6.		
7.		
8.		
9.		
10.		

LO 3,4 48. Loraine, Denis, and Janine Bland started a business providing bookkeeping and accounting services on January 1, 1997. During January the following transactions took place:

a) Loraine, Denis, and Janine each provided $5,000, cash in return for which they were issued with 5,000 shares of capital stock with a $1 par value.

b) An office and furniture were rented. Rent of $2,000 cash was paid for the month of January.

c) Services of $20,000 were performed for **customers**; 75% was paid in cash and the remainder was still outstanding at the end of January.

d) Office stationery supplies of $500 were bought. The supplies were bought on credit, and at the end of the month no payment had yet been made to the supplier. The supplies were used immediately they were acquired.

e) A computer was bought at the end of the month for $2,000 cash.

f) Loraine, Denis, and Janine had agreed that each would receive a monthly salary of $5,000. Salaries were paid at the end of the month.

Required

1. Complete the table below showing the impact of each transaction on the accounting equation.

	Assets			=	Liabilities +	Owners' Equity	
	Cash	*Computer*	*Accounts Receivable*		*Accounts Payable*	*Capital Stock*	*Retained Earnings*
a)							
Bal.				=			
b)							
Bal.				=			
c)							
Bal.				=			
d)							
Bal.				=			
e)							
Bal.				=			
f)							
Bal.				=			

2. Prepare a trial balance on January 31, 1997, an income statement for the month of January and a balance sheet as of January 31, 1997. On the basis of the statements you have prepared, do you think that the business is viable with the present arrangements?

Critical Thinking Problem

LO 4 49. Pacioli Company's summary transactions for its first year of operations to December 31, 1997, are summarized below.

1. Stockholders invested $250,000 cash in exchange for 250,000 common shares with a par value of $1 each.
2. Software inventory was bought over the year totaling $180,000. All purchases were made on credit.
3. Office furniture was bought for $36,000 cash on February 1, 1997. The furniture has a three-year life and zero residual value.
4. Pacioli paid its creditors $150,000 in cash.
5. The first year's rental of $60,000 on a retail store was paid on January 1, 1997.
6. During the year total sales were $400,000, of which $80,000 were in cash and the remainder were on credit.
7. Pacioli received $70,000 from accounts receivable.
8. Wages and salaries of $62,000 were paid during the year.
9. Utilities for the year of $10,000 were paid in cash.

Pacioli's bookkeeper prepared journal entries for these transactions and posted them to ledger accounts. He asks you for help to find his $10,000 mistake when his trial balance did not balance.

		Debit $	Credit $
1.	Cash	250,000	
	Capital stock		250,000
	Receipt of cash in exchange for stock issue		
2.	Software inventory	180,000	
	Accounts payable		180,000
	Purchase of software inventory on credit		
3.	Office furniture	36,000	
	Cash		36,000
	Purchase of furniture for cash		
4.	Accounts payable	150,000	
	Cash		150,000
	Cash payment to creditors		
5.	Cash	60,000	
	Rent expense		60,000
	Cash payment for rent		
6.	Cash	80,000	
	Accounts receivable	220,000	
	Sales		400,000
	Cash and receivables from sales		
7.	Accounts receivable	70,000	
	Cash		70,000
	Cash received from accounts receivable		

8.	Wages and salaries expense	62,000	
	Cash		62,000
	Cash paid for wages and salaries		
9.	Utilities expense	10,000	
	Cash		10,000
	Cash paid for utilities		

CASH

	Debit		Credit
1.	250,000	3.	36,000
5.	60,000	4.	150,000
6.	80,000	8.	62,000
7.	70,000	9.	10,000
e.b.	202,000		

CAPITAL STOCK

	Debit		Credit
		1.	250,000

ACCOUNTS PAYABLE

	Debit		Credit
4.	250,000	2.	180,000
6.	320,000		
e.b.	290,000		

RENT EXPENSE

	Debit		Credit
		5.	60,000

OFFICE FURNITURE

	Debit		Credit
3.	36,000		

ACCOUNTS RECEIVABLE

	Debit		Credit
		7.	70,000

UTILITIES EXPENSE

	Debit		Credit
9.	10,000		

WAGES EXPENSE

	Debit		Credit
		8.	52,000

SOFTWARE INVENTORY

	Debit		Credit
2.	180,000		

SALES

	Debit		Credit
		6.	400,000

Trial balance on 12/31/97	**Debit**	**Credit**
Cash	$ 202,000	
Rent expense		$ 60,000
Sales		400,000
Wages expense	52,000	
Utilities expense	10,000	
Accounts receivable		70,000
Office furniture	36,000	
Software inventory	180,000	
Capital stock		250,000
Accounts payable	290,000	
	$770,000	$780,000

Required

The bookkeeper has made errors both in the journal entries, and the posting to, and balancing of, ledger accounts. Help him by correcting his accounting entries. Prepare a corrected trial balance.

Solutions

Fill in the Blanks

1. account
2. chart of accounts
3. subsidiary ledger
4. internal
5. journal
6. trial balance
7. source documents
8. external
9. debited
10. compound
11. debited
12. dual effect
13. credited, debited
14. debits, credits
15. $200,000

True/False

		COMMENT/EXPLANATION
16.	True	
17.	True	
18.	False	Although not all recognizable events generate a standard source document, some form of documentation must be generated for all transactions. generate source documents.
19.	False	All transactions must be recorded in journal entries.
20.	True	
21.	False	A credit is simply a shorthand way of saying that there is an increase in a liability or owners' equity account or a decrease in an asset account.
22.	True	
23.	False	A T account is so called because it is in the shape of a T.
24.	True	
25.	True	
26.	False	The increase in cash equals the reduction in accounts receivable, so the net effect on total assets is zero.
27.	False	Stockholders' equity is unaffected by a bond issue.
28.	False	The net effect on total assets is zero and the current ratio does not change.
29.	False	Since liabilities are unaffected by the stock issue, but total assets increase, the debt-to-total-assets ratio increases.
30.	True	

Multiple Choice

31. c
32. b
33. b
34. a
35. c
36. c
37. d
38. a
39. b
40. a
41. b
42. d
43. a
44. a
45. c

Problems 46 and 47

ECONOMIC EVENT	ACCOUNTING ENTRY	SOURCE DOCUMENTS	INFORMATION
1.	F	Receipt from post office	Total cost of stamps used
2.	H		
3.	B	Checks received from stockholders	Total of checks received
4.	A	Checks received from bondholders	Total of checks received
5.	A	Invoice from supplier	Amount of purchase
6.	G	Receipt from vendor	Cost of computer
7.	H		
8.	F	Lists of bondholders and interest paid to each	Total interest paid
9.	F	Lists of stockholders and dividends paid to each	Total dividends paid
10.	D	Invoice or statement from creditor	Amount of invoice or statement

Problem 48

1.

	Assets			=	Liabilities +	Owners' Equity	
	Cash	*Computer*	*Accounts Receivable*		*Accounts Payable*	*Capital Stock*	*Retained Earnings*
a)	$+15,000	$	$		$	$ +15,000	$
Bal.	15,000			=		15,000	
b)	-2,000						-2,000
Bal.	13,000			=		15,000	-2,000
c)	+15,000		+5,000				+20,000
Bal.	28,000		5,000	=		15,000	18,000
d)					+500		-500
Bal.	28,000		5,000	=	500	15,000	17,500
e)	-2,000	+2,000					
Bal.	26,000	2,000	5,000	=	500	15,000	17,500
f)	-15,000						-15,000
Bal.	11,000	2,000	5,000	=	500	15,000	2,500

Trial balance on January 31, 1997	**Debit**	**Credit**
Cash	$11,000	
Computer	2,000	
Accounts receivable	5,000	
Accounts payable		$ 500
Capital stock		15,000
Retained earnings		2,500
Totals	**$18,000**	**$18,000**

2. **Income statement for the month of January 1997**

Service revenues		$20,000
Costs and expenses:		
Salary expense	$15,000	
Rent expense	2,000	
Stationery expense	500	
Total expenses		17,500
Net income		$2,500

Balance sheet on January 31, 1997

Cash	$11,000	Accounts payable		$ 500
Accounts receivable	5,000	*Stockholders' equity*		
Current assets	16,000	Capital stock	$15,000	
Computer	2,000	Retained earnings	2,500	
				17,500
Total assets	$18,000	**Total liabilities and stockholders' equity**		$18,000

The income statement shows a small positive net income after the owners' salaries have been paid. The future viability of the enterprise depends on whether or not revenues will grow so that this level of salary payments can be maintained. If these salaries cannot be paid from future revenues, the owners will have to decide whether the salary payments they are receiving from the new company are comparable with what they could earn elsewhere. If they are, then they should probably accept an alternative job offer; if they are not, they should consider reducing the salaries they are receiving from the company to a level comparable to their alternative employment.

Critical Thinking Problem 49

The following are the corrected entries for Pacioli for the year ended 12/31/97:

		Debit	Credit
1.	Cash	250,000	
	Capital stock		250,000
	Receipt of cash in exchange for stock issue		
2.	Software inventory	180,000	
	Accounts payable		180,000
	Purchase of software inventory on credit		
3.	Office furniture	36,000	
	Cash		36,000
	Purchase of furniture for cash		
4.	Accounts payable	150,000	
	Cash		150,000
	Cash payment to creditors		
5.	Rent expense	60,000	
	Cash		60,000
	Cash payment for rent		

6.	Cash	80,000	
	Accounts receivable	320,000	
	Sales		400,000
	Cash and receivables from sales		
7.	Cash	70,000	
	Accounts receivable		70,000
	Cash received from accounts receivable		
8.	Wages and salaries expense	62,000	
	Cash		62,000
	Cash paid for wages and salaries		
9.	Utilities expense	10,000	
	Cash		10,000
	Cash paid for utilities		

CASH

	Debit		Credit
1.	250,000	3.	36,000
6.	80,000	4.	150,000
7.	70,000	5.	60,000
		8.	62,000
		9.	10,000
e.b.	82,000		

CAPITAL STOCK

	Debit		Credit
		1.	250,000

ACCOUNTS PAYABLE

	Debit		Credit
4.	150,000	2.	180,000
		e.b.	30,000

RENT EXPENSE

	Debit		Credit
5.	60,000		

OFFICE FURNITURE

	Debit		Credit
3.	36,000		

ACCOUNTS RECEIVABLE

	Debit		Credit
6.	320,000	7.	70,000
e.b.	250,000		

UTILITIES EXPENSE

	Debit		Credit
9.	10,000		

WAGES EXPENSE

	Debit		Credit
8.	62,000		

SOFTWARE INVENTORY

	Debit		Credit
2.	180,000		

SALES

	Debit		Credit
		6.	400,000

Trial Balance on 12/31/97	**Debit**	**Credit**
Cash	82,000	
Accounts receivable	250,000	
Software inventory	180,000	
Office furniture	36,000	
Accounts payable		30,000
Capital stock		250,000
Sales		400,000
Rent expense	60,000	
Wages expense	62,000	
Utilities expense	10,000	
	$680,000	$680,000

Chapter 4

Income Measurement and Accrual Accounting

This chapter continues the exploration of the accounting process started in Chapter 3 by considering how income is measured and accounted for. You have two overall goals in this chapter. First, understand the conceptual framework for measuring income and how, within that framework, accounting for income is carried out. Second, review the entire accounting process, called the accounting cycle, from the initial step of recording an event through to the final step of preparing financial statements.

Learning Objectives

LO 1 Explain the significance of recognition and measurement in the preparation and use statements.
LO 2 Explain the difference between the cash, and accrual basis of accounting.
LO 3 Describe the revenue recognition principle and explain its application in various situations
LO 4 Describe the matching principle and the various methods for recognizing revenue.
LO 5 Identify the four major types of adjustments, and determine their impact on the accounting
LO 6 Explain the steps in the accounting cycle and the significance of each step.
LO 7 Explain why and how closing entries are made at the end of the period.
LO 8 Understand how to use a worksheet as the basis for preparing financial statements.

Key Textbook Exhibits

Exhibit 4-3 shows the income statement and partial cash flow statement for the Glengarry Health Club. Note how the cash measure of performance differs from the accrual-based measure, and make sure you understand the reason for the difference between them.

Exhibit 4-4 gives an illustration of the relationship between costs, assets, and expenses. When costs are incurred, assets are created and the use of the assets generates expenses. For example, a piece of equipment will be used over several periods, and spreading the cost of that asset over the asset's useful life (through charging depreciation) results in depreciation expense for each period.

Exhibit 4-5 summarizes the types of adjustments that are necessary to implement the accrual basis of accounting. Make sure you fully understand these.

Exhibit 4-7 summarizes the steps in the complete accounting cycle. Note that these steps are carried out in every period for which financial statements are prepared, and that the cycle is continually repeated repeatedly.

Review of Key Concepts

LO 1 In measuring income, consideration must be given to both recognition and measurement. **Recognition** refers to the process by which accountants depict the effects of economic events on the entity. Implicit in the process of recognition is the need for accountants to choose which economic events to recognize.

Once an event is recognized, it is then necessary to **measure** it, to quantify its impact on the entity. In measuring assets, two conceptual issues must be addressed:

- *The basis of measurement must be decided.* Two possible measures of value are **historical cost** (the original cost of the item) and **current value** (the amount that could be received now if the asset were sold). The choice between them involves a trade-off between reliability and relevance - historical cost is more reliable, but current value is likely to be more relevant to many decisions.
- *The monetary unit may not have a stable value.* Inflation, or a rise in the general level of prices in the economy, may result in distortions in the accounting numbers reported.

Test Your Understanding!

Question: A company owns two pieces of land that both appear in its balance sheet at historical cost. One piece of land was bought twenty years ago, the other last year, and for each, the company paid $100,000. Both pieces of land are therefore shown in the balance sheet at $100,000. Does this mean that they are equally valuable today?

Answer: Probably not. Land that was bought twenty years ago is unlikely to be worth $100,000 today. Inflation (an increase in the general price level) could have increased its value over twenty years, and, in addition, there could have been increases or decreases in its value that were related to the particular piece of land (development potential, discovery of oil, deterioration in the area, etc.). Consequently, the historical costs that appear in the balance sheet cannot be used as reliable measures of current value.

LO 2 The **measurement of income** provides a way to communicate information about how the business has performed over the period. Two possible ways of measuring income are the **accrual basis** and the **cash basis**. The two methods differ in when revenue and expenses are recognized. For an income statement prepared on the cash basis, revenues and expenses are recognized when the associated cash is received or paid. For an income statement prepared on an accrual basis, revenue is recognized when it is earned, and expense is recognized when it is incurred.

LO 3 Under the accrual basis of income measurement, revenues are recognized according to the **principle of revenue recognition**, which requires that two conditions must be met. First, the revenues must have been earned; i.e., the costs associated with generating the revenues must have been incurred or be capable of being reliably estimated. Second, the revenues must have been realized or be realizable; i.e., cash or claims to cash must have been received in exchange for the goods or service.

LO 4 Under the **matching principle**, costs for a period are matched against the revenues they have helped to generate during that period. The determining factor, therefore, in charging an expense in any period is whether it can be matched against revenue. Expenses can come from two sources: from using an asset and from incurring a liability.

Test Your Understanding!

Question: A retail store has the following information about sales of Product A for January 1995:

Sales to customers on credit (no cash was received in January)	$20,000
Cash sales to customers	$10,000
Inventory of Product A - January 1, 1995	$0
Cash purchases during January	$40,000
Inventory of Product A - January 31, 1995	$10,000

How much revenue would be recognized under the cash basis of income recognition? How much under the accrual basis? What expenses would be recognized under each basis of income recognition?

Answer:

	Cash basis	Accrual basis
Revenues	$10,000	$30,000
Expenses	$40,000	$30,000

Under the cash basis of accounting, only the cash received for sales would be recognized. Under the accrual basis, all sales would be recognized provided (1) the costs associated with generating the revenues have been incurred or can be reliably estimated and (2) claims to cash have been received. The expenses recognized under each method would also vary. Under the cash basis, all cash paid for purchases ($40,000) is charged as an expense for the month; under the accrual basis, the matching principle results in only those goods that were sold during the period being expensed. Goods on hand at the end of the period ($10,000) are not, so the expense (called cost of goods sold) is the difference between the goods purchased and the closing inventory ($40,000 - $10,000).

LO 5 **Adjustments** are journal entries made at the end of the accounting period that ensure the proper matching of costs and revenues for companies using the accrual basis of accounting. They are not necessary for companies using a cash basis. There are four distinct types of adjustments corresponding to when the cash for an expense or revenue is paid or received during the accounting period. Note that these adjustments never involve the cash account.

Deferred expense

When cash is paid for an expense before the expense is incurred, an asset account is created at the time of payment. At the end of the period, this asset must be reduced (credited) and an expense account increased (debited) by the amount of the cost that has expired over the period. The adjusting entry involves

	Debit	Credit
Debit expense	xxx	
Credit asset		xxx

To illustrate, Pacioli Company made a cash payment of $500 on July 1, 1997, to pay the premium on a one-year fire insurance policy. On that date, the following journal entry was made to record the payment. The entry resulted in the creation of an asset account, prepaid insurance.

		Debit	Credit
7/1/97	Prepaid insurance	500	
	Cash		500

On December 31, 1997, at the end of the accounting period, an adjusting entry must be made to reduce the asset account by the amount of the insurance policy used up during the accounting period. In this case, the company has used six months of a twelve-month policy and therefore exactly half, or $250, of the policy benefit has been used. The adjusting entry both reduces the asset and increases (or creates) an insurance expense account.

12/31/97	Insurance expense	250	
	Prepaid insurance		250

Deferred revenue

Similarly, when cash is received before revenue is earned, a liability account is created. At the end of the period, the liability must be reduced (debited) and a revenue account increased (credited) by the amount of the revenue that has been earned during the period. The adjusting entry involves

Debit liability	xxx	
Credit revenue		xxx

Pacioli Company received $25,000 from a customer on December 1, 1997 for work that was to be done over the next two months. The following journal entry was made to record the receipt of cash. Note that the journal entry creates a liability account called "revenues received in advance."

12/1/97	Cash	25,000	
	Revenue received in advance		25,000

On December 31, 1997, exactly half of the work has been completed and therefore an adjusting entry is needed to record the amount of revenue that has been earned. The adjusting entry both reduces the liability account and increases (or creates) the revenue account.

12/31/97	Revenue received in advance	12,500	
	Revenue		12,500

Accrued liability

When expense is incurred before cash is paid, an entry to record the amount owed must be made. A liability account must therefore be increased (credited), and an expense account must be increased (debited) The adjusting entry involves

Debit expense	xxx	
Credit liability		xxx

Pacioli Company owes its employees $2,000 in unpaid wages on December 31, 1997. The adjusting entry creates a liability account called wages payable and increases (or creates) wages expense.

12/31/97	Wages expense	2,000	
	Wages payable		2,000

Accrued asset

When revenue is earned before cash is received, an entry to record the amount to be received must be made. An asset account is therefore increased (debited), and a revenue account is increased (credited). The adjusting entry involves

Debit asset	xxx	
Credit revenue		xxx

On December 1, 1997, Pacioli Company accepted a $10,000 note receivable from a customer. Interest on the note is 6% per annum, and it will be paid on the maturity of the note on February 1, 1995. Interest on the note for the month of December has not been paid. The adjusting entry to record the interest due on the note increases (or creates) an interest receivable account and an interest revenue account.

12/31/97	Interest receivable	50	
	Interest revenue		50
	(6% x 10,000 x 1/12)		

Adjusting entries are extremely important in testing your understanding of the logic of the accounting process. Make sure you fully understand them.

Test Your Understanding!

Question: Can you identify two features that are common to the four types of adjustments?

Answer: All four types of adjustments involve a balance sheet account (asset or liability) and an income statement account (revenue or expense). In addition, none of the four entries involves cash.

LO 6 The accounting cycle is the name given to the entire accounting process, which starts with the recording of an economic event in a source document and ends with the preparation of a set of financial statements. The steps in the accounting cycle can be represented as follows:

	Step	Performed
1.	Collect and analyze information from source documents	Continuously
2.	Journalize transactions	Continuously
3.	Post transactions to accounts in the ledger (daily or weekly)	Periodically
4.	Prepare worksheet	End of period
5.	Prepare financial statements	End of period
6.	Record and post adjustments	End of period
7.	Close the accounts	End of period

Step 7 involves closing the accounts so that financial statements can be prepared. A key element in this last step is deciding which accounts should be reported in the income statement and which in the balance sheet. Balance sheet accounts are called **real accounts** because they are permanent in nature. Revenue and expense accounts, which are reported in the income statement, are called **nominal or temporary accounts** because they are closed at the end of the period. The closing process results in both the net income or loss for the period being calculated, and return to zero of the balances in all temporary accounts ready for the start of the new cycle.

LO 7 At the end of the accounting cycle, **closing entries** are used (1) to close all revenue and expense accounts (**nominal** or **temporary** accounts) to an income summary account so that the temporary accounts start the new period with zero balances, and (2) to transfer the net income or loss from the income summary to the retained earnings account. The steps in the closing process are as follows:

Step 1 Close revenue and expense accounts to income summary:

Debit revenue accounts	xxx	
Credit income summary		xxx
Debit income summary	xxx	
Credit expense accounts		xxx

Note that if revenues exceed expenses, the company has positive net income and the balance on income summary at this point is a credit; if expenses exceed revenues, the company has a net loss and the balance on income summary at this point is a debit.

Step 2 Close income summary to retained earnings:

If the company has made a profit:

Debit income summary	xxx	
Credit retained earnings		xxx

Or, if the company has made a loss:

Debit retained earnings	xxx	
Credit income summary		xxx

Step 3 Close the dividend account to retained earnings:

Debit retained earnings	xxx	
Credit dividends		xxx

To illustrate the use of closing entries, assume that the following is an extract from the adjusted trial balance of Platox Company on December 31, 1997.

	$ Debit	**$ Credit**
Retained Earnings		50,000
Sales		200,000
Cost of Goods Sold	150,000	
Wages Expense	20,000	
Utilities Expense	5,000	
Rent Expense	3,000	
Dividend	10,000	

Step 1 Close revenue and expense accounts to income summary:

		Debit	Credit
12/31/97	Sales	200,000	
	Cost of goods sold		150,000
	Wages expense		20,000
	Utilities expense		5,000
	Rent expense		3,000
	Income summary		22,000

Step 2 Close income summary to retained earnings:

		Debit	Credit
12/31/97	Income summary	22,000	
	Retained earnings		22,000

Step 3 Close the dividend account to retained earnings:

		Debit	Credit
12/31/97	Retained earnings	10,000	
	Dividend		10,000

The T account for retained earnings is as follows:

RETAINED EARNINGS

12/31/97	10,000	b.b.	50,000
		12/31/97	22,000
		e.b.	62,000

LO 8 Worksheets can be used to prepare financial statements by recording adjusting and closing entries. Typically, but not necessarily, worksheets have ten columns: two for the unadjusted trial balance, two for recording adjusting entries, two for the adjusted trial balance, two for recording the closing entries, and two for the balance sheet.

Review of Key Terms

Accrual basis	A system of accounting in which revenues are recognized when earned and expenses when incurred.
Accrued liability	A liability resulting from the recognition of an expense before the payment of cash.
Accrued revenue	An asset resulting from the recognition of revenue before the receipt of cash.
Adjusting entries	Journal entries made at the end of a period by companies using the accrual basis of accounting.
Cash basis	A system of accounting that recognizes revenue when cash is received and expenses when cash is paid.
Closing entries	Journal entries made at the end of a period to return the balance in all nominal accounts to zero and to transfer the net income or loss and the dividends of the period to retained earnings.
Current value	The amount of cash or cash equivalent that could be received now by selling an asset.
Deferred expense	An asset resulting from the payment of cash before incurring the expense.
Deferred revenue	A liability resulting from the receipt of cash before the recognition of revenue.
Expenses	The use of assets or incurring of liabilities in delivering goods and services.
Historical cost	The original cost of an asset.
Installment method	The method by which revenues are recognized at the time cash is collected.
Matching principle	The association of revenue for a period with all the costs expended in generating that revenue.
Nominal accounts	The name given to revenue, expense, and dividend accounts because they are temporary and are closed at the end of the period.
Percentage-of-completion method	The method used by contractors to recognize revenues before the completion of a long-term contract.
Production method	The method whereby revenue is recognized when a commodity is produced rather than when it is sold.
Real accounts	The name given to balance sheet accounts because they are permanent and are not closed at the end of the period.
Recognition	The process of recording an item in the financial statements as an asset, liability, revenue, expense, or the like.
Revenue recognition principle	Revenues are recognized on the income statement when they are realized, or realizable, and earned.
Revenues	Increases in assets or reductions in liabilities from delivering or producing goods or services.
The accounting cycle	A series of steps performed each period that results in the preparation of a set of financial statements.

Practice Test
Questions and Problems

Complete each of the following statements:

LO 3 1. The principle of revenue recognition requires that revenues must have been both ______________ and ______________.

LO 4 2. Under the ______________, costs for a period are matched against the revenues they helped to generate during the period.

LO 5 3. The four types of adjustments are ______________, ______________, ______________, and ______________.

LO 6 4. The entire accounting process from the recording of an economic event to the preparation of financial statements is called the ______________.

LO 3 5. ______________ is the method used by contractors to recognize revenues before the completion of a long-term contract.

LO 1 6. ______________ is the original cost of an asset; ______________ is the amount of cash or cash equivalent that could be received now by selling the asset.

LO 6 7. Financial statements prepared for any period less than a year are called ______________.

LO 1 8. ______________ is the process of recording an item in the financial statements as an asset, liability, equity, revenue, or expense.

LO 5 9. Adjusting entries are ______________ transactions and therefore never involve ______________.

LO 5 10. ______________ is used to refer to a situation where cash has either been paid or received, but where recognition of the revenue or expense is delayed to a later time.

LO 4 11. ______________ involve the use of assets or incurring of liabilities in delivering goods and services.

LO 3 12. ______________ is used to refer to a situation in which no cash has yet been paid or received, but it is necessary to recognize an expense and the associated liability, or a revenue and the associated asset.

LO 3 13. ______________ is the name given to allocating the cost of a long-term asset over its life.

LO 6 14. ______________ is the name given to revenue, expense, and dividend accounts because they are temporary and are closed at the end of the period.

LO 1 15. The ______________ is the original cost of an asset.

Indicate whether each of the following statements is true or false:

LO 5 16. Adjustments are concerned with ensuring that the cash account is up to date at the end of the period.

LO 7 17. An adjusting entry does not include an entry to the cash account.

LO 1 18. Current value is both more relevant and more reliable than historical cost.

LO 5 19. Deferred expense is an asset that results from the payment of cash before the expense is incurred.

LO 3 20. Expenses may come both from using an asset and by incurring a liability.

LO 7 21. Failing to adjust for depreciation in a period will overstate net income in that period and understate total assets at the end of the period.

LO 2 22. If a company has positive net income during a period, its retained earnings balance on the balance sheet will increase from the previous year.

LO 4 23. If a company only ever makes cash sales, then revenues and reported income are identical under both the cash and accrual bases of accounting.

LO 1 24. Inflation may have a significant impact on the validity of reported income.

LO 7 25. Revenue and expense accounts are also known as nominal or permanent accounts.

LO 7 26. Statements prepared monthly, quarterly, or at other intervals less than a year in duration are called internal statements, since they are not provided to stockholders.

LO 3 27. The figure for revenue or sales in the financial statements measures the cash received from customers during the accounting period.

LO 6 28. The only steps in the accounting cycle that are carried out continuously throughout the accounting period are collecting and analyzing information from source documents, and journalizing transactions.

LO 3 29. The percentage of completion method is the method by which revenues are recognized at the time cash is collected.

LO 3 30. The revenue recognition method by which revenues are recognized at the time a commodity is produced rather than when it is sold is called the installment method.

For each of the following questions, circle the alternative that best answers the question:

LO 3 31. The following information is available for Company A during March 1995:

Cash sales to customers	$150,000
Inventory of Product A - March 1, 1995	$0
Cash purchases during March	$120,000
Inventory of Product A - March 31, 1995	$20,000

The net income reported under the accrual basis of accounting for Company A for the month of March, 1995 was

a) $150,000
b) $120,000
c) $30,000
d) $50,000

LO 2 32. On the morning of June 27, 1997, you purchased a sweater (that was originally priced at $120) on sale for $50 cash. In the afternoon, you accepted an offer of $80 for it, which you will receive on July 1, 1997. You are certain that you will receive the money. For the day of June 27, 1997, your net income and cash flow, respectively, were

a) $30 and $30
b) $70 and $30
c) $0 and -$50
d) $30 and -$50

LO 6 33. After closing is complete,

a) all temporary accounts have a zero balance.
b) the net income or net loss and the dividends for the period have been transferred to the retained earnings account.
c) all accounts with a non-zero balance will be communicated in the balance sheet.
d) All of the above are correct.

LO 6 34. The net income for the period is $400, and dividends paid amount to $600. Which of the following statements is TRUE?

a) The company paid out more in dividends than the cash it generated from its operations.
b) The company paid out more in dividends than it earned in income.
c) The company paid out less in dividends than it earned in income.
d) The company paid out less in dividends than the cash it generated from its operations.

LO 6 35. A revenue or sales account is

a) a temporary account that is closed at the end of the accounting period.
b) communicated on the income statement.
c) an increase in retained earnings.
d) All of the above are correct.

LO 6 36. Which of the following accounts is closed at the end of the accounting period but is NOT found in the income statement?

a) Sales revenue
b) Accounts receivable
c) Dividends paid
d) Rent expense

LO 5 37. Which of the following could NOT be an adjustment?

a) Increase insurance expense, decrease prepaid insurance
b) Increase rent expense, decrease prepaid rent
c) Decrease accounts payable, decrease cash
d) Increase depreciation expense, increase accumulated depreciation

LO 5 38. During the adjusting process, failing to enter an adjustment for supplies inventory used during the period would

a) overstate the liabilities and understate net income.
b) understate liabilities and overstate net income.
c) overstate assets and net income.
d) understate assets and net income.

LO 2 39. During 1997, Smite Company paid $12,000 to its landlord for rent. On January 1, 1997, prepaid rent was $3,000 and on December 31, 1997, prepaid rent was $4,000. Rent expense for 1997 was

a) $10,000
b) $11,000
c) $12,000
d) $13,000

LO 4 40. Which of the following statements is TRUE?

a) For commodities, revenue may be recognized before the point of sale.
b) For installment sales, revenue is recognized before cash has been received.
c) For long-term contracts, revenue should be recognized when cash payments are received from the customer.
d) For franchising operations, revenue from initial franchise fees may be recognized before the franchiser has made substantial performance of its obligations.

LO 5 41. Ceres Company fails to make an adjusting entry for depreciation at the end of the accounting period. The effect of this is that

a) the current ratio at the end of the period is overstated.
b) the debt-to-equity ratio is overstated.
c) the profit margin is overstated.
d) both b) and c) are correct.

LO 5 42. During 1997, Smilla Company's income statement reported salary expense of $28,000. On January 1, 1997, the balance on the salaries payable account was $8,000, and on December 31, 1997, the balance was $4,000. The cash paid in salaries during 1997 was

a) $24,000
b) $32,000
c) $36,000
d) $32,000

LO 5 43. The net book value of Jura Corporation's plant and machinery was $20,000 on January 1, 1997, and was $30,000 on December 31, 1997. During the year the company bought plant and machinery for $14,000, and did not sell any of its existing plant or machinery. The depreciation expense for 1997 was

a) $4,000
b) $24,000
c) $16,000
d) $6,000

LO 5 44. Isaly Company's balance on its inventory account on January 1, 1997 was $3,000, and on December 31, 1997 it was $1,000. All purchases were for cash, and it paid $54,000 cash to its suppliers during the year. The cost of goods sold on its income statement was

a) $52,000
b) $56,000
c) $55,000
d) $57,000

LO 5 45. Adjusting entries are an application of

a) the revenue recognition principle.
b) conservatism.
c) the matching principle.
d) relevance.

Answer each of the following problems:

LO 5,6 46. On January 1, 1997, Drymen Company was incorporated as a management-consulting firm. During the year the following summary events occurred:

1. Stockholders invested $170,000 cash, in exchange for capital stock.
2. Two years' rent of $19,200 was paid in advance on January 1, 1997.
3. Supplies of $3,500 were purchased on credit and used immediately.
4. Office furniture, fixtures, and equipment were purchased for $30,000 cash.
5. Fees earned during the year were $115,000, of which $70,000 was on credit and the remainder was for cash.
6. Utilities expense for the year amounted to $1,700 and was paid in cash.
7. Salaries of $33,000 were paid in cash during the year.
8. On July 1, the firm purchased a comprehensive three-year insurance policy for $6,000 cash.
9. The firm provided services of $15,000 for a client. These fees are in addition to the fees identified in item 5. For these services, Drymen accepted a $15,000 note receivable on August 1, 1997. The note has an interest rate of 10%, and both the interest and the capital are due to be paid in one year.
10. Drymen Company paid in full for the supplies purchased in item 3.
11. Legal expenses of $1,500 were paid in cash.
12. Cash collections on accounts receivable were $35,000.
13. Cash dividends of $10,000 were paid.

Additional information:

a) Interest on the note receivable must be accrued.
b) The necessary amount of prepaid insurance must be written off.
c) Prepaid rent must be written off.
d) The office furniture, fixtures, and equipment have a five-year life and zero salvage value.
e) Salaries of $2,300 were earned but unpaid at year-end.
f) Fees of $2,000 were earned at year-end, for which the receivable and the revenue have not yet been recorded.

Required

1. Prepare the journal entries for the year, and post them to T accounts.
2. Prepare an unadjusted trial balance.
3. Prepare the adjusting entries, and post them to the ledger accounts.
4. Prepare an adjusted trial balance.
5. Prepare closing entries, and post them to the ledger accounts.
6. Prepare a post-closing trial balance.
7. Prepare an income statement and classified balance sheet as of December 31, 1997.

LO 5 47. A company is drawing up its annual accounts for the year ended December 31, 1997. The following information must be taken into account:

a) The company owns equipment that originally cost $50,000 three years ago. The company depreciates equipment over a five-year period, assuming straight line depreciation, and zero salvage value.

b) On October 1, 1997, the company contracted to carry out maintenance on an empty building for one year. Payment in advance of $5,000 for the first six months of the contract was received on October 1, 1997. It was expected that revenue would be earned evenly over the six months.

c) Annual property taxes of $4,800 are due to be paid on January 31, 1998. The taxes relate to the year February 1, 1997, to January 31, 1998.

d) The company owns $100,000 of corporate bonds, and a full year's interest at 6% will be received on March 31, 1998. No entry has yet been made for this interest receipt.

Required

1. Identify what type of adjustment is needed for each item.

2. Show the effect of each adjustment on the accounting equation.

3. Give the adjusting journal entries.

Critical Thinking Problem

LO 5 **48.** What would be the effect on the reported income and balance sheet if the adjustments for the Pacioli Company in **LO 5** on pages 65 and 66 above were not made before the closing process? Analyze the impact using the following table. Note that if net income is overstated or understated, then owners' equity will also be overstated or understated by the same amount, since owners' equity is contributed capital plus retained earnings.

	Effect on Income Statement	Effect on Balance Sheet
A.	Revenue: Expense: Net income:	Assets: Liabilities: Owners' equity:
B.	Revenue: Expense: Net income:	Assets: Liabilities: Owners' equity:
C.	Revenue: Expense: Net income:	Assets: Liabilities: Owners' equity:
D.	Revenue: Expense: Net income:	Assets: Liabilities: Owners' equity:

Solutions

Fill in the Blanks

1. earned, realized (or realizable)
2. matching principle
3. accrued liability, accrued asset, deferred expenses, deferred revenues
4. accounting cycle
5. percentage-of-completion
6. historical cost, current value
7. interim statements
8. recognition
9. internal, cash
10. deferral
11. expenses
12. accrual
13. depreciation
14. nominal or temporary
15. historical cost

True/False

		COMMENT/EXPLANATION
16.	False	Adjustments ensure the correct application of the accrual basis of accounting.
17.	True	
18.	False	Since it can be derived from the original transaction, historical cost is more reliable than current value. However, for many decisions, current value is more relevant than historical cost since it reflects current economic conditions.
19.	True	
20.	True	
21.	False	Failing to adjust for depreciation will overstate both net income and net assets.
22.	False	If dividends in the year are greater than net income, the retained earnings balance will decline.
23.	False	A company with only cash sales will report identical revenues under both the cash and accrual bases of accounting. However, the expenses under both methods may differ, and so reported income under the two methods may be different.
24.	True	
25.	False	Revenue and expense accounts are nominal or temporary accounts.
26.	False	Statements provided covering a period of less than a year are called interim statements.
27.	False	Revenue is the amount of sales made either for cash or on credit.
28.	True	
29.	False	The percentage-of-completion method recognizes revenues in proportion to the relationship between incurred costs and total project costs.
30.	False	The production method is the revenue recognition method used when revenues from commodities are recognized at the point of production rather than sale.

Multiple Choice

31.	d	39.	b
32.	d	40.	a
33.	d	41.	d
34.	b	42.	a
35.	d	43.	a
36.	c	44.	b
37.	c	45.	c
38.	c		

Problem 46

Part 1

	Account	Debit	Credit
(1)	Cash	170,000	
	Capital stock		170,000
(2)	Prepaid rent	19,200	
	Cash		19,200
(3)	Supplies expense	3,500	
	Accounts payable		3,500
(4)	Furniture, fixtures & equipment	30,000	
	Cash		30,000
(5)	Cash	45,000	
	Accounts receivable	70,000	
	Sales		115,000
(6)	Utilities expense	1,700	
	Cash		1,700
(7)	Salaries expense	33,000	
	Cash		33,000
(8)	Prepaid insurance	6,000	
	Cash		6,000
(9)	Note receivable	15,000	
	Sales		15,000
(10)	Accounts payable	3,500	
	Cash		3,500
(11)	Legal expenses	1,500	
	Cash		1,500

	Account	Debit	Credit
(12)	Cash	35,000	
	Accounts receivable		35,000
(13)	Dividends	10,000	
	Cash		10,000

3. Adjusting entries

	Account	Debit	Credit
(a)	Interest receivable	625	
	Interest revenue		625
	(5/12 x 10% x 15,000 = $625)		
(b)	Insurance expense	1,000	
	Prepaid insurance		1,000
	(1/2 x 1/3 x 6,000)		
(c)	Rent expense	9,600	
	Prepaid rent		9,600
	(19,200 x 1/2)		
(d)	Depreciation expense	6,000	
	Accumulated depreciation		6,000
	(1/5 x 30,000)		
(e)	Salaries expense	2,300	
	Salaries payable		2,300
(f)	Accounts receivable	2,000	
	Sales		2,000

5. Closing entries

	Account	Debit	Credit
(i)	Sales	132,000	
	Interest revenue	625	
	Rent expense		9,600
	Utilities expense		1,700
	Salary expense		35,300
	Insurance expense		1,000
	Supplies expense		3,500
	Legal expense		1,500
	Depreciation		6,000
	Income summary		74,025
(ii)	Income summary	74,025	
	Retained earnings		74,025
(iii)	Retained earnings	10,000	
	Dividends		10,000

CASH

	Debit		Credit
1.	170,000	2.	19,200
5.	45,000	4.	30,000
12.	35,000	6.	1,700
		7.	33,000
		8.	6,000
		10.	3,500
		11.	1,500
		13.	10,000
e.b.	145,100		

ACCOUNTS PAYABLE

	Debit		Credit
10.	3,500	3.	3,500

FURNITURE

	Debit		Credit
4.	30,000		

UTILITIES EXPENSE

	Debit		Credit
6.	1,700	(i)	1,700

INTEREST REVENUE

	Debit		Credit
(i)	625	a)	625

LEGAL EXPENSE

	Debit		Credit
11.	1,500	(i)	1,500

DEPRECIATION EXPENSE

	Debit		Credit
d)	6,000	(i)	6,000

NOTE RECEIVABLE

	Debit		Credit
9.	15,000		

PREPAID RENT

	Debit		Credit
2.	19,200	c)	9,600
e.b.	9,600		

CAPITAL STOCK

	Debit		Credit
		1.	170,000

SALES

	Debit		Credit
		5.	115,000
		9.	15,000
		f)	2,000
(i)	132,000	e.b	132,000

RENT EXPENSE

	Debit		Credit
c)	9,600	(i)	9,600

ACCOUNTS RECEIVABLE

	Debit		Credit
5.	70,000	12.	35,000
f)	2,000		
e.b.	37,000		

SALARIES EXPENSE

	Debit		Credit
7.	33,000		
e)	2,300		
e.b.	35,300	(i)	35,300

INSURANCE EXPENSE

	Debit		Credit
b)	1,000	(i)	1,000

SUPPLIES EXPENSE

	Debit		Credit
3.	3,500	(i)	3,500

ACCUMULATED DEPRECIATION

	Debit		Credit
		d)	6,000

INTEREST RECEIVABLE

	Debit		Credit
a)	625		

PREPAID INSURANCE

	Debit		Credit
8.	6,000	b)	1,000
e.b.	5,000		

SALARIES PAYABLE

		e)	2,300

DIVIDENDS

13.	10,000	(iii)	10,000

RETAINED EARNINGS

(iii)	10,000	(ii)	74,025
		e.b.	64,025

INCOME SUMMARY

(ii)	74,025	(i)	74,025

Calculations

(a) 5/12 x 10% x 15,000 = $625

(b) 1/2 x 1/3 x 6,000 = $1,000

(c) 19,200 x 1/2 = $9,600

(d) 1/5 x 30,000 = $6,000

Income Statement for year ended December 31, 1997

Sales		$132,000
Interest revenue		625
		132,625
Expenses		
Supplies	$3,500	
Salaries	35,300	
Rent	9,600	
Utilities	1,700	
Insurance	1,000	
Depreciation	6,000	
Legal	1,500	
		58,600
Net Income		$74,025

Statement of retained earnings for year ended December 31, 1997

Opening retained earnings balance	-0-
Net income for current year	74,025
	74,025
Less dividends	10,000
Closing retained earnings balance	$64,025

Balance sheet as of December 31, 1997

Current assets			
Cash		$ 145,100	
Accounts receivable		37,000	
Interest receivable		625	
Note receivable		15,000	
Prepaid rent		9,600	
Prepaid insurance		5,000	
Total current assets			$ 212,325
Furniture, fixture & equipment	$ 30,000		
Less accumulated depreciation	(6,000)		24,000
			$236,325
Liabilities & stockholders' equity			
Current liabilities			
Salaries payable			$ 2,300
Stockholders' equity			
Capital stock		$ 170,000	
Retained earnings		64,025	
			234,025
			$236,325

Parts 2,4,6	Unadjusted		Adjusting entries		Adjusted		Closing entries		Post closing	
	Dr	Cr.	Dr	Cr.	Dr	Cr.	Dr	Cr.	Dr	Cr.
Furniture, fixtures & equipment	30,000				30,000				30,000	
Accumulated depreciation				6,000		6,000				6,000
Prepaid rent	19,200			9,600	9,600				9,600	
Prepaid insurance	6,000			1,000	5,000				5,000	
Accounts receivable	35,000		2,000		37,000				37,000	
Note receivable	15,000				15,000				15,000	
Interest receivable			625		625				625	
Cash	145,100				145,100				145,100	
Capital stock		170,000				170,000				170,000
Retained earnings							10,000	74,025		64,025
Dividends	10,000				10,000			10,000		
Accounts payable										
Salaries payable				2,300		2,300				2,300
Sales		130,000		2,000		132,000	132,000			
Interest revenue				625		625	625			
Rent expense			9,600		9,600			9,600		
Utilities expense	1,700				1,700			1,700		
Salary expense	33,000		2,300		35,300			35,300		
Insurance expense			1,000		1,000			1,000		
Supplies expense	3,500				3,500			3,500		
Legal expense	1,500				1,500			1,500		
Depreciation expense			6,000		6,000			6,000		
Income summary							74,025	74,025		
Total	300,000	300,000	21,525	21,525	310,925	310,925	216,650	216,650	242,325	242,325

Problem 47

1 and 2

Adjustment	**Type**	**Effect on accounting equation**				
		Assets	=	**Liabilities**	+	**Owners' equity**
a)	Deferred expense	- 10,000				- 10,000
b)	Deferred revenue			- 2,500		+ 2,500
c)	Accrued liability			+ 4,400		- 4,400
d)	Accrued asset	+ 4,500				+ 4,500

3

		Debit	Credit
a)	Depreciation expense	10,000	
	Accumulated depreciation		10,000
	To record depreciation for year to December 31, 1997		
b)	Unearned revenues	2,500	
	Maintenance revenues		2,500
	To record recognition of revenues received in advance		
c)	Property tax expense	4,400	
	Property tax payable		4,400
	To record property taxes due for eleven months to December 31, 1997		
d)	Interest receivable	4,500	
	Interest revenue		4,500
	To record interest revenue for nine months to December 31, 1997		

Critical Thinking Problem 48

The table below summarizes the impact on the income statement and balance sheet of failing to make the adjusting entries for Pacioli Company.

	Effect on Income Statement		Effect on Balance Sheet	
A.	Revenue:	no effect	Assets:	overstated by 250
	Expense:	understated by 250	Liabilities:	no effect
	Net income:	overstated by 250	Owners' equity:	overstated by 250
B.	Revenue:	understated by 12,500	Assets:	no effect
	Expense:	no effect	Liabilities:	overstated by 250
	Net income:	understated by 12,500	Owners' equity:	understated by 12,500
C.	Revenue:	no effect	Assets:	no effect
	Expense:	understated by 2,000	Liabilities:	understated by 2,000
	Net income:	overstated by 2,000	Owners' equity:	overstated by 2,000
D.	Revenue:	understated by 50	Assets:	understated by 50
	Expense:	no effect	Liabilities:	no effect
	Net income:	understated by 50	Owners' equity:	understated by 50

Chapter 5

Merchandise Accounting and Internal Control

This chapter discusses the accounting issues associated with inventory, particularly in relation to merchandising companies. The need for an efficient system of internal control to safeguard the assets of the company and ensure the validity of its financial reports is also discussed. Your overall objectives in this chapter are to understand the measurement and accounting issues associated with purchasing and sales, and to gain an understanding of the role and key elements of an internal control system.

Learning Objectives

LO 1 Understand how wholesalers and retailers account for sales of merchandise.
LO 2 Explain the differences between the periodic and perpetual inventory systems
LO 3 Understand how wholesalers and retailers account for cost of goods sold.
LO 4 Explain the importance of internal control to a business.
LO 5 Describe the basic internal control procedures.
LO 6 Describe the various documents used in recording purchases of merchandise and their role in controlling cash disbursements.

Key Textbook Exhibits

Exhibits 5-4 illustrates the cost of goods sold model for a merchandiser.

Exhibit 5-6 summarizes the issues related to transportation costs and transfer of title.

Exhibit 5-8 illustrates the types of business document needed for the purchasing function. Make sure you understand the role of each of the documents and how and where it fits into the entire purchasing process.

Review of Key Concepts

LO 1 For retailers and wholesalers, it is necessary when recording sales to recognize the impact of sales returns and allowances, trade and quantity discounts and credit terms on the total sales recorded.

- **Sales returns and allowances** are recorded in a separate *contra* revenue account. This account has a debit balance and allows the company to monitor the level of returns and allowances.
- **Trade discounts and quantity discounts**, unlike sales returns and allowances, are not recorded in the accounts, and the net amount is recorded as revenue.
- **Sales discounts** are offered by many companies to encourage early payment by customers. They can be accounted for in one of two ways. The gross method initially records sales at the gross amount. If a customer subsequently takes advantage of the discount, the amount of the discount is credited to a contra revenue account called sales discounts. For example, on July 1, 1997, a sale of $5,000 is made with terms that allow for a discount of 3% if payment is made within 10 days of the sale, and, if the discount is not taken, the full amount must be paid within 30 days. (Note that this is often written as 3/10, net 30.) If the company uses the gross method, the journal entries are as follows:

		Debit	Credit
7/1/97	Accounts receivable	5,000	
	Sales		5,000
	Sale of goods on account		

If the discount is taken and the customer pays on July 8, 1997:

		Debit	Credit
7/1/97	Cash	4,850	
	Sales discounts	150	
	Accounts receivable		5,000
	Receipt of cash for goods sold on account		

If the discount is not taken and the customer pays on July 31, 1997:

		Debit	Credit
7/31/97	Cash	5,000	
	Accounts receivable		5,000
	Receipt of cash for goods sold on account		

LO 1 The calculation for **cost of goods sold** for a retailer or wholesaler is as follows:

	Beginning inventory	Goods on hand at the beginning of the period
+	**Purchases**	Goods bought during the period
=	**Cost of goods available for sale**	
-	**Ending inventory**	Goods not sold during the period
=	**Cost of goods sold**	

LO 2 Inventory is accounted for under either the perpetual or the periodic inventory system.

- Under the **perpetual inventory system**, the inventory account is continually updated whenever a sale occurs. At the same time as the revenue associated with a sale is recorded, an entry is made which reduces the asset Inventory and increases the cost of goods sold. At any point during the accounting period, the inventory account balance represents the goods that are available for sale. For example, assume in the illustration above that the cost of the goods sold was $3,500. The following additional entry would be made when the sale of $5,000 was recorded:

		Debit	Credit
7/1/97	Cost of goods sold	3,500	
	Inventory		3,500
	Cost of goods sold for $5,000		

- Under the **periodic inventory system**, the inventory account is updated only once, at the end of the accounting period. It is necessary to open a separate purchases account in which all purchases made by the company are recorded. A physical count of goods is taken at the end of the period and the difference between the cost of goods available for sale (equal to purchases plus beginning inventory) and the cost of goods from the physical count is the figure used for cost of goods sold. The inventory account is then updated with the total purchases of the period and the ending inventory for the period. During the period therefore, the inventory account balance cannot be relied upon to provide the goods available for sale.

LO 3 For retailers and wholesalers, when recording purchases it is necessary to recognize the impact of purchase returns and allowances, purchase discounts, and transportation costs on the total purchases recorded.

- **Purchase returns and allowances** are recorded in a separate account, which is a contra account to the purchases account.
- **Purchase discounts** are accounted for under either the **gross method** or the **net method,** which parallel the methods used for sales discounts. To illustrate the gross method, assume that on December 1, 1997, Company Z buys $3,000 of consumable supplies on terms of 4/5, net 30. When the goods are purchased, the impact on the accounting equation is as follows

		Debit	Credit
12/1/97	Consumable expenses	3,000	
	Accounts payable		3,000
	Purchase of consumables on account		

If the discount is taken and the account is paid within five days:

		Debit	Credit
12/5/97	Accounts payable	3,000	
	Purchase discounts		120
	Cash		2,880
	Receipt of cash for goods sold on account		

- **Transportation costs** can be either the responsibility of the seller (the goods are FOB, or free on board, destination point) or the responsibility of the buyer (FOB shipping point). Where the transportation costs are the responsibility of the buyer, they must be added to the costs of the goods purchased. If they are FOB shipping point, they become the property of the buyer as soon as they leave the shipping point and are therefore included in the buyer's inventory at year-end. Similarly, where goods are in transit at year-end and are FOB destination point, they are not included in the buyer's inventory at year-end.

LO 4 An **internal control system** consists of the policies and procedures necessary to ensure that the entity's overall objective is being met by the safeguarding of its assets and the reliability of its accounting records. Management has the primary responsibility for the reliability of the financial statements and many companies employ a full-time internal audit staff to monitor and evaluate the internal control system. The independent public accountant's responsibility, on the other hand, is primarily to determine whether the accounts are presented fairly. The audit committee of the board of directors provides the contact between the stockholders and the external auditors.

LO 5,6 The **internal control structure** of an organization consists of three elements: the control environment, the accounting system, and internal control procedures. In addition, business documents are a key determinant in the success of both the accounting system and the internal control system.

- The **control environment** refers to the pervasive attitude towards internal control within the organization. Determining factors include personnel policies and practices, management style and the activities of the audit committee.
- The **accounting system**, whether it is automated or manual, must be capable of supporting the internal control procedures established. In particular, it must be capable of handling both the volume and the complexity of the business's transactions.
- **Internal control procedures** include both **administrative controls,** which are concerned with efficient operation and adherence to management policies, and **accounting controls,** which are concerned with safeguarding assets and ensuring the reliability of the financial statements. The key internal control procedures are as follows

Proper Authorizations

Management authorizes certain individuals to carry out certain tasks and can then hold these individuals responsible for the outcome of their actions. For example, only one individual in a retail store may authorize refunds.

Segregation of Duties

The physical custody of assets should be separated from the accounting for them. For example, the same individual should not be responsible for both delivering goods to a customer and receiving the cash for the goods.

Independent Verification

The work of one department or individual should act as a check on the work of another. For example, the physical count of inventory in a perpetual inventory system acts as a check on the records of both the storeroom and the individual in the accounting department who maintains the inventory account.

Safeguarding Assets and Records

Adequate safeguards must be in place to protect assets and accounting records from losses of various kinds. For example, changes in computer code should only be made by properly authorized individuals and who can provide the appropriate password.

Independent Review and Appraisal

Both the independent auditors and the internal audit staff should regularly review, appraise, and report on the effectiveness of the internal control system.

Review of Key Terms

Accounting control A procedure concerned with safeguarding the assets or the reliability of the financial statements.

Accounting system The methods and records used to accurately report an entity's transactions and to maintain accountability for its assets and liabilities.

Administrative control A procedure concerned with efficient operation of the business and adherence to managerial policies.

Audit committee A subset of the board of directors that acts as a direct contact between the stockholders and the independent accounting firm.

Board of directors The group composed of key officers of a corporation and outside members responsible for the general oversight of the affairs of the entity.

Cost of goods available for sale Beginning inventory plus cost of goods purchased.

Cost of goods sold Cost of goods available for sale minus ending inventory.

FOB destination point Terms that require the seller to pay for the cost of shipping the merchandise to the buyer.

FOB shipping point Terms that require the buyer to pay the shipping costs.

Foreign Corrupt Practices Act Legislation intended to increase the accountability of management for accurate records and reliable financial statements.

Internal audit The department responsible for monitoring and evaluating the internal control system.

Internal control procedures Policies and procedures necessary to ensure the safeguarding of an entity's assets, the reliability of its accounting records, and the accomplishment of overall company objectives.

Internal control structure The policies and procedures established to provide assurance that entity objectives are achieved.

Invoice The form sent by the seller to the buyer as evidence of a sale.

Invoice approval form A form the accounting department uses before making payment to document the accuracy of all the information about a purchase.

Net sales Sales revenue less sales returns and allowances and sales discounts.

Periodic inventory system The system in which the inventory account is updated only at the end of the period.

Perpetual inventory system The system in which the inventory account is increased at the time of each purchase of merchandise and decreased at the time of each sale.

Purchase discounts The contra purchases account used to record reductions in purchase price for early payment to the supplier.

Purchase order The form sent by the purchasing department to the supplier.

Purchase requisition The form a department uses to initiate a request to order merchandise.

Purchase returns and allowances The contra purchases account used in a periodic inventory system when a refund is received from a supplier or a reduction is given in the balance owed to the supplier.

Purchases The account used in a periodic inventory system to record acquisitions of merchandise.

Quantity discount A reduction in selling price for buying a large number of units of a product.

Receiving report	A form used by the receiving department to account for the quantity and condition of merchandise received from a supplier.
Report of management	A written statement in the annual report indicating the responsibility of management for the financial statements.
Sales discounts	The contra revenue account used to record discounts given customers for early payment of their accounts.
Sales returns and allowances	The contra revenue account used to record both refunds to customers and reductions of their accounts.
Trade discount	A reduction in selling price offered to a special class of customers.
Transportation-in	The adjunct account used to record freight costs paid by the buyer.

Practice Test
Questions and Problems

Complete each of the following statements:

LO 1 1. The major difference between a retailer's and a service organization's income statement is the inclusion of ________________, which on the retailer's income statement is deducted from net sales to get gross margin.

LO 1 2. A ________________ is offered to customers who buy large quantities; a ________________ is offered to particular types of customer; a ________________ is offered to customers who pay early.

LO 1 3. ________________ can be thought of as a pool of costs distributed between goods that were sold and goods in ending inventory.

LO 2 4. The ________________ inventory system allows greater control over inventory at a greater cost.

LO 3 5. When goods are shipped FOB ________________, it is the responsibility of the seller to pay for transportation costs.

LO 4 6. ________________ controls focus on the efficiency with which an organization is run, ________________ controls focus on safeguarding assets and the reliability of the financial statements.

LO 4 7. The internal control structure consists of three basic elements, ________________, ________________, and ________________.

LO 5 8. ________________ refers to the type of internal control procedure that results in the work of one department acting as a check on the work of another.

LO 1 9. The shorthand way of identifying invoice terms that provide for a 2% discount if the invoice is paid within 10 days, or the full amount to be paid within 30 days is ________________.

LO 6 10. The ________________ is used by the accounting department to document the accuracy of the purchase requisition, the purchase order, and the receiving report.

LO 1 11. A company buys goods for $3,000, 2/8, net 30, and pays on the fifteenth day after the sale. The amount the company pays is ________________.

LO 1 12. The ________________ of recording sales discounts assumes that customers will not normally take advantage of the discount offered.

LO 4 13. The ________________ is a subset of the board of directors that acts as a direct contact between the stockholders and the independent accounting firm.

LO 4 14. The ________________ is a written statement in the annual report indicating the responsibility of management for the financial statements.

LO 4 15. The ________________ is the department responsible for monitoring and evaluating the internal control system.

Indicate whether each of the following statements is true or false:

LO 2 16. The gross method of accounting for sales discounts is more realistic if customers routinely take advantage of the discounts.

LO 4 17. No system of internal control, however well designed, can be completely foolproof.

LO 1 18. If we add purchases and cost of goods sold and deduct opening inventory, we find the closing inventory.

LO 2 19. Point-of-sales terminals have resulted in more retailers adopting periodic inventory systems.

LO 3 20. When goods are shipped FOB shipping point, freight costs are added to the net purchases for the period.

LO 5 21. The external auditor need not be concerned with assessing the effectiveness of the internal control system, since that is the responsibility of the internal audit staff.

LO 6 22. A purchase order can be used as a source document for recording a purchase and a liability.

LO 5 23. If the cash receipts are greater than the amount recorded on the cash register tape, the excess cash should be kept until the next day to cover any shortage on the next day's receipts.

LO 5 24. An adequate system of internal control would require one person to prepare and sign checks and a different person to mail them.

LO 5 25. Serial numbering of business documents such as checks provides an important internal control device.

LO 2 26. A physical count of inventory is carried out only under the periodic inventory system.

LO 2 27. When the perpetual inventory system is used, cost of goods sold is updated every time a sale is made.

LO 2 28. Under both the periodic and the perpetual systems, ending inventory is entered in the accounts after a physical count.

LO 5 29. If a company employs an external auditor, it need not employ an internal audit staff.

LO 2 30. When a customer returns merchandise, the sales account is debited or reduced by that amount.

For the following questions, circle the alternative that best answers the question:

LO 2 31. Jenny Department Store uses a periodic inventory system. What is the impact on the financial statements of an overstatement of ending inventory?

a) Current year's net income will be overstated.
b) Next year's net income will be overstated.
c) Next year's ending inventory will be overstated.
d) Next year's ending inventory will be understated.

LO 3 32. Which of the following statements correctly defines the calculation of net purchases?

a) Gross purchases less purchase returns and allowances less purchase discounts plus transportation-in
b) Gross purchases less purchase returns and allowances less purchase discounts less transportation-in
c) Gross purchases plus purchase returns and allowances less purchase discounts plus transportation-in
d) Gross purchases plus purchase returns and allowances plus purchase discounts less transportation-in

LO 1 33. In 1997, Alpha Corporation's closing inventory of $20 million was higher than its opening inventory by $5 million. Its net purchases for 1997 were $200 million. What was Alpha's cost of goods sold for the year?

a) $195 million
b) $220 million
c) $215 million
d) $185 million

LO 3 34. If goods are purchased FOB shipping point, which of the following costs should not be included in ending inventory?

a) Transportation-in
b) Transportation-out
c) Import duties on imported goods
d) Wages paid to warehouse staff in receiving department

LO 2 35. Which of the following is not a feature of periodic inventory systems?

a) Provide up to date information on inventory for management control
b) Cheaper to maintain than perpetual inventory system
c) Require a physical count of inventory at the end of the period
d) Require opening of separate purchases account to record acquisitions of goods during the accounting period

LO 5 36. Which of the following is not a type of internal control procedure?

a) Segregation of duties
b) Independent verification
c) Proper authorizations
d) Review by external auditor

LO 5 37. Which of the following pairs of duties could be carried out by one person and still maintain the integrity of the internal control system?

a) Preparing and signing checks
b) Making cash sales and recording them in the journal
c) Preparing and mailing purchase orders
d) Ordering and receiving inventory

LO 5 38. Which of the following does not act as a control mechanism for cash received by a merchandising company?

a) Cash register displays visible to customers
b) Cash register tapes locked into the till
c) Prenumbered cash register receipts
d) All of the above

LO 6 39. Which of the following documents is sent to the supplier when a purchase is made?

a) Invoice approval form
b) Receiving report
c) Purchase order
d) Purchase requisition

LO 7 40. Which of the following groups provides direct contact between the stockholders and the independent audit firm?
a) The board of directors
b) The company management
c) The internal auditors
d) The audit committee

LO 1 41. A build up of inventory can indicate that
a) the company's products are less desirable.
b) The prices of the products are undesirable.
c) either a) or b).
d) neither a) nor b).

LO 2 42. Alpha Company uses a perpetual inventory system, and at the end of the year, its cost of goods sold account has a balance of $230,000, and its inventory account has a balance of $40,000. A physical count of its inventory indicates that its closing inventory balance is in fact $30,000. Which of the following errors could have led to this overstatement of inventory?
a) Failure to record the cost of a sale in the cost of goods sold and inventory accounts
b) Failure to record a sale in the sales account
c) Recording a sale twice in the sales account
d) Recording the cost of a sale twice in the cost of goods sold and inventory accounts

LO 1,3 43. The normal account balances for sales returns and sales discounts are, respectively,
a) a credit balance and a debit balance.
b) a debit balance and a credit balance.
c) both debit balances.
d) both credit balances

LO 1,3 44. The normal account balances for purchase returns and purchase discounts are, respectively,
a) both debit balances.
b) both credit balances
c) a credit balance and a debit balance.
d) a debit balance and a credit balance.

LO 2 45. Which of the following statements is true?
a) The periodic inventory method provides an up-to-date figure for cost of goods sold throughout the accounting period.
b) Point-of-sales terminals in retail stores have led to an increased use of periodic inventory systems.
c) Under the periodic system, the inventory account is updated each time a sale is made.
d) The ending inventory under the periodic inventory system is found by physically counting the units on hand at the end of the period.

Answer each of the following problems:

LO 5 46. The following information is available for DJIMI Discount Warehouse. Fill in the blanks in the table.

	12/31/1995	12/31/1996	12/31/1997
Opening inventory	35,000	?	?
Purchases	100,000	120,000	?
Purchase discounts	3,000	?	6,000
Cots of goods available for sale	?	158,000	170,000
Cost of goods sold	?	100,000	?
Ending inventory	40,000	?	65,000

LO 3 47. Perry's Parlous Plants operates a periodic inventory system and is preparing its accounts for the year ended December 31, 1997. Complete the following table for items that were in transit at the year-end, showing how the company should deal with each item:

TRANSACTION	PAY FREIGHT COSTS?	RECORD PURCHASE OR SALE IN 1997 INCOME STATEMENT?	INCLUDE IN INVENTORY IN BALANCE SHEET ON 12/31/1997?
Purchase from Petula Phlox; FOB shipping point			
Purchase from Georgia Geraniums; FOB destination point			
Sale to Freddes Firs; FOB destination point			
Purchase from Randy Roses Geraniums; FOB shipping point			

LO 4,5 48. For the following situations, indicate whether or not you believe that the system of internal control is adequate and, if not, what you would do to improve it.

1. Mr. W is a computer programmer for a small grocery chain. Since he is the only computer-literate member of staff, he is responsible both for designing changes to the computerized accounting system and for programming them into the system.

2. Ms. K is the accountant for a large discount warehouse. She is known to be a workaholic and has not taken a day off work (even for vacations) for three years. She personally oversees all cash transactions, calculating the total cash takings each day, preparing the bank pay-in slips, and personally lodging cash payments in the bank.

3. Mr. S is the Receiving Department manager for the same discount warehouse. He is known to be frequently absent from his job and to allow his workers to work without supervision. He is proud of the fact that several of them can imitate his signature so that he does not personally have to sign for all the deliveries that are made.

4. Ms. L supervises the booking office of a railroad station and has agreed that cash, which appears to be more than recorded takings, should be put in a drawer and used for future shortages. At the end of each month, if there is any cash left in the drawer, it is reported in the monthly returns to the head office, and the drawer is emptied for the beginning of the next month.

Critical Thinking Problem

LO 1 49. Consider the information in Problem 46. What has happened to the firm's inventory level over the three years? What additional information would you need before you could comment on the advisability of this trend?

Solutions

Fill in the Blanks

1. cost of goods sold
2. quantity discount, trade discount, sales discount
3. cost of goods available for sale
4. perpetual
5. destination point
6. administrative, accounting
7. control environment, accounting system, control procedures
8. independent verification
9. 2/10, net 30
10. invoice approval form
11. \$3,000
12. gross method
13. audit committee
14. report of management
15. internal audit department

True/False

		COMMENT/EXPLANATION
16.	False	The net method is more appropriate.
17.	True	
18.	False	Closing inventory equals opening inventory plus purchases minus cost of goods sold.
19.	False	Point-of-sales terminals make using a perpetual inventory systems easier.
20.	True	
21.	False	The external auditor must be satisfied himself as to the effectiveness of the internal control system because the validity of the accounting system depends on it.
22.	False	Receipt of the goods or an invoice from the supplier is the basis of the purchaser's recognition of a liability.
23.	False	All shortages should be reported on a daily basis so that any pattern indicating fraud can be identified.
24.	False	The preparation and signature of checks should be separated.
25.	True	
26.	False	A physical count is also carried out under the perpetual system to act as a check on the closing balance on the inventory account.
27.	True	
28.	False	Under the perpetual system, the inventory account is continually updated after each sale and therefore ending inventory can be found as the closing balance on the inventory account. As was pointed out above, this balance is confirmed by a physical count carried out at the end of the period.
29.	False	Both are normally needed. The external auditor carries out an examination of the internal control procedures of the entity. Therefore, the more effective the internal audit staff, the more reliance the external auditor can place on the information derived from the accounting system.
30.	False	The sales returns account, which is a contra sales account, is debited.

Multiple Choice

31. a
32. a
33. a
34. b
35. a
36. d
37. c
38. d
39. c
40. d
41. c
42. a
43. c
44. b
45. d

Problem 46

	12/31/1995	12/31/1996	12/31/1997
Opening inventory	35,000	40,000	58,000
Purchases	100,000	120,000	118,000
Purchase discounts	3,000	2,000	6,000
Cots of goods available for sale	132,000	158,000	170,000
Cost of goods sold	92,000	100,000	105,000
Ending inventory	40,000	58,000	65,000

Problem 47

Transaction	Pay freight costs?	Record purchase or sale in 1997 income statement?	Include in inventory in balance sheet on 12/31/1997?
Purchase from Petula Phlox; FOB shipping point	Yes	No	Yes
Purchase from Georgia Geraniums; FOB destination point	No	No	No
Sale to Freddes Firs; FOB destination point	Yes	No	Yes
Purchase from Randy Roses Geraniums; FOB shipping point	No	Yes	No

Problem 48

1. The principal of segregation of duties would suggest that Mr. W should not run the entire computer system, since he would have the opportunity to manipulate it to his own benefit. As an illustration of what someone in that position can do, a programmer for a bank wrote into a program, which calculated interest to be charged on loans, a small routine that credited all the roundings in the calculation to his own account. It was not until several hundred thousand dollars found their way into his account that his fraud was discovered.
2. No one person, no matter how senior, should be allowed to have full control of cash receipts and bank lodgments. Ms. K could easily steal some cash and there would be no record, other than those prepared by her, to identify how much money should be paid into the bank. A further suspicious situation is her reluctance to take time off. Many frauds have been discovered when illness kept the individual concerned out of the office for a few days, and other staff members could get access to records normally kept under close control.

3. Mr. S's department sounds like a disaster waiting to happen. It is hard to see whether any internal control procedures are either in place or being followed. No one should sign someone else's signature, since it completely defeats the purpose of having someone in a senior position sign for deliveries. Perhaps the best solution is to suggest that Mr. S find other employment.
4. Any cash shortages and excesses should be reported on a daily basis, preferably analyzed by employee. In this way, it will be apparent if there is any pattern in the shortages of the office as a whole, or by any individual.

Critical Thinking Problem 49

The inventory levels have increased steadily over the three years. In general, firms wish to control the amount of inventory they are carrying, since it represents a significant investment. In addition, inventories can become obsolete, and the firm may be unable to realize what it paid for them. For these reasons, the firm should examine whether or not it can reduce its inventory levels. There are, however, circumstances where increasing inventories are necessary. In particular, if the company's sales are increasing, additional inventories may be needed to provide enough safety stock for the new sales level. This might be the case here since the cost of goods sold has increased, suggesting a higher level of sales activity. To confirm this, the sales figures for the three years would be needed.

Chapter 6

Inventories and Cost of Goods Sold

This chapter continues the exploration of accounting for inventory started in Chapter 5 by discussing the various methods that are used to find the cost of inventory. You have two overall aims in this chapter. First, understand the assumptions underlying the different methods used for inventory costing, and how each method is applied in practice. Second, understand the impact of different methods on reported income and the balance sheet.

Learning Objectives

LO 1 Identify the forms of inventory held by different types of businesses and the types of cost incurred.

LO 2 Explain the relationship between the valuation of inventory and the measurement of income.

LO 3 Analyze the effects of an inventory error on various financial statement items.

LO 4 Apply the inventory costing methods of specific identification, weighted average, FIFO, and LIFO using a periodic system.

LO 5 Analyze the effects of different costing methods on inventory, net income, income taxes, and cash flow.

LO 6 Apply the lower of cost or market rule to the valuation of inventory.

LO 7 Explain why and how the cost of inventory is estimated in certain situations.

LO 8 Analyze the management of inventory turnover.

LO 9 Explain the effects of inventory transactions on the statement of cash flows.

LO 10 Explain the differences between a periodic and a perpetual inventory system.

LO 11 Apply the inventory costing methods using a perpetual system.

Key Textbook Exhibits

Exhibit 6-1 contains an illustration of the types of costs and inventories held by merchandising and manufacturing enterprises.

Exhibit 6-4 summarizes the impact over two years of an overstatement or understatement of first year closing inventory. You should not try to learn this by rote, but rather understand the principle behind this exhibit.

Exhibits 6-12 through 6-15 illustrate the use of the perpetual inventory system. Work through the examples so that you understand why the choice of inventory system and the inventory costing method can lead to different figures for ending inventory and cost of goods sold.

Review of Key Concepts

LO 1 Inventory held by merchandising enterprises differs from inventory held by manufacturing enterprises in terms of both the costs incurred in acquiring the inventory, and the types of inventory held.

- For a merchandiser, goods purchased for resale are normally the only type of inventory held. The costs associated with merchandise inventory are simply those required to buy the inventory (including transportation-in, if appropriate).
- Inventory for a manufacturer consists of three distinct categories: raw materials, work in process and finished goods. A manufacturer incurs three types of cost: direct material, direct labor, and manufacturing overhead.

The costs included in each type of inventory for each type of enterprise are summarized below:

Retailer/Wholesaler	Manufacturer		
Merchandise Inventory	**Raw Materials**	**Work in Process**	**Finished Goods**
Cost to purchase	Cost to purchase	Cost of the materials, direct labor, and overhead used in the manufacture of unfinished items	Total cost of materials, direct labor, and overhead used to manufacture goods completed but not yet sold

LO 2,3 One of the most fundamental concepts in accounting is the relationship between asset valuation and income measurement. Since assets are unexpired costs, and expenses are expired costs, reducing the value of an asset results in an increase in expenses, with a consequent reduction in income. This general point can be illustrated by exploring the relationship between inventory valuation and income measurement.

Cost of goods sold is found from

Beginning Inventory + Purchases - Ending Inventory = Cost of Goods Sold

The valuation of ending inventory therefore determines the cost of goods sold. In addition, we find net earnings from

Sales - Cost of Goods Sold - Other Expenses = Net Earnings

Given revenue for the period, net earnings are determined by cost of goods sold. The higher is cost of goods sold, the lower is net earnings, and vice versa. As we have seen above, cost of goods sold is a function of the valuation of ending inventory. Reported income is therefore directly related to the valuation of ending inventory.

Test Your Understanding!

Question: Suppose a company can use one of two different inventory valuation methods. Method One gives a higher ending inventory than Method Two. Will reported income be higher or lower under Method One than under Method Two? Can you find a general rule about how reported income is related to cost of goods sold and to ending inventory?

Answer: Under Method One, ending inventory is higher, so cost of goods sold will be lower. Therefore, reported income will be higher under Method One than under Method Two.

The general rule is that reported income is inversely related to cost of goods sold, and directly related to ending inventory.

We can use the general rule just derived to explore the impact that errors in inventory valuation will have on reported income. Suppose Company A makes a mistake in valuing its inventory in Year 1, the first year of its operations. The error results in the ending inventory in Year 1 being recorded as $10,000 rather than $5,000, the correct amount. Also assume that at the end of Year 2, the inventory is correctly recorded at $15,000. Assume that sales, beginning inventory, purchases, and operating expenses for Company A are as presented in the following table. The effect of the error can be analyzed as follows:

Effects of Inventory Error in Year 1 on Reported Income and Retained Earnings

Year 1	**Reported**		**Corrected**	
Sales		$100,000		$100,000
Cost of Goods Sold				
Beginning Inventory	$ 10,000		$ 10,000	
Add: Purchases	50,000		50,000	
Cost of Goods Available for Resale	60,000		60,000	
Less: Ending Inventory	10,000		5,000	
Cost of Goods Sold		50,000		55,000
Gross Margin		50,000		45,000
Less: Operating Expenses		10,000		10,000
Net Income		$ 40,000		$ 35,000
Retained Earnings				
Balance - Beginning of Year		$ 0		$ 0
Add: Net Income for Year		40,000		35,000
Balance - End of Year		$ 40,000		$ 35,000

Year 2	**Reported**		**Corrected**	
Sales		$120,000		$120,000
Cost of Goods Sold				
Beginning Inventory	$ 10,000		$ 5,000	
Add: Purchases	60,000		60,000	
Cost of Goods Available for Resale	70,000		65,000	
Less: Ending Inventory	15,000		15,000	
Cost of Goods Sold		55,000		50,000
Gross Margin		65,000		70,000
Less: Operating Expenses		10,000		10,000
Net Income		$ 55,000		$ 60,000
Retained Earnings				
Balance - Beginning of Year		$ 40,000		$ 35,000
Add: Net Income for Year		55,000		60,000
Balance - End of Year		$ 95,000		$ 95,000

As we can see, an overstatement of the valuation of ending inventory in Year 1 results in an overstatement of income for that year. In the following year, the beginning inventory will be overstated. Since the ending inventory for the second year is correct, second year income is understated by the amount of the original error. Note also that although the retained earnings balance at the end of the first year will be overstated by $5,000, the balance on retained earnings at the end of the second year will be correct. The impact of the error therefore dissipates in the second year.

Test Your Understanding!

Question: Can you work through the above argument for the case where Company A erroneously **understates** its ending inventory in Year 1? What will be the impact on the income and retained earnings for both periods, assuming that the ending inventory for Year 2 is correct?

Answer: An understatement of the valuation of ending inventory in Year 1 will result in an understatement of income for that period. Retained earnings will be understated at the end of Year 1. In the following year, the beginning inventory will be understated. If the ending inventory for the second period is correct, second period income will be overstated by the amount of the original error, and the balance on retained earnings at the end of the second year will be correct. Again, the impact of the error dissipates in the second year.

LO 4 In some types of business, for example car dealerships, it is possible to **specifically identify** items in ending inventory. In this case, the cost of goods sold and the purchase price of ending inventory are clearly identifiable. In most businesses, however, this inventory costing method is not feasible. An inventory costing method must be chosen on the basis of an assumption about how inventory costs flow through the organization. There are three commonly used inventory costing methods:

- **Weighted Average Cost Method** The weighted average cost for each period is calculated by dividing cost of goods available for sale during the period (purchases plus beginning inventory) by the units available for sale. This weighted average cost is assigned to all units available for sale during the period, including ending inventory.
- **First-in, First-out Method (FIFO)** This method assumes that the first units sold during the period are the units that were purchased first. Ending inventory cost therefore consists of the items that were most recently purchased.
- **Last-in, First-out Method (LIFO)** In contrast to FIFO, LIFO assumes that the first units sold are those that have been purchased most recently. Ending inventory cost therefore consists of items that may have been purchased several periods before.

To illustrate the use of each method, assume that beginning inventory and purchases during January 1994 for the Alpat Company were as in the following table. Alpat uses a periodic inventory system, and during the year sold 9,000 units at a selling price of $20 per unit.

		UNITS	COST PER UNIT
Beginning inventory		2,500	$10
Purchases:	January 1	3,000	$11
	January 11	2,500	$12
	January 25	2,000	$15

The total cost of goods available for sale and the total number of units available for sale during the period is found first.

		NUMBER OF UNITS	COST PER UNIT	TOTAL COST
Beginning inventory		2,500	$10	$25,000
Purchases:	January 1	3,000	$11	$33,000
	January 11	2,500	$12	$30,000
	January 25	2,000	$15	$30,000
Goods available for sale		10,000		$118,000
Sales		9,000		
Ending inventory		1,000		

Weighted Average Cost Method

Average cost per unit is $11.80 and is found by dividing total cost of goods available for sale ($118,000) by the total units of goods available for sale (10,000 units).

	UNIT COST	UNITS	TOTAL COST
Ending inventory	$11.80	1,000	$11,800
Cost of goods sold	$11.80	9,000	$106,200

First-In, First-Out (FIFO)

Under FIFO, it is assumed that the oldest units are sold first. Ending inventory is therefore assumed to come from the last purchase on January 25. Cost of goods sold is found by subtracting the ending inventory value from the total cost of goods available for sale.

	UNIT COST	UNITS	TOTAL COST
Ending inventory	$15	1,000	$15,000
Cost of goods sold ($118,000 - $15,000)		9,000	$103,000

Last-In, First-Out (LIFO)

Under LIFO, the latest units purchased are assumed to be sold first. Ending inventory is therefore assumed to come from beginning inventory. Cost of goods sold is found by subtracting the ending inventory value from the total cost of goods available for sale.

	UNIT COST	UNITS	TOTAL COST
Ending inventory	$10	1,000	$10,000
Cost of goods sold ($118,000 - $10,000)		9,000	$108,000

The impact of the different inventory valuation methods on income can be see from the following table. In this example, where prices are rising, FIFO leads to lower cost of goods sold, higher gross margin, and higher ending inventory than LIFO.

	AVERAGE COST	FIFO	LIFO
Sales (9,000 units @ $20)	$180,000	$180,000	$180,000
COGS	106,200	103,000	108,000
Gross margin	73,800	77,000	72,000
Ending inventory	$11,800	$15,000	$10,000

Test Your Understanding!

Question: Must a firm that uses LIFO sell first the goods it bought most recently?

Answer: No. The cost flow assumptions of each of these inventory costing methods do not necessarily match physical flows of inventory. To reduce spoilage and obsolescence, most organizations sell the oldest inventory first. However, irrespective of the physical flows, they may choose to assume a last-in first-out cost flow.

LO 5 The overriding consideration in the choice of an inventory costing method should be the ability of the method to accurately reflect the net income of the period. The following factors, however, also enter into an individual firm's choice:

- **Cash Flow and Taxes** In a period of rising prices, LIFO can result in higher cost of goods sold and lower reported earnings than under FIFO. Relative to FIFO, taxes can therefore be deferred under LIFO.
- **LIFO Conformity Rule** If LIFO is used for tax reporting, the IRS requires that the company also use LIFO for reporting to stockholders.
- **LIFO Liquidation** If in any period, the number of units sold exceeds the number of units purchased, the number of units in ending inventory is lower than in beginning inventory. The difference in units is part of the goods sold during the period. Where LIFO is used as the inventory costing method, these units may have been carried in inventory at their original cost, which could be very much lower than units being bought now. In this case, cost of goods sold will be lower because it contains these units. This is known as LIFO Liquidation and it can result in a relatively low cost of goods sold and a high reported (and taxable) income.
- **Replacement Cost of Inventory** The use of replacement cost for both cost of goods sold and inventory results in better economic measures of both income and inventory valuation. At a time of rising prices and increasing or stable inventory levels, LIFO results in the best approximation of replacement cost of goods sold, and therefore of economic income in the income statement. FIFO results in the closest approximation to valuing inventory at replacement cost in the balance sheet.

LO 6 Where the cost of inventory exceeds its market value, inventory should be marked to market by writing the value of inventory down to replacement cost. This **lower of cost or market rule** can be applied to the total inventory, to individual items, or to groups of inventory. At the end of each period, using one of the costing methods above, the cost of inventory is compared with the market price (replacement cost) of inventory. If market is less than cost, the inventory is written down to the lower amount.

For example, assume that Company A is preparing its accounts for the year ending December 31, 1997. The cost of inventory under LIFO is $25,000, but the company estimates that the replacement cost of the inventory is $20,000. The following adjusting entry is made. Note that the effect of this entry is to reduce the asset inventory and the owners' equity.

Dec. 31	Loss on decline in value of inventory	5,000	
	Inventory		5,000
	To record decline in value of inventory.		

LO 7 In some circumstances, it is necessary to estimate the value of inventory and two principal methods are used.

Gross Profit Method

The gross profit method is used in a periodic inventory system to value inventory that has been destroyed or lost and cannot be counted. The validity of the method critically depends on reliable estimation of the gross profit ratio. To illustrate this method, assume that on March 31, 1994, Islay Corporation's warehouse was destroyed by fire, and an estimate of the lost inventory is needed for an insurance claim. The following information is available:

Inventory, March 1, 1994	$150,000
Purchases during March	$350,000
Sales, March	$500,000
Gross margin is 40% of revenue.	

Cost of goods sold is found by multiplying the cost of sales margin by net sales. Since gross margin is 40% of revenue, cost of sales is (100% - 40%) = 60% of revenue.

Sales	$500,000
Cost of sales %	60%
Cost of goods sold	$300,000

The ending inventory value is found by deducting cost of goods sold from cost of goods available for sale (beginning inventory plus purchases).

Beginning inventory, March 1	$150,000
Plus Purchases	350,000
Goods available for sale	500,000
Less Cost of goods sold	300,000
Ending inventory, March 31	$200,000

Retail Inventory Method

The retail inventory method is used to estimate the cost of inventory in retail organizations where a count of inventory using the retail prices rather than costs is substantially easier. To illustrate, the following information is available for Mull Inc. for the month of June, 1994.

	COST	RETAIL
Inventory, June 1	$10,000	$13,500
Plus Purchases in June	$40,000	$61,500
Total	$50,000	$75,000

The ratio of cost to retail price is determined from beginning inventory and purchases for the period.

Ratio of cost to retail = $50,000/ $75,000

= 67%

The retail price of the ending inventory is determined by a physical count. The ratio of cost to retail is applied to the retail price of ending inventory to estimate the cost of ending inventory.

Inventory, June 30 at retail	=	$15,000
Inventory, June 30 at cost	=	$15,000 x 67%
	=	$10,000

LO 8 Inventory is one of the largest assets on the balance sheet of many enterprises. Adequate inventory is essential to efficient manufacturing, since lack of inventory can result in expensive shutdowns. Further, the availability of inventory to fill orders can be a major factor in ensuring good relations with customers. On the other hand, too much inventory can cause unnecessary storage costs, tie up capital unnecessarily, and increase the risk that inventory becomes obsolete. Management of inventory is therefore a critical part of management's task. When analyzing the financial statements, two ratios, inventory turnover and number of days' sales in inventory, can help in understanding the effectiveness of the company's inventory management. Inventory turnover gives the number of times on average inventory is bought and sold during the year. The number of days' sales in inventory gives how many days one average inventory stays in the enterprise before it is sold. Inventory turnover and number of days' sales in inventory are defined as follows:

$$\text{Inventory Turnover Ratio} = \frac{\text{Cost of Goods Sold}}{\text{Average Inventory}}$$

$$\text{Number of Days' Sales in Inventory} = \frac{\text{Number Of Days In The Period}}{\text{Inventory Turnover Ratio}}$$

To illustrate the calculation of these ratios, assume that Company D's cost of goods sold for Year 3 was $200,000, its beginning inventory at the beginning of Year 3 was $50,000, and its ending inventory at the end of Year 3 was $70,000.

$$\text{Inventory Turnover Ratio} = \frac{\text{Cost of Goods Sold}}{\text{Average Inventory}} = \frac{\$240{,}000}{(\$50{,}000 + \$70{,}000)/2} = 4 \text{ times}$$

$$\text{Number of Days' Sales in Inventory} = \frac{\text{Number of Days in the Period}}{\text{Inventory Turnover Ratio}} = \frac{360}{4} = 90 \text{ days}$$

In deciding whether these ratios represented good inventory management by Company D, we would need to compare them with Company D's previous years' ratios, as well as with inventory turnover and number of days' sales in inventory ratios of other companies in the same industry as Company D.

LO 9 If a company uses the direct method for its cash flow statement, the cash paid to suppliers of inventory will be shown as a use of cash. Where the company uses the indirect method, cash flow from operations is found by adjusting net income for increases or decreases in both the Inventory and Accounts Payable accounts. The adjustments to be made to net income to find cash flow from operations areas follows:

ITEM	ADJUSTMENT TO NET INCOME
Increase in inventory	Deduct from net income
Decrease in inventory	Add to net income
Increase in accounts payable	Add to net income
Decrease in accounts payable	Deduct from net income

Test Your Understanding!

Question: Assume that Company C's balance sheets for Year 9 and Year 10 contain the following account balances. What adjustments would be made to Company C's Year 10 net income of $50,000 to find cash flow from operations for Year 10?

Company C - Balance Sheet	*Year 9*	*Year 10*
Inventory	$10,000	$15,000
Accounts Payable	$40,000	$60,000

Answer: The following adjustments would be made:

Net Income	$50,000
Less: Increase in inventory	(5,000)
Plus: Increase in accounts payable	20,000

LO 10,11 Two systems of inventory management are found in practice: perpetual inventory systems and periodic inventory systems. The following table summarizes the differences between the two methods. Note that all inventory costing methods (LIFO, FIFO, etc.) can be used with each system. If either LIFO or average cost is used, the cost of goods sold and net income may be different under the periodic and perpetual systems.

Feature	Periodic Inventory System	Perpetual Inventory System
Count of inventory	Carried out at the end of each period and critical to allocation of cost between ending inventory and cost of goods sold.	Carried out at the end of each period to confirm valuation of ending inventory.
Purchases	Recorded in Purchases Account that is closed at the end of the period.	Recorded direct to Inventory Account.
Sales	Under both systems, the Sales account is credited, and Cash or Accounts Receivable debited, with the sale price.	
Cost of goods sold	No entry is made for the cost of goods sold at the time the sale is made.	The inventory account is updated each time a sale is made. Cost of goods sold is credited to Inventory account and debited to Cost of Goods Sold account each time.
FIFO	The valuation of ending inventory is the same under both systems.	
LIFO	Cost of goods sold and ending inventory are based on the cost of the last units sold for the entire period.	Cost of goods sold is based on the last units purchased at the time of each sale. Cost of goods sold and ending inventory will therefore differ from the corresponding figures calculated under the periodic system.
Average cost	Cost of goods sold and ending inventory are based on the average cost of goods available for sale for the period as a whole.	The average cots of goods sold is calculated at the time of each purchase. Therefore, for this inventory costing method, the ending inventory and cost of goods sold will differ under the periodic and perpetual inventory systems.

Review of Key Terms

Consignment	A legal arrangement in which inventory owned by one entity is turned over to another entity for sale.
FIFO method	An inventory costing method that assigns the most recent costs to ending inventory.
Finished goods	The inventory of a manufacturer that is complete and ready for sale.
Gross profit method	A technique used to establish an estimate of the cost of inventory stolen, destroyed, or otherwise damaged, or the amount of inventory on hand at an interim date.
Inventory profit	That portion of the gross profit resulting from holding inventory during a period of rising prices.
Inventory turnover ratio	A measure of the number of times inventory is sold during the period.
LIFO conformity rule	An IRS requirement that if LIFO is used on the tax return, it must also be used in reporting income to stockholder.
LIFO liquidation	The result of selling more units than are purchased during the period, which can have negative tax consequences if a company is using LIFO.
LIFO method	An inventory costing method that assigns the most recent costs to cost of goods sold.
LIFO reserve	The excess of the value of a company's inventory stated at FIFO, compared with the inventory value stated at LIFO.
Lower of cost or market (LCM) rule	A conservative approach to valuing inventory, which is an attempt to anticipate declines in the value of inventory before its actual sale.
Merchandise inventory	The account wholesalers and retailers use to report inventory held for sale.
Moving average method	The name given to an average cost method when it is used with a perpetual inventory system.
Number of days' sales in inventory	A measure of how long it takes to sell inventory.
Raw materials	The inventory of a manufacturer before the addition of any direct labor or manufacturing overhead.
Replacement cost	The current cost of a unit of inventory.
Retail inventory method	A technique used by retailers to convert the retail value of inventory to a cost basis.
Specific identification method	An inventory costing method that relies on matching unit costs with the actual units sold.
Weighted average cost method	An inventory costing method that assigns the same unit cost to all units available for sale during the period.
Work in process	The cost of unfinished products in a manufacturing company.

Practice Test
Questions and Problems

Complete each of the following statements:

LO 1 1. A manufacturer's inventory is composed of three elements: _____________, _____________, and _____________.

LO 2 2. Cost of goods available for sale is found by adding _____________ to _____________; cost of goods sold is found by deducting _____________ from cost of goods available for sale.

LO 3 3. Most art galleries operate on a _____________ basis, whereby art owned by the artist is turned over to the gallery to sell, with the gallery and the artist splitting the profits from any sales and any unsold pieces being returned to the artist.

LO 6 4. Where the market price of inventory is lower than its historic cost, the _____________ rule is applied.

LO 7 5. Inventory value can be estimated in the case of a fire or loss by using the ____________ method.

LO 7 6. The _________________ method is often used by retailers to value inventory for interim statements by converting the retail value of inventory to cost.

LO 7 7. The __________________ ratio is calculated by dividing cost of goods sold by average inventory for the period and is used to measure how often the company replaces its inventory each year.

LO 4 8. The __________________ method assigns the same unit cost to all units available for sale during the period.

LO 5 9. The excess of the value of a company's inventory stated at FIFO, compared with LIFO, is called the _____________.

LO 5 10. When a company using LIFO sells more units in a period than it purchases, some of the units sold will come from older inventory with a relatively low unit price; this situation results in a low cost of goods sold figure and high gross margin and is referred to as _____________.

Use the following information to answer questions 11 through 15:

Terra Corporation makes the following purchases in the month of July, 1997:

Date	**Number of Units Purchased**	**Unit Cost**
July 3	100	$15
July 15	100	$10
July 23	100	$5

The beginning inventory on July 1 was 200 units at a price per unit of $20, and the company had 200 units on hand on July 31.

LO 5 11. The company sold _____________ units during the month of July.

LO 5 12. Under the weighted average cost method, the average cost assigned to all units available for sale during the period is $_______________ per unit.

LO 5 13. The inventory costing method that produces the highest cost of goods sold in these circumstances is _____________ .

LO 5 14. The inventory costing method that produces the highest ending inventory in these circumstances is _____________ .

LO 5 15. At a time of falling prices, net income under FIFO will be ________________ than under LIFO.

Indicate whether each of the following statements is true or false:

LO 2 16. The cost of goods sold is inversely related to the value of ending inventory.

LO 5 17. Where a company pays tax, short-term cash flow under LIFO will be higher than under other inventory costing methods at a time of rising prices.

LO 7 18. A department store will normally have a higher inventory turnover ratio than a supermarket.

LO 3 19. If a counterbalancing inventory error is made over two accounting periods, the net effect of the error on retained earnings should be zero by the end of the second period.

LO 6 20. Inventory must always be reported at historic cost.

LO 9 21. To find cash flow from operations using the indirect method, increases in inventory should be added to net earnings.

LO 7 22. No interim figures for cost of goods sold and ending inventory are readily available from the accounting records under the periodic system of inventory.

LO 11 23. LIFO will lead to identical cost of goods sold, but different inventory values, under the periodic system and the perpetual system.

LO 1 24. Of the three types of cost incurred by manufacturers, only direct labor and manufacturing overhead form part of work in process.

LO 3 25. If an art gallery sells paintings on consignment, the gallery need not pay the painter for unsold paintings.

LO 10 26. Under the perpetual inventory method, no physical count of inventory need be carried out at the end of the accounting period, since this system provides up-to-date information about cost of goods sold and inventory values.

LO 9 27. When the direct method for the cash flow statement is used, a decrease in inventory is deducted from net income to find cash flow from operations.

LO 9 28. When the indirect method for the cash flow statement is used, a decrease in accounts payable is added to net income, and an increase in accounts payable is deducted from net income to find cash flow from operations.

LO 10 29. Under the average cost method, the valuation of ending inventory is the same under both the perpetual and the periodic systems.

LO 4 30. A disadvantage of LIFO is that it could result in physical deterioration of inventory, since the latest purchases are sold first.

For each of the following questions, circle the alternative that best answers the question.

LO 3 31. Jenny Department Store uses a periodic inventory system What is the impact on the financial statements of an overstatement of ending inventory?

Current year's net income will be overstated.

Next year's net income will be overstated.

Next year's ending inventory will be overstated.

Next year's ending inventory will be understated.

LO 5 32. If a company uses the LIFO cost flow assumption for its federal income tax return

a) it must use FIFO on its financial statements.
b) it must use LIFO on its financial statements.
c) it may use any inventory cost flow assumption for its financial statements.
d) LIFO cannot be used for federal tax return computations.

LO 5 33. Mr. Albert works for a supermarket chain, and his bonus is calculated as a percentage of gross profit (sales minus cost of goods sold). To maximize his bonus, which of the following cost flow assumptions would Mr. Albert prefer if inventory prices and levels are rising?

a) LIFO.
b) FIFO.
c) Average cost.
d) Inventory cost flow assumption does not affect gross profit.

LO 5 34. During a period of steeply rising prices, a company adopts a new method of production, resulting in a dramatic reduction in inventories The effect of this on reported earnings and inventory turnover in the year the change takes place is to

a) increase earnings and decrease inventory turnover.

b) increase earnings and increase inventory turnover.

c) decrease earnings and decrease inventory turnover.

d) decrease earnings and increase inventory turnover.

LO 5 35. If the market value of inventory is lower than its cost, then application of the lower of cost or market rule would

a) increase earnings and decrease current ratio.

b) increase earnings and increase current ratio.

c) decrease earnings and decrease current ratio.

d) decrease earnings and increase current ratio.

LO 7 36. In which of the following situations would the retail inventory method be an appropriate way to estimate inventories for companies using the periodic inventory system?

a) A supermarket that has kept records of purchases at both retail and cost prices carries out a physical count of the retail price of the goods on its shelves.

b) A department store has a fire and loses part of its inventory.

c) A company wishes to estimate the value of inventory for interim financial statements.

d) All of the above.

LO 3 37. Which of the following should NOT be included in inventory cost for a car dealership?

a) The costs of transporting the cars from the factory to the dealership

b) Excise and sales taxes

c) The salary cost of the salesman who sells the vehicle

d) The cost of modifications to the vehicles made by the dealer before the vehicle is offered for sale

LO 5 38. Which of the following statements about LIFO liquidation is FALSE?

a) LIFO liquidation occurs when a company using LIFO sells more units during the period than it buys.

b) LIFO liquidation results in a high tax bill for the company if prices are rising.

c) A company can avoid LIFO liquidation by buying inventory at the end of the year.

d) LIFO liquidation results in inventory from previous periods, with relatively low prices being included in cost of goods sold when prices are falling.

LO 5 39. Assume that a bond covenant states that a company's ratio of debt to equity may not rise above 1:1. Currently the company's ratio of debt to equity is 0.9:1 To ensure compliance with its bond covenant, which of the following cost flow assumptions would the company prefer if inventory prices are falling?

a) LIFO.
b) FIFO.
c) Average cost.
d) The company would not be able to influence its ratio of debt to equity by its inventory cost flow assumption.

LO 7 40. A high inventory turnover ratio could result from

a) collection policies that ensure prompt payment of customers' accounts.
b) a high gross margin.
c) inventory levels being carefully monitored to ensure that they are not too high relative to the volume of sales.
d) the physical flow of inventory ensuring that the oldest units are sold first.

Use the following information to answer questions 41 through 43:

Sidlaw Corporation has the following information for its inventory for the month of August, 1997.

Date	Number of Units Purchased	Unit Cost
August 8	150	$21
August 20	?	?
August 30	100	$24

The beginning inventory on August 1 was 100 units at a price per unit of $20, and the company had 100 units in inventory on August 31. Sales for the month were 400 units. Although a purchase took place on August 20, information is not available about how many units were purchased or the cost per unit.

LO 4 41. The number of units purchased on August 20 was

a) 50
b) 250
c) 150
d) 100

LO 4 42. If the FIFO cost of goods sold for August is $8,600, the cost per unit of the goods purchased on August 20 is

a) $21
b) $22
c) $23
d) $24

LO 4 43. The ending inventory under LIFO is

a) $2,000
b) $2,400
c) $2,100
d) $2,300

LO 8 44. A company's cost of goods sold is $300,000, its inventory turnover for the year is 20, and its beginning inventory at the beginning of Year 10 was $10,000. Its ending inventory at the end of Year 10 is

a) $ 10,000
b) $ 20,000
c) $100,000
d) $ 17,500

LO 9 45. A company has the following balances on its balance sheets at the beginning and end of Year 5:

Inventory	
December 31, Year 4	$25,000
December 31, Year 5	$30,000
Accounts payable	
December 31, Year 4	$10,000
December 31, Year 5	$ 8,000

The company uses the indirect method for its cash flow statement and to find the cash flow from operations, the following adjustments must be made to net income:

a) Deduct $5,000 from net income and add $2,000 to net income.
b) Deduct $5,000 from net income and deduct $2,000 from net income.
c) Add $5,000 to net income and add $2,000 to net income.
d) Add $5,000 to net income and deduct $2,000 from net income.

Answer each of the following problems:

LO 7 46. On January 31, 1994, Surfers Store in Santa Teresa was destroyed by an earthquake. Inventory worth $10,000 was subsequently salvaged from the ruins. An estimate of the lost inventory is needed for an insurance claim. The following information is available:

Inventory January 1, 1994	$ 75,000
Purchases during January	$250,000
January sales	$300,000

Cost of sales is 75% of revenue.

Required

1. Using the gross profit method, estimate the amount of inventory lost in the earthquake, and the loss on inventory after the insurance recovery.

2. If the insurance company finally pays $80,000, give the journal entry for, and show the effect on the accounting equation of, recording the inventory loss and the receipt of cash from the insurance company.

LO 11 47. The following is an extract from the Statement of Cash Flows for Toys "R" Us, Inc.

Consolidated Statements of Cash Flows TOYS"R"US, INC. AND SUBSIDIARIES			
(In $ millions)	*February 3, 1996*	*January 28, 1995*	*January 29, 1994*
CASH FLO WS FROM OPERATING ACTIVITIES			
Net earnings	$148.10	$531.80	$483.00
Adjustments to reconcile net earnings to net cash provided by operating activities:			
Restructuring and other charges	396.6	-	-
Depreciation and amortization	191.7	161.4	133.4
Deferred income taxes	-66.7	-14.5	36.5
Changes in operating assets and liabilities:			
Accounts and other receivables	-10.8	-17.4	-29.1
Merchandise inventories	-193.1	-221.6	-278.9
Prepaid expenses and other operating assets	-15.7	-31.7	-39.5
Accounts payable, accrued expenses and other liabilities	-150.5	183.5	325.1
Income taxes payable	-49.3	-2	26.6
Total adjustments	102.2	57.7	174.1
Net cash provided by operating activities	$ 250.3	$ 589.5	$ 657.1

Required

1. Does TOYS "R" US use the direct or indirect method to prepare the operating section of the statement of cash flows?

2. Did inventories increase or decrease during 1996, 1995, and 1994? If the opening balance in the inventory account was $1,000 on January 30, 1993, what were the balances on the inventory account on the balance sheets on February 3, 1996, January 28, 1995, and January 29, 1994?

LO 4 48. Clare Corporation's inventory records show the following for the year ended December 31, 1994:

	Units	Unit Cost($)
Beginning inventory	1,000	$40
Purchases:		
March 31	600	43
May 27	800	49
August 26	700	50
October 19	1,000	56
December 15	900	60

Clare uses a periodic inventory system and during the year sold 4,500 units at a selling price of $60 per unit. Expenses other than cost of goods sold amounted to $40,000 for the year, and the tax rate is 40%.

Required

1. Compute cost of goods sold and ending inventory under each of the following three methods:

   Weighted average

   FIFO

   LIFO

2. Prepare income statements for Clare Corporation under each of the three methods.

3. If Clare wishes to pay the least amount of taxes for 1994, which method would you recommend?

4. Suppose you were considering investing in Clare and learned that Clare had switched from LIFO to FIFO. What would be the effect on reported net income of the switch? Would that affect your decision whether or not to invest in the company? Why?

Critical Thinking Problem

LO 5 49. The footnotes to the financial statements of Company X for the year ended December 31, 1996, contain the following statements:

"Inventories are stated generally at the lower of cost or market. The cost of all inventories is determined by the last-in, first-out method. As a result of decreases in inventories over the year, certain LIFO inventory quantities were liquidated. These inventory adjustments favorably affected income before taxes."

Required

1. Explain how liquidating LIFO inventories can favorably affect income before taxes, and explain the effect the LIFO liquidation would have on Company X's 1996 tax liability.

2. How could Company X have avoided a LIFO liquidation?

Solutions

Fill in the Blanks

1. raw materials, work in process, finished goods
2. opening inventories, purchases, closing inventories
3. consignment
4. lower of cost or market
5. gross profit
6. retail inventory
7. inventory turnover
8. average cost
9. LIFO reserve
10. LIFO liquidation
11. 300 units
12. $14
13. FIFO
14. LIFO
15. lower

True/False

		COMMENT/EXPLANATION
16.	True	
17.	True	
18.	False	Supermarkets sell many perishable items and must therefore turn over much of their inventory within days. Department stores' sales tend to be seasonal, and their inventory may turn over only every few weeks or even months.
19.	True	
20.	False	If the replacement cost of inventory is lower than its historic cost, the inventory is written down to its replacement cost.
21.	False	Increases in inventory should be deducted from net earnings to find cash flow from operations, because an increase in inventory implies that cash is being expended in the buildup of inventory.
22.	True	
23.	False	Cost of goods sold and ending inventory are inextricably linked. A change in one results in a change in the other. Ending inventory values under LIFO will differ between a perpetual and a periodic inventory system, but that also means that cost of goods sold under the two systems will also differ.
24.	False	All three cost components, direct materials, direct labor, and manufacturing overhead, form part of work in process.
25.	True	
26.	False	A physical count is carried out at the end of each period under the perpetual inventory system to confirm valuation of ending inventory.
27.	False	Under the direct method, cash flow from operations is not found by adjusting net income.
28.	False	A decrease in accounts payable is deducted from net income, and an increase is added to net income.
29.	False	Since the average cost is calculated after every purchase under the perpetual system, the average cost can vary over the period and will differ from the average cost under the periodic system, which is calculated only once at the end of the period.
30.	False	The physical flow of goods and the assumption made about cost flows are different.

Multiple Choice

31.	a	39.	a
32.	b	40.	c
33.	b	41.	c
34.	b	42.	c
35.	c	43.	a
36.	a	44.	b
37.	c	45.	b
38.	d		

Problem 46

1.

Sales	$300,000
Gross profit %	75%
Cost of goods sold	$225,000
Beginning inventory	$ 75,000
Plus Purchases	250,000
Goods available for sale	325,000
Less Cost of goods sold	225,000
Ending inventory	100,000
Less Inventory recovered	10,000
Inventory lost in earthquake	90,000
Less Cash paid by insurance company	80,000
Loss on inventory after insurance recovery	$ 10,000

2.

Cash	80,000	
Loss on inventory	10,000	
Inventory		90,000

To record decline in value of inventory resulting from earthquake.

Assets =	Liabilities +	Owners' Equity
+80,000		-10,000
-90,000		

Problem 47

1. TOYS "R" US uses the indirect method for preparing its cash flow statement, since cash flow from operations is found by adjusting net income from operations.

2. Inventories increased in all three years. The inventory balances can be found by adding the increase in inventory each year to the beginning inventory balance for that year.

Balance - Inventory Account, January 30, 1993	$1,000.0
Plus: Increase in inventory to January 29, 1994	278.9
Balance - Inventory Account, January 29, 1994	1,278.9
Plus: Increase in inventory to January 28, 1995	221.6
Balance - Inventory Account, January 28, 1995	1,500.5
Plus: Increase in inventory to February 3, 1996	193.1
Balance - Inventory Account, February 3, 1996	$1,693.6

Problem 48

1.	Number of units	Cost per unit	Total cost
Beginning inventory	1,000	$40	$40,000
Purchases 3/31/94	600	$43	$25,800
5/27/94	800	$49	$39,200
8/26/94	700	$50	$35,000
10/19/94	1,000	$56	$56,000
12/15/94	900	$60	$54,000
Total	5,000		$250,000
Less: Sales	4,500		
Ending inventory	500		

	Unit cost	Units	
Average cost per unit			$50
Ending inventory	$50	500	$25,000
Cost of goods sold	$50	4,500	$225,000
LIFO			
Ending inventory	$40	500	$20,000
Cost of goods sold		4,500	$230,000
($250,000 - 20,000)			
FIFO			
Ending inventory	$60	500	$30,000
Cost of goods sold		4,500	$220,000
($250,000 - 30,000)			

2.	Average cost	FIFO	LIFO
Sales	$ 270,000	$ 270,000	$ 270,000
COGS	225,000	220,000	230,000
Gross margin	45,000	50,000	40,000
Expenses	40,000	40,000	40,000
Income before taxes	5,000	10,000	0
Tax payable	2,000	4,000	0
Income after taxes	$3,000	$6,000	$0

3. Clare would pay the least taxes under LIFO.

4. The effect would be to increase net income from $0 under LIFO to $6,000 under FIFO. In deciding whether or not to invest in the company, remember that this is an accounting rather than an economic change and that the fundamental economic situation of the company has not altered. A number of empirical studies have been done to see whether the stock prices of companies switching from LIFO to FIFO rise when the change is announced. The evidence is somewhat mixed, but there does not seem to be support for the view that investors are fooled by this type of accounting change.

Critical Thinking Problem 49

1. In a period of rising prices, the inventory balance on the balance sheet will contain costs relating to periods when prices were substantially lower than current prices. When inventory levels drop, some of these low costs will be included in the cost of goods sold. As a result, reported income is higher than if LIFO liquidation had not taken place. Company X's 1996 tax liability would be higher than if the LIFO liquidation had not taken place.
2. Company X could have avoided a LIFO liquidation by ensuring that inventory levels did not drop over the year - in other words, by buying enough inventory to cover usage.

Chapter 7

Cash and Receivables

This chapter discusses accounting for cash and receivables, which constitute the most common types of current assets other than inventory. You have two main aims in this chapter. First, you should understand the nature of cash and gain insights into the management and accounting issues associated with it. Second, you should address the various valuation issues associated with short-term receivables such as accounts receivable and notes receivable.

Learning Objectives

- **LO 1** Identify and describe the various forms of cash reported on a balance sheet.
- **LO 2** Understand the accounting for investments of idle cash in financial instruments such as certificates of deposit.
- **LO 3** Understand the various techniques that companies use to control cash.
- **LO 4** Understand how to account for accounts receivable, including bad debts.
- **LO 5** Understand how to account for interest-bearing notes receivable.
- **LO 6** Understand how to account for non-interest-bearing notes receivable.
- **LO 7** Explain various techniques that companies use to accelerate the inflow of cash from sales.
- **LO 8** Explain the effects of transactions involving liquid assets on the statement of cash flows.

Key Textbook Exhibits

Exhibit 7-4 provides an illustration of a bank reconciliation statement. Note the types of adjustments that are made to both the bank account balance and the book balance.

Exhibits 7-5 and 7-6 illustrate the use of estimating uncollectible accounts using an aging schedule. Note how the "percent uncollectible" increases with the age of the debts.

Exhibit 7-7 illustrates the relationships between the parties involved in the credit card sales. Note how the use of the credit card simplifies the collection procedure for the seller.

Review of Key Concepts

LO 1 The cash figure shown in the balance sheet contains not only cash held by the company in the form of currency on hand and in checking, savings and money market accounts, but also **cash equivalents**. Cash equivalents are investments that are readily convertible to known amounts of cash and that have a maturity when acquired of less than three months; examples include commercial paper, treasury bills, and money market funds.

LO 2 A business's cash requirements are often seasonal, with certain times of the year requiring larger cash balances than others. Companies deal with cash shortages by borrowing on a short-term basis. Similarly, since cash balances are largely unproductive, companies usually try to invest any excess cash to earn interest or provide a return. Various vehicles for this type of short-term investment are available, but the most common are certificates of deposit (CDs), debt securities, and equity securities.

Since a penalty is paid for early withdrawal of a CD, the money invested in CDs may not be immediately available. So, whether CDs are classified as a cash equivalent or as a short-term investment depends on whether there are fewer than ninety days to the maturity date.

When an accounting period ends before a CD matures, the interest to the end of the accounting period must be accounted for. For example, assume that on December 1, 1997, Company X invests $6,000 excess cash in a 90-day CD at an annual rate of 5%. At this time, a CD asset account is created and cash is reduced by $5,000. At the company's financial year end on December 31, interest on the CD has been earned but not yet received. Since interest for 30 days has been earned, the amount of interest is

5% x $6,000 x 30/360 = $25

The adjustment to record this is

		Debit	Credit
12/31/97	Interest receivable	25	
	Interest revenue		25
	Interest receivable on certificate of deposit		

The $25 interest revenue will appear in the income statement for the year ended December 31, 1997. On February 28, 1998, the principal and full 90 days of interest at $75 is received (5% x $6,000 x 90/360). The entry to record this is

		Debit	Credit
2/28/98	Cash	6,075	
	Interest receivable		25
	Interest revenue		50
	Short-term investment: CD		6,000
	Repayment of interest and principal on certificate of deposit		

The interest Receivable account is therefore closed and the interest revenue of $50 will be reported in the income statement for the year ended December 31, 1998. This series of entries ensures proper matching of interest revenues to the time period when they were earned.

Equity investments can be classified as short-term investments or long-term investments, depending on the marketability of the investment and the intent of the company. **Trading securities**, which are purchased with the intention of selling them in the near future, are always classified as current assets. **Available-for-sale securities** are marketable, but the intent of the company dictates whether they are classified as short-term or long-term.

LO 3 At the end of each period, the company receives a statement from the bank for each of its accounts. The balance on the statement rarely matches the account balance maintained in the company's ledger because the bank and the company are not completely synchronized in their recording of transactions. As its name suggests, a **bank reconciliation** is carried out to explain the difference between the two figures. Two main types of adjustment which must be made in a bank reconciliation:

- **Transactions recorded by the company and not yet recorded by the bank.** For example, **outstanding checks** are checks that the company has issued and that have not yet been processed through the company's bank account. In addition, **deposits in transit** are deposits that the company made (usually just before the end of the accounting period) that are not yet reflected in the account balance.
- **Transactions recorded by the bank and not yet recorded by the company.** For example, the bank enters charges for service and interest on balances directly into the customer's account. Similarly, if the bank is acting as a collecting agent on behalf of the company, it will credit collections direct to the company's account.

Although it is possible to use several formats when preparing a bank reconciliation, the principal behind each is identical. The bank account balance must be increased by any deposits in transit and reduced by checks in transit; the book balance must be increased by any interest paid or collections made by the bank and decreased by any charges or NSF checks (checks where the payee's account balance cannot cover the amount of the check). Mistakes can be made both by the bank and by the company, and the bank reconciliation procedure is often the means whereby these are found. Once the reconciliation is complete, entries are made in the accounts to record the adjustments made to the book balance.

Test Your Understanding!

Question: Why doesn't the company record adjustments made to the bank account balance in its accounts?

Answer: Basically, the company is responsible only for maintaining its own set of accounts. The bank maintains its own accounts and will record any items that the company has already recorded and it has not (for example, checks in transit).

LO 3 A **petty cash fund** is used for small cash payments. An individual is given responsibility for maintaining the fund and is provided with an initial sum of money. Payments are made from this sum against receipts, and at the end of the period, the total of the receipts should equal the money paid out. The fund is replenished by this amount to bring it up to the original sum, and an adjustment is made both to record the replenishment and to recognize the various expenditures incurred.

LO 4 The balance of accounts receivable on the balance sheet represents the sum of many individual accounts. In order to better manage these individual accounts, a **subsidiary ledger** is often maintained to record separate transactions for each individual debtor. In the general ledger, a **control account** summarizes the total transactions that take place in the subsidiary ledger.

LO 4 Companies can rarely collect all money owed to them by their customers and must account for amounts that are uncollectible. The two main methods for accounting for bad debts are the **direct write-off** and the **allowance** methods.

- The **direct write-off method** is carried out after a particular amount proves uncollectible. The account receivable involved is reduced by the uncollectible amount and the bad debt expense account is increased. Because the expense is recognized only after the account proves uncollectible, this method fails to provide proper matching of expenses and revenues in the time period in which the revenues are earned. Unless the amounts involved are immaterial, the direct write-off method is therefore unacceptable under GAAP.
- The **allowance method** in effect *predicts* how much of the accounts receivable balance will prove uncollectible and creates an allowance for doubtful accounts as a *contra* account to accounts receivable. The allowance method therefore better matches the revenues and costs in a period. Two main methods are used to estimate the amount of the allowance:

Percentage of Net Credit Sales. On the basis of past experience, the company estimates the percentage of net credit sales that will prove uncollectible. To illustrate, assume that net credit sales for a period are $100,000 and that the company estimates 2% of these will prove uncollectible. The estimate of uncollectible accounts for the current period is calculated as follows:

% of uncollectibles x net credit sales for the period = 2% of $100,000
= $2,000

The following adjustment is made to record this:

	Debit	Credit
Bad debts expense	2,000	
Allowance for doubtful accounts		2,000
Increase in allowance for bad debts		

Percentage of Accounts Receivable. For this method, again on the basis of past experience, the company estimates what percentage of the closing accounts receivable balance will be uncollectible. To illustrate, assume that the accounts receivable balance is $2,500,000 and that the company estimates 1% of these will prove uncollectible. The account balance for the *contra* allowance for doubtful accounts is calculated as follows:

% of uncollectibles x accounts receivable balance = 1% of $2,500,000
= $25,000

The allowance account is increased to this amount and the difference increases bad debts expense. To continue the above example, if the current balance on the Allowance account is $24,000, the adjustment to increase the balance by the required amount is as follows:

	Debit	Credit
Bad debts expense	1,000	
Allowance for doubtful accounts		1,000
Increase in allowance for bad debts		

The percentage of accounts receivable method can be modified by classifying accounts receivable into different groups, according to how long they have been outstanding. This is known as an **aging schedule**. A different percentage is used for each group, with the percentage increasing as the period of the debt gets longer.

Under the allowance method, when a debt actually becomes uncollectible, both the customer's account and the allowance account are reduced by the amount of the uncollectible account. If an amount that has previously been written off is subsequently recovered, the entry is reversed. The customer's account and the allowance for doubtful account are both increased.

- A basic ratio, which gives users insights into how well a company manages its accounts receivables, is the accounts receivables turnover calculated as follows:

$$\text{Accounts receivables turnover} = \frac{\text{Net credit sales}}{\text{Average accounts receivable}}$$

Test Your Understanding!

Question: Company A has an accounts receivable turnover of 30 times a year; Company B has an accounts receivable turnover of 5 times per year. Is Company A six times as effective at managing its accounts receivable as Company B?

Answer: Probably not. The two companies might be in very different industries. Even if they are in the same industry, Company A and Company B might have very different proportions of credit sales. However, even if the two companies are very similar, you cannot conclude that Company A is more effective at handling its accounts receivable. The high turnover could be a signal that Company A's credit policies are overly strict and that the company may be losing lucrative sales. It does appear that Company B should consider whether or not its credit department is operating effectively so that it is not losing the use of cash for long periods.

LO 5,6 **Notes receivable** are promises to pay money in the future. There are two main types: **interest-bearing notes** and **non-interest-bearing notes** (or discounted notes).

- For an interest-bearing note, the interest payable is explicitly stated, and its accounting treatment for interest due but unpaid at the end of the accounting period is directly analogous to the example given above for a CD.
- For a non-interest-bearing note, the principal (the cash or value of goods received when the note was issued) is less than the maturity value (the cash that must be paid when the note matures). Although no interest rate is specifically stated on the note, interest is effectively paid since more money is paid at the end than is received at the beginning. Suppose, for example, that a note is received by Company A from a customer for goods with a net sales value of $3,000. The note will mature in 3 months, and the maturity value is $3,150. The implicit interest in this agreement is $150 for three months, equivalent to $600 in a full year. The implicit *annual* interest rate is therefore $600 or 20% of $3,000. The adjustment to record the receipt of the note is as follows:

	Debit	Credit
Note receivable	3,150	
Sales revenue		3,000
Discount on notes receivable		150
To record receipt of note receivable		

The discount on notes receivable account is a *contra* account to the notes receivable account. As interest on the note is earned, this account is reduced and interest revenue is increased. If the accounting period ended one month after the note was received, the entry to record the interest earned on the note would be as follows:

	Debit	Credit
Discount on notes receivable	50	
Interest revenue		50
Interest revenue on note receivable		

Test Your Understanding!

Question: What would be the current balance on the notes receivable account in the balance sheet and how would the payment on the maturity of the note be recorded?

Answer: At this point, the notes receivable balance would be $3,150, with the *contra* account, discount on notes receivable, having a balance of $100. The net balance would therefore be $3,050. When the cash payment of $3,150 is received on maturity, the adjustment would be as follows:

	Debit	Credit
Cash	3,150	
Discount on notes receivable	100	
Notes receivable		3,150
Interest revenue		100

LO 7 Companies can speed up the flow of cash from sales in several ways. With **credit card sales**, the company receives payment directly from the credit card company and avoids the uncertainties and costs associated with multiple cash collections. However, the credit card company does charge a collection fee and so the system, while increasing the speed of cash collection, is not costless. Companies can also accelerate the receipt of cash by **discounting notes receivable**, either immediately after the note is received or after it has been outstanding but before maturity. Again this method is not costless, since the amount received for the note will be less than the total amount that would have been received at maturity. When the note is discounted, cash is increased, notes receivable is reduced, and the difference between the principal and the amount received increases interest revenue.

LO 8 If a company uses the direct method for its cash flow statement, the cash collected from customers is shown as a source of cash. When the company uses the indirect method, cash flow from operations is found by adjusting net income for increases or decreases in the accounts receivable balance. For example, if accounts receivable increase over the period, the sales figure exceeds the cash received from sales. To find cash flow from operations, the increase in accounts receivable must be deducted from net income.

Review of Key Terms

Aging schedule	A form used to categorize the various individual accounts receivable according to the length of time each has been outstanding.
Allowance method	A method of estimating bad debts on the basis of either the net credit sales of the period or the amount of accounts receivable at the end of the period.
Bank reconciliation	A process whereby the bank statement balance and the book balance are reconciled.
Bank statement	A document that summarizes the activity in a bank account.
Cash equivalent	Investments that are readily convertible to known amounts of cash and that have an original maturity to the investor of three months or less.
Control account	The general ledger account that is supported by a subsidiary ledger.
Credit memoranda	A list of all items other than deposits that are shown in the bank statement as increases in the company's bank account.
Debit memoranda	A list of items other than canceled checks that are shown as deductions on the bank statement.
Debt securities	Securities issued by corporations as evidence of borrowing.
Deposit in transit	A sum of money or check that is recorded in the company's books as deposited in the bank account but has not yet been processed by the bank.
Direct write-off method	The recognition of bad debts expense at the point when an account is written off as uncollectible.
Discounted note	An alternative name for a non-interest-bearing promissory note.
Discounting	The process of selling a promissory note.
Equity securities	Securities issued by corporations as evidence of part ownership in the company, such as common stock and preferred stock.
Interest	The difference between the principal amount of a promissory note and its maturity value.
Interest-bearing note	A promissory note in which the interest rate is explicitly stated.
Maker	The party to a promissory note who agrees to repay the money at some future date.
Maturity date	The date when a promissory note is due.
Maturity value	The amount of cash to be paid by the maker to the payee on the maturity date of a promissory note.
Non-interest-bearing note	A promissory note in which interest is not explicitly stated but is implicit in the agreement.
Note payable	A liability resulting from the signing of a promissory note.
Note receivable	An asset resulting from the acceptance of a promissory note from another company.

Outstanding check A check written by the company but not yet charged to the company's account by the bank.

Payee The party to a promissory note who will receive the money at some future date.

Petty cash fund A fund that is set up to provide for minor cash disbursements and is replenished to its starting balance on a regular basis, expenditure from the fund being recorded in the books at the time the fund is replenished

Principal The amount of cash, or the fair value of the products or services, received by the maker when a promissory note is issued

Promissory note A written promise to repay a definite sum of money on demand or at a fixed or determinable date in the future

Subsidiary ledger The detail for a number of individual items that collectively make up a single general ledger account

Term The length of time a promissory note is outstanding

Practice Test
Questions and Problems

Complete each of the following statements:

LO 1 1. ________________ securities are purchased with the intention of selling them in the near future and are always classified as current assets.

LO 1 2. ________________ are investments that are readily convertible to known amounts of cash and have a maturity when acquired of less than three months.

LO 3 3. ________________ are checks for which the payee does not have sufficient money in his or her bank account to honor the check.

LO 4 4. The ________________ method requires the company to estimate what proportion of its net sales will be uncollectible and to use this to identify the current period's allowance for doubtful accounts.

LO 4 5. Under the allowance method when individual accounts are recognized as uncollectible, the ________________ account is debited and the ________________ account is credited with the amount of the uncollectible debt.

LO 4 6. The ratio of net credit sales to accounts receivable gives insights into how well a company manages its accounts receivable and is called ________________.

LO 4 7. The ________________ account is the *contra* account to notes receivable, in which the effective interest on a non-interest-bearing note is recorded.

LO 8 8. Under the indirect method for the cash flow statement, if a company's accounts receivable balance has decreased over the year, cash flow from operations is found by ________________ the change in accounts receivable to net income.

LO 4 9. __________________ is the procedure whereby accounts receivable are classified according to how long they have been outstanding.

LO 2 10. If a company's cash needs are seasonal, __________________ are accommodated by short-term borrowing.

LO 3 11. A process whereby the bank statement balance and the book balance are reconciled is called a __________________.

LO 1 12. __________________ are issued by corporations as evidence of borrowing. __________________ are issued by corporations as evidence of part ownership in the company, such as common stock and preferred stock.

LO 3 13. A fund that is set up to provide for minor cash disbursements and that is replenished to its starting balance on a regular basis is called a __________________. Expenditure from the fund is recorded in the books at the time the fund is replenished.

LO 5 14. The amount of cash, or the fair value of the products or services, received by the maker when a promissory note is issued is the __________________; the amount of cash to be paid by the maker to the payee on the maturity date of a promissory note is the __________________.

LO 5 15. The length of time a promissory note is outstanding is known as the __________________; the date that a promissory note is due is the __________________.

Indicate whether each of the following statements is true or false:

LO 3 16. In a bank reconciliation, checks and deposits in transit are deducted from the bank statement balance.

LO 4 17. Expenditures from the petty cash fund are recorded in the ledger only when the fund is replenished.

LO 8 18. If accounts receivable decrease over the year, then sales are greater than cash collected from customers.

LO 4 19. The direct write-off method for uncollectible accounts results in an understatement of current income and an overstatement of future income.

LO 4 20. Under the allowance method, when an account is written off as uncollectible, the current ratio decreases.

LO 7 21. A firm with a current ratio greater than one will increase its current ratio by discounting its non-current notes receivable.

LO 2 22. Available for sale securities are always classified as current assets.

LO 4 23. The link between a subsidiary ledger and the general ledger is provided by a control account.

LO 6 24. As its name suggests, no interest is paid or earned on a non-interest-bearing note.

LO 3 25. A bank reconciliation need be carried out only when errors are found in the ledger cash account.

LO 4 26. Both the direct write-off method and the allowance method of accounting for bad debts expense are acceptable under GAAP.

LO 5 27. For interest-bearing notes, interest earned but not yet collected is not recognized until the note matures.

LO 1 28. Cash equivalents such as commercial paper, money market funds, and T-bills are included with cash on the balance sheet.

LO 6 29. Discounting a note receivable involves selling the note to a third party to accelerate the inflow of cash.

LO 8 30. Purchases and sales of short-term investments do not appear as a separate item on the statement of cash flows.

For the following questions, circle the alternative that best answers the question:

LO 1 31. Which of the following would NOT be included in the cash balance in a balance sheet prepared on January 1, 1997?

a) Coin and currency balances
b) Balances in checking accounts
c) Balances in petty cash accounts
d) A CD maturing on May 1, 1997

LO 4 32. A petty cash fund of $200 is established on January 1, 1997. At the end of January, the cash in the Petty Cash fund is $23 and receipts supporting payments from the fund totaling $170 are available. The journal entry at the end of January to replenish the fund is

		Debit	Credit
a)	Miscellaneous expenditure	170	
	Cash		170
b)	Miscellaneous expenditure	193	
	Cash over/short	7	
	Cash		200
c)	Miscellaneous expenditure	177	
	Cash		170
	Cash over/short		7
d)	Miscellaneous expenditure	170	
	Cash over/short	7	
	Cash		177

LO 3 33. In a bank reconciliation, bank charges are
a) added to the book balance.
b) subtracted from the book balance.
c) added to the bank balance.
d) subtracted from the bank balance.

LO 3 34. In a bank reconciliation, it was discovered that a check written for $600 for payment of utilities expense had mistakenly been recorded in the ledger as $660. Which of the following is the correct adjusting entry to correct this mistake in the ledger?

a)	Cash	60	
	Rent expense		60
b)	Rent expense	60	
	Cash		60
c)	Rent expense	600	
	Cash		600

d) Since the correct amount has been debited to the bank account, no adjustment is necessary in the ledger.

LO 4 35. The face amount of accounts receivable for Company A is $50,000. It is estimated that 2% of these will prove uncollectible, that customers will take advantage of cash discounts of $1,000, and that sales of $2,000 will be returned. The net realizable value of accounts receivable is
a) $50,000
b) $49,000
c) $48,000
d) $46,000

LO 4 36. Under the direct write-off method, writing off an account as uncollectible will
a) increase both the current ratio and net income.
b) decrease both the current ratio and net income.
c) increase the current ratio and decreases net income.
d) decrease the current ratio and increases net income.

LO 4 37. Company B uses the percentage of sales method of accounting for doubtful accounts. Its allowance for doubtful accounts on January 1, 1997, was $6,000, and on December 31, 1997, was $4,500. During the year, sales were $500,000 and an allowance of 1% of sales was made for doubtful accounts. Accounts written off as uncollectible during 1997 amounted to
a) $1,500
b) $4,500
c) $5,000
d) $6,500

LO 6 38. Company Y received a six-month non-interest-bearing note in payment for net sales of $20,000 on December 1, 1997. The note will mature in 3 months with a maturity value of $21,000. Company Y's financial year ends on December 31, 1997. The entry to record the receipt of the note on December 1 is

	Account	Debit	Credit
a)	Note receivable	21,000	
	Discount on note receivable		1,000
	Sales revenue		20,000
b)	Note receivable	20,000	
	Sales revenue		20,000
c)	Note receivable	20,000	
	Interest receivable	1,000	
	Sales revenue		21,000
d)	Note receivable	21,000	
	Sales revenue		21,000

LO 6 39. Company Y received a six-month non-interest-bearing note in payment for net sales of $20,000 on December 1, 1997. The note will mature in 3 months with a maturity value of $21,000. Company Y's financial year ends on December 31, 1997. The entry to record interest earned on the note on December 31 is

	Account	Debit	Credit
a)	Discount on note receivable	333	
	Interest revenue		333
b)	Interest receivable	333	
	Interest revenue		333
c)	Interest receivable	333	
	Note receivable		333

d) None of the above.

LO 7 40. If a company's collection period for accounts receivable is unacceptably long, which of the following statements is FALSE?

a) The company may need to borrow to meet its accounts payable.
b) The company may offer cash discounts to increase the collection period.
c) The company may discount its notes receivable to increase cash flow.
d) Cash flow from operations may be lower than expected for the firm's sales.

Use the following information to answer questions 41 through 43:

On November 1, 1997, Zen Corporation invested $20,000 of excess cash in a 90-day certificate of deposit. The CD matures on January 31, 1998, and has an annual interest rate of 12%.

LO 1 41. At the financial year end on December 31, 1997, the company makes the following entry relating to the CD:

	Account	Debit	Credit
a)	Interest receivable	400	
	Interest revenue		400
b)	Short-term investments: CD	200	
	Interest revenue		200
c)	Short-term investments: CD	400	
	Interest revenue		400

d) No entry is necessary until the interest is received on January 31, 1998.

LO 1 42. On January 31, 1998, the CD matures and the company makes the following entry:

		Debit	Credit
a)	Cash	20,600	
	Short-term investments: CD		20,600
b)	Cash	20,600	
	Short-term investments: CD		20,000
	Interest revenue		600
c)	Cash	20,600	
	Short-term investments: CD		20,000
	Interest revenue		200
	Interest receivable		400
d)	Cash	20,600	
	Short-term investments: CD		20,000
	Interest revenue		400
	Interest receivable		200

LO 2 43. The revenue recognized by Zen in the year to December 31, 1997, and the year to December 31, 1998, was

a) 0, $600.
b) $200, $400.
c) $400, $200.
d) $600, 0.

LO 7 44. Soho Restaurant accepts Diners Club credit cards. During the week ended July 4, 1997, the total Diners Club credit card sales were $25,000. Diners Club pays the amount due to Soho on July 7 after deducting a 4% collection fee. The entry to record the receipt of cash from Diners Club on July 7 was:

		Debit	Credit
a)	Cash	25,000	
	Accounts receivable - Diners Club		25,000
b)	Cash	25,000	
	Collection fee expense		1,000
	Accounts receivable - Diners Club		24,000
c)	Cash	24,000	
	Collection fee expense	1,000	
	Accounts receivable - Diners Club		25,000
d)	Cash	24,000	
	Collection fee expense	1,000	
	Sales revenue		25,000

LO 4 45. Which of the following statements is TRUE?

a) The direct write-off method can result in understatement of the accounts receivable balance on the balance sheet.
b) The main difference between the direct write-off method and the allowance method is the timing of the recognition of bad debts.
c) Under the allowance method, when bad debts are written off, the allowance account is debited and bad debt expense is credited.
d) The main difference between the percentage of net credit sales method and the percentage of accounts receivable method is the percentage used in calculating the allowance for doubtful debts.

Answer each of the following problems:

LO 3 46. For the month ended December 31, 1997, the following information relating to the cash account of Delta Dentists is available:

a) According the bank statement, the balance on the checking account on December 31, 1997 is $140,326.

b) The cash account on the company books shows a balance of $148,072.

c) Delta made a deposit of $25,326 on December 31 which is not included in the bank statement.

d) The following checks were issued by Delta during December but have not yet appeared on the bank statement:

Check No.	Amount
1147	$7,350
1156	8,400
1270	1,526

e) The bank collected interest on notes receivable on behalf of the company. The bank statement shows that $500 was collected during December.

f) Two NSF checks were returned with the May statement. These were from customers Smith and Jones for $242 and $162, respectively.

g) Interest earned on the checking account was $256; $48 of bank charges were charged to the account.

h) It was discovered that a check for $250 written by Delta to Molar X-Rays was erroneously recorded in the Mortar Fillings account in the ledger.

Required

Prepare a bank reconciliation for Delta for the month of December and list some advantages to the company of preparing a bank reconciliation.

LO 5 47. Match Corporation accepted a nine-month interest-bearing note for $28,000 from Box Company on July 1, 1997, for sales of $25,000. Match Company prepares its accounts to December 31 each year.

Required

1. What is the effective rate of interest on the note?

2. Prepare the journal entries for Match over the life of the note, assuming the note is held to maturity and paid in full on the due date.

3. What are the net balances for the note receivable on July 1, 1997 and on December 31, 1997?

4. Prepare journal entries on October 1, 1997, assuming Match discounts the note on that day for $25,200.

LO 2 48. The following information appears on Alpha Corp.'s balance sheet for years ended December 31, 1997, and December 31, 1996.

	December 31, 1997	December 31, 1996
9-month certificates of deposit	$ 50	$ 151
IBM stock, acquired on 12/1/1996*	0	265
U.S. Treasury notes	704	494
Cash	45	94
Receivables less allowances	947	803
Inventories	685	620

* When the company acquired the IBM stock, it intended to sell it in January, 1997. The company carried out its intention to sell the stock early in January 1997.

Required

1. Identify which items constitute cash equivalents, and suggest the order in which they should appear in the balance sheet.

2. Where should the non-cash equivalents appear on the balance sheet?

3. What is the amount and direction of change in the company's cash and cash equivalent balances over the year? Is the company as liquid at the end of the year as it was at the beginning? What additional information would you want to know to help you to judge whether or not the change was significant?

Critical Thinking Problem

LO 8 49. The following table gives the cash flow statement of Compaq Computers for the years ended December 31, 1994, 1995, and 1996.

CONSOLIDATED STATEMENT OF CASH FLO WS

Year ended December 31, in millions	1996	1995	1994
Cash flows from operating activities:			
Cash received from customers	$17,939	$13,910	$9,986
Cash paid to suppliers and employees	-13,639	-12,437	-9,778
Interest and dividends received	110	53	22
Interest paid	-91	-100	-65
Income taxes paid	-911	-543	-319
Net cash provided by (used in) operating activities	3,408	883	-154
Cash flows from investing activities:			
Purchases of property, plant and equipment, net	-342	-391	-357
Purchases of short-term investments	-1,401		
Proceeds from short-term investments	328		
Acquisition of businesses, net of cash acquired	-22	-318	
Other, net	-26	6	-51
Net cash used in investing activities	-1,463	-703	-408
Cash flows from financing activities:			
Issuance of common stock pursuant to stock option plans	112	79	100
Tax benefit associated with stock options	91	60	53
Issuance of long-term debt			300
Net cash provided by financing activities	203	139	453
Effect of exchange rate changes on cash	27	-45	-47
Net increase (decrease) in cash and cash equivalents	2,175	274	-156
Cash and cash equivalents at beginning of year	745	471	627
Cash and cash equivalents at end of year	$2,920	$745	$471
Reconciliation of net income to net cash provided by(used in) operating activities			
Net income	$1,313	$789	$867
Depreciation and amortization	285	214	169
Provision for bad debts	155	43	36
Purchased in-process technology		241	
Deferred income taxes	-371	-17	-184
Loss on disposal of assets	5	2	2
Exchange rate effect	14	33	46
Increase in accounts receivable	-210	-863	-926
Decrease (increase) in inventories	1,004	-135	-882
Decrease (increase) in other current assets	5	-41	-55
Increase in accounts payable	586	479	248
Increase (decrease) in income taxes payable	131	-61	173
Increase in other current liabilities	491	199	352
Net cash provided by (used in) operating activities	$3,408	$883	($154)

Required

Use the table to answer the following questions:

1. Does Compaq use the direct or indirect method for presentation of the cash flow statement?

2. How much cash was collected from customers each year?

3. By how much did accounts receivable increase in each of the three years?

4. If we were to assume that all accounts receivable related to sales, what would the firm's revenues be in each of the three years?

Solutions

Fill in the Blanks

1. trading
2. cash equivalents
3. not sufficient funds
4. allowance
5. allowance for doubtful accounts, accounts receivable
6. accounts receivable turnover
7. discounts on notes receivable
8. adding
9. aging
10. cash shortages
11. bank reconciliation
12. debt securities, equity securities
13. petty cash fund
14. principal, maturity value
15. term, maturity date

True/False

		COMMENT/EXPLANATION
16.	False	Checks and deposits in transit are deducted from the bank statement balance.
17.	True	
18.	False	When cash collected is greater than sales, the additional cash received reduces the balance on the accounts receivable account.
19.	False	The direct write-off method results in uncollectible accounts receivable relating to the current period's sales being written off in the future. Therefore, the method results in an understatement of future income and an overstatement of current income.
20.	False	When the allowance method is used, writing off uncollectible accounts reduces the allowance for doubtful accounts account, not accounts receivable.
21.	True	
22.	False	Available-for-sale securities are marketable, but the intent of the company dictates whether or not they are classified as short-term or long-term.
23.	True	
24.	False	A non-interest-bearing note has an implicit rather than an explicit interest rate.
25.	False	A bank reconciliation statement should be carried out irrespective of whether or not errors are found or suspected.
26.	False	Only the allowance method is acceptable under GAAP.
27.	False	Interest is recognized when earned, not received.
28.	True	
29.	True	
30.	False	Purchases and sales of short-term securities are regarded as significant events and are therefore reported separately on the statement of cash flows.

Multiple Choice

31.	d	39.	a
32.	d	40.	b
33.	b	41.	a
34.	a	42.	c
35.	d	43.	c
36.	b	44.	c
37.	d	45.	b
38.	a		

Problem 46

Bank reconciliation December 31, 1997

Balance in bank statement		$ 140,326
Plus deposit in transit		25,326
		$165,652
Less Checks in transit		
1147	$7,350	
1156	8,400	
1270	1,526	
		17,276
Adjusted balance		$148,376
Balance in cash account		$148,072
Plus Interest collected on notes	500	
Interest on bank accounts	256	
		756
		148,828
Less NSF checks	242	
	162	
charges	48	
		452
Adjusted cash balance		$148,376

Journal entries

		Debit	Credit
7/1/97	Note receivable	28,000	
	Sales		25,000
	Discount on note		3,000
	To record receipt of note receivable		

		Debit	Credit
12/31/97	Cash	500	
	Interest revenue		500
	To record interest collected on note by bank		

		Debit	Credit
12/31/97	Cash	256	
	Interest revenue		256
	To record interest earned on checking account		

		Debit	Credit
12/31/97	Jones account	242	
	Smith account	162	
	Cash		404
	To record NSF checks		

		Debit	Credit
12/31/97	Bank charges expense	48	
	Cash		48
	To record charges from bank		

		Debit	Credit
12/31/97	Morton Fillings	250	
	Molar X-Rays		250
	To correct error in accounts payable		

Benefits to Delta include increased control over cash, the opportunity to find errors, the opportunity to ascertain NSF checks and to amend credit policies accordingly, and the opportunity to assess actual cash available so that shortages and excesses can be dealt with.

Problem 47

1. **Effective interest rate calculation**

Implicit interest	=	\$28,000 - \$25,000	=	\$3,000
Period of note			=	9 months
Interest for full year	=	$\$3,000 \times \frac{12}{9}$	=	\$4,000
Effective annual interest rate	=	$\frac{\$4,000}{\$25,000} \times 100\%$	=	16%

2. **Journal entries**

		Debit	Credit
7/1/97	Note receivable	28,000	
	Sales		25,000
	Discount on note		3,000
	To record receipt of note receivable		

		Debit	Credit
12/31/97	Discount on note	2,000	
	Interest revenue		2,000
	To record interest earned on note receivable		

		Debit	Credit
3/31/98	Discount on note	1,000	
	Cash	28,000	
	Note receivable		28,000
	Interest revenue		1,000
	To record receipt of note receivable		

3. **Balance sheet entries**

	July 1, 1997	*December 31, 1997*
Note receivable	$28,000	$28,000
Less discount on note	(3,000)	(1,000)
Net book value	$25,000	$27,000

4. Note discounted on October 1, 1997

Maturity value of note	=	$28,000
Proceeds of discount	=	$25,200

Journal entry

		Debit	Credit
10/1/97	Cash	25,200	
	Discount on note	3,000	
	Note receivable		28,000
	Interest revenue		200
	To record discounting of note receivable		

Problem 48

1. Cash equivalents - possible order

	December 31, 1997	**December 31, 1996**
Cash	$ 45	$ 94
U.S. Treasury notes	704	494
IBM stock	0	265
Total	*749*	*853*

2. The following non-cash equivalents should appear on the balance sheet under current assets:

	December 31, 1997	**December 31, 1996**
9 month certificates of deposit	$ 50	$ 151
Receivables less allowances	947	803
Inventories	685	620

3. The cash equivalents have reduced by $104, or 12.2%, over the year. The company is not therefore as liquid at the end of the year as it was at the beginning. The additional information that would be helpful is the level of sales (if the company's activities are

lower, then the cash requirements may be lower), credit terms offered to customers and by suppliers, and whether other short-term sources of cash are available.

Critical Thinking Problem 49

1. Compaq uses the direct method for its cash flow statement.

2. Cash received from customers:

1996	1995	1994
$17,939	$13,910	$9,986

3. Increase in accounts receivable

1996	1995	1994
$210	$863	$926

4. If a company uses the direct method for its cash flow statement, the cash collected from customers is shown as a source of cash. If accounts receivable increase over the period, the sales figure exceeds the cash received from sales. To find the sales figure, the increase in accounts receivable is added to cash received from customers to obtain the following estimates for sales of the period:

1996	1995	1994
$18,149	$14,773	$10,912

The actual sales for those years were:

1996	1995	1994
$18,109	$14,755	$10,866

The difference could be due to the fact that not all accounts receivable balances related to sales transactions, but to other short-term receivables.

Chapter 8

Operating Assets: Property, Plant, and Equipment, Natural Resources, and Intangibles

This chapter explores the accounting issues associated with long-term assets. Both tangible and intangible assets are discussed and your aim in this chapter is to understand the different accounting methods used for each type of asset.

Learning Objectives

LO 1	Understand the balance sheet disclosures for long-term operating assets.
LO 2	Determine the acquisition cost of an operating asset.
LO 3	Explain how to calculate the acquisition cost of assets purchased for a lump-sum.
LO 4	Describe the impact of capitalizing interest as part of the acquisition cost of an asset.
LO 5	Compare depreciation methods and understand the factors affecting the choice of method.
LO 6	Understand the impact of a change in the estimate of the asset life or residual value.
LO 7	Determine which expenditures should be capitalized as asset costs and which should be treated as expenses.
LO 8	Analyze the effect of the disposal of an asset at a gain or loss.
LO 9	Understand the balance sheet presentation of intangible assets.
LO 10	Describe the proper amortization of intangible assets.
LO 11	Explain the impact that long-term assets have on the statement of cash flows.

Key Textbook Exhibits

Table 8-1 compares the straight-line and the double declining-balance methods. Note how the accelerated method (double declining-balance) results in higher initial depreciation charges and how the book value varies as a result.

Exhibit 8-7 provides definitions of the most common intangible assets.

Review of Key Concepts

LO 1 Operating assets are used to produce the goods and services the company sells, and are essential to the long-term viability of the company. There are two main types of operating assets - tangible assets that have physical form, such as plant, machinery, land, and buildings; and intangible assets such as patents, goodwill, and trademarks.

LO 2 The first issue to be resolved in accounting for tangible assets is how they should be valued. Under U.S. GAAP, historic cost is the basis of valuation for long-term assets. The historic cost or acquisition cost should include all costs necessary to acquire the asset and prepare it for its intended use. Taxes, transportation charges, installation costs, and any necessary repairs or upgrades incurred at the time of the asset's purchase can be included.

LO 3 Sometimes assets are bought as a group at a price different from what would have been paid if the assets had been bought individually. When this happens, the acquisition cost of the group should be prorated to the individual items on the basis of their individual market prices. For example, if land and buildings are acquired together, the cost of the land should be separated from the cost of the building, using the respective market prices. This procedure is necessary because each asset may have a different economic life and may therefore need to be written off over a different period.

LO 4 When money is borrowed to acquire an asset, interest expense is incurred. The question arises of whether or not this interest should be included in the acquisition cost of the asset. Interest is normally regarded as part of the financing decision rather than as part of the acquisition decision, and is therefore not normally included in the acquisition cost. There is one exception to this. When interest is used to finance the construction rather than the purchase of an asset, part of that interest can be included in the cost of the asset or **capitalized**. The proportion of interest that is capitalized is the interest on the average expenditure over the period. The logic behind this is that since construction takes place progressively over the period, the interest charges are also incurred progressively over the period. Therefore, the interest related to the construction is based on the average expenditure over the period.

LO 5 By their nature, long-term assets are used over more than one accounting period and the cost of the asset must be spread over the assets' useful lives. The allocation process is called **depreciation.** The underlying principle is that cost allocation should closely match the decline in the asset's usefulness.

Test Your Understanding!

Question: Your brother buys a new car for $20,000 and comments that as soon as he drove it out of the car dealership, it depreciated by $2,000. Does he mean the same thing as an accountant does when he talks about depreciation?

Answer: No. He is implying that the car's **value**, or what he could get if he resold the car, has dropped by $2,000. Accountants are not attempting to find the market value of assets that they depreciate; rather, they are spreading the asset's cost over its useful life.

LO 5 Since allocation of cost is a matter of judgment; several methods of depreciation have been developed. We look at three:

- The **straight-line method** assumes that the asset's usefulness declines uniformly over its life, and an equal amount is written off the asset each year. The amount that is written off each year is found from

$$\frac{\text{Acquisition cost - Residual value}}{\text{Number of years of life}}$$

- The **units-of-production** method allocates cost on the basis of how many units of production are produced by the asset in a particular accounting period. The charge per unit is found from:

$$\frac{\text{Acquisition cost - Residual value}}{\text{Total number of units produced over the asset's entire life}}$$

- The **double declining-balance** method bases the depreciation on double the rate of depreciation under the straight-line method. This rate is applied to the net book value of the asset at the beginning of the year. Note that when calculating the rate to be charged, salvage value is ignored. For example, suppose a machine has a four-year life, an original cost of $10,000, and an estimated residual value of $1,000. The percentage straight-line depreciation rate is first calculated:

$$\frac{100\%}{4} = 25\%$$

The straight-line rate is doubled to find the rate under the double declining-balance method:

$$2 \times 25\% = 50\%$$

The rate to be applied under the double declining balance method is therefore 50%. The depreciation for this machine over its life is shown below. Note that Year 4's depreciation of $250 is not 50% of $1,250. It is a balancing figure resulting in an ending book value that equals the residual value of $1,000.

Year	Rate	Book value - beginning	Depreciation	Book value - end
1	50%	$10,000	$5,000	$5,000
2	50%	5,000	2,500	2,500
3	50%	2,500	1,250	1,250
4	50%	1,250	250	1,000

Test Your Understanding!

Question: Which parameters of the of the above depreciation methods (acquisition cost, residual value, number of years of life, total number of units produced over the entire life) are known with certainty when the asset is purchased?

Answer: Only the acquisition cost is known with certainty when the asset is purchased. All the other parameters must be estimated. Judgment plays a large part in determining depreciation charges and the resulting book values of long-term assets.

LO 5 Although the total depreciation written off over the life of the asset is identical under each method, the timing of the write-off over individual accounting periods varies greatly, resulting in substantially different reported income under each method. The double declining-balance method results in higher depreciation charges in the early years. This type of method is therefore called an accelerated method, and these methods are appropriate when the usefulness of the asset declines substantially in the early years. The most commonly used method is straight-line, which produces the highest reported net income in the early years.

LO 6 Since depreciation charges are based on estimates of acquisition cost, residual value, and asset life, it is possible that these estimates could be reevaluated and changed during the life of an asset. If that happens, depreciation already written off is not reassessed. Rather, the remaining book value at the time of the reevaluation is written off over the remaining life on the basis of the new estimates. For example, suppose a machine was bought for $100,000. When it was bought, the useful life was estimated to be 5 years, with no residual value. If straight-line depreciation is used, $20,000 is charged to depreciation each year. By the end of year 2, the net book value of the asset is $60,000. Now suppose that at the beginning of year 3 the company decides to replace the machine at the end of its fourth year of life, and that it can be sold at that time for $5,000. New annual depreciation charges for years 3 and 4 are calculated as follows:

$$\frac{\text{Closing book value - New estimated residual value}}{\text{Remaining life}} = \frac{60{,}000 - 5{,}000}{2} = \$27{,}500$$

LO 7 Whether expenditure on assets is capitalized (added to the asset's cost) or expensed (charged immediately to income) can have a major impact on reported earnings. For example, suppose that major repairs costing $10,000 are carried out on an asset with an original cost of $25,000 and a book value of $10,000. If the repairs are expensed, then income will be reduced by the total amount of repairs in the year the repair is carried out. If, however, the costs of the repairs are capitalized, the impact on the income statement will be spread over the remaining life of the asset. The capitalized cost is depreciated along with the remaining book value. In this case, the impact on the current income statement is much less dramatic. In general, if an expenditure increases the life of the asset or its productivity, it should be capitalized. Otherwise, it should be written off to the income statement in the period it is incurred.

LO 8 When an asset is sold, the difference between the book value of the asset and the sale price should be recognized as a gain or a loss on sale. The loss or gain on sale is shown on the income statement under other income and expense.

Natural resources, such as coalfields, oil wells, and timberlands, are assets that are carried in the Property, Plant, and Equipment category of the balance sheet. They are originally recorded at cost, and the cost is written off over the life of the asset in a way similar to the way depreciation is expensed for other long-term assets. The process is usually referred to as **depletion**, and the calculation is based on the portion of the natural resource that was consumed during the current year.

LO 9 Intangible assets are assets that have no physical form but still provide future economic benefits to the company. The most common types of intangibles are goodwill, patents and trademarks, copyrights, and organization costs. The costs of research and development, however, are not capitalized under U.S. GAAP but instead are expensed in the period when they are incurred. As with physical assets, intangibles are presented in the balance sheet at historic cost minus amortization (where amortization is the word used for depreciation of an intangible). The only intangibles that appear on the balance sheet, therefore, are the ones that are the result of a purchase transaction.

Test Your Understanding!

Question: The Coca Cola company did not purchase its famous trademark, which is easily its greatest asset. Would you expect to see it appear on the balance sheet as an intangible asset?

Answer: No. Only intangibles that are the result of a purchase transaction will appear on the balance sheet.

LO 10 Intangibles should be amortized over their life in a way directly analogous to the depreciation of fixed assets. The main issue in amortizing intangibles is defining the period over which they should be amortized. There are significant international differences in the amortization of intangibles; for example, goodwill is amortized over a maximum of 40 years under U.S. GAAP but over a much shorter period in other countries.

LO 11 Several ratios can be used to gain insight into the type and use of fixed assets. The average life and average age of long-term assets are both useful measures of how long the company can expect to use its assets. The asset turnover ratio is a measure of how productively the company uses its assets.

$$\text{Average age} = \frac{\text{Accumulated depreciation}}{\text{Depreciation expense}}$$

$$\text{Average life} = \frac{\text{Historic cost of assets}}{\text{Depreciation expense}}$$

$$\text{Asset turnover} = \frac{\text{Net sales}}{\text{Average total assets}}$$

In the statement of cash flows, the cash paid or received in the acquisition or sale of assets are shown under investing activities. When the indirect method is used, it is necessary to make two adjustments to net income to find cash from operations. First, since depreciation is a non-cash expense that has been deducted in calculating net income, it must be added back to net income to find cash from operations. Second, the gain or loss on sale has also been added to or deducted in finding net income. However, the sale of fixed assets is reported under investing activities and therefore the gain or loss must be deducted from, or added back to, net income to find cash flow from operations.

Review of Key Terms

Accelerated depreciation	A term that refers to several methods by which a higher amount of depreciation is recorded in the early years of an asset's life and a lower amount is recorded in the later years.
Acquisition cost	An amount that includes all of the costs normally necessary to acquire an asset and prepare it for its intended use.
Book value	The original acquisition cost of an asset minus the amount of accumulated depreciation.
Capital expenditure	A cost that improves an operating asset and is added to the asset account.
Capitalization of interest	The process of treating the cost of interest on constructed assets as a part of the asset cost rather than as an expense.
Change in estimate	A change in the life of an asset or in its expected residual value.
Depreciation	The allocation of the original acquisition cost of an asset to the periods benefited by its use.
Double declining-balance method	A method by which depreciation is recorded at twice the straight-line rate but the depreciable balance is reduced in each period.
Gain on sale of asset	An account whose amount indicates how much the selling price on an asset's disposal exceeds its book value.
Goodwill	The amount indicating that the purchase price of a business exceeded the total fair market values of the identifiable net assets at the time the business was acquired.
Intangible asset	A long-term asset that has no physical properties, for example patents, copyrights, and goodwill.
Land improvements	Additions made to a piece of property such as paving or landscaping a parking lot. The costs are treated separately from land for purposes of recording depreciation.
Loss on sale of asset	An account whose amount indicates how much the book value of an asset exceeds the reselling price received on the asset's disposal.
Natural resources	Assets that are consumed during their use, for example coal or oil.
Organization costs	Costs that are incurred at the initial formation of a corporation and are treated as an intangible asset.
Research and development costs	Expenditures incurred in the discovery of new knowledge and the translation of research into a design or plan for a new product.
Revenue expenditure	A cost that keeps an operating asset in its normal operating condition and is treated as an expense of the period.
Straight-line depreciation	A method by which the same dollar amount of depreciation is recorded in each year of asset use.
Units-of-production method	A method by which depreciation is determined by the number of units the asset can produce.

Practice Test Questions and Problems

Complete each of the following statements:

LO 10 1. ____________________ is calculated by dividing the property, plant, and equipment cost by depreciation expense; it indicates how long the company intends to keep its assets on average.

LO 10 2. ____________________ is calculated by dividing accumulated depreciation by depreciation expense; it indicates how long, on average, the company has owned its long-term assets.

LO 4 3. When interest costs for financing the construction of an asset are capitalized, the amount of interest is based on the ____________________ over the construction period.

LO 10 4. ____________________ is a measure of how many dollars of assets are necessary for every dollar of sales.

LO 11 5. When the indirect method of presentation is used for the statement of cash flows, depreciation expense is presented in the ____________________ section and acquisitions and sales of long-term assets appear in the ____________________ section.

LO 2 6. The ____________________ of a long-term asset includes all the costs necessary to acquire the asset and prepare it for its intended use.

LO 5 7. ____________________ is the allocation of the acquisition cost of a long-term asset over its expected life.

LO 5 8. The ____________________ method of depreciation assumes that an asset's usefulness declines steadily over time.

LO 9 9. ____________________ is calculated by deducting the market value of the individual net assets from the purchase price of an acquired business; it must be written off over not more than forty years.

LO 10 10. ____________________ is the process of writing off intangibles over their lives.

LO 5 11. An asset is acquired for $6,000 on January 1, Year 1. It is expected to have a five-year life and residual value of $1,000. The depreciation expense in Year 4 is ____________________ if the company uses straight-line depreciation.

LO 5 12. An asset is acquired for $6,000 on January 1, Year 1. It is expected to have a five-year life and residual value of $1,000. The depreciation expense in Year 1 is ____________________ if the company uses the double declining-balance method of depreciation.

LO 5 13. An asset is acquired for $6,000 on January 1, Year 1. It is expected to have a five-year life and residual value of $1,000. The net book value of the asset at the beginning of Year 3 is ____________________ if the company uses the double declining-balance method of depreciation.

LO 5 14. An asset is acquired for $6,000 on January 1, Year 1. It is expected to have a five-year life and residual value of $1,000. The asset is fully depreciated to its expected residual value, and is sold at the end of Year 5 for ____________________ at a loss of $750.

LO 5 15. An asset is acquired for $6,000 on January 1, Year 1. It is expected to have a five-year life and residual value of $1,000. After two years, the asset is sold for $3,000, and the company uses the double declining-balance method of depreciation. The company makes a ____________________ of ____________________ on the sale of the asset.

Indicate whether each of the following statements is true or false:

LO 9 16. All expenditures for research and development can be capitalized under U.S. GAAP.

LO 6 17. Long-lived assets can be revalued to market value during their life.

LO 5 18. An accelerated depreciation method results in increased cash flow to the company because of the tax shield provided by the method.

LO 5 19. The cost of land must be amortized over a period not exceeding forty years.

LO 1 20. Car manufacturers typically have a higher ratio of long-lived assets to total assets than advertising agencies.

LO 7 21. When a piece of machinery is bought, the cost of installing it in the factory must be expensed and cannot be added to the cost that is capitalized and depreciated.

LO 5 22. Accelerated methods of depreciation are most appropriate when the market value of the asset decreases most in the early years of the asset's life.

LO 5 23. Depreciation expense recognition results in an increased debt/equity ratio.

LO 9 24. Not all intangible assets that have value to the company appear on the balance sheet; the balance sheet shows the cost of intangibles, not their value.

LO 7 25. The cost of replacing a vehicle's engine is never capitalized, since it represents maintenance of an existing asset.

LO 5 26. If an asset has a ten-year life, and zero residual value, and the double declining-balance method of depreciation is used, its net book value at the end of five years will be less than half of its original cost.

LO 7 27. Improvements that significantly extend the asset's life are treated separately from the asset for the purposes of charging depreciation.

LO 5 28. Irrespective of the method used, the total depreciation charged over an asset's life should equal the difference between its original cost and its estimated residual value.

LO 8 29. An asset with a net book value of $3,000 and accumulated depreciation of $4,000 is sold for $8,000 at a loss of $1,000.

LO 9 30. According to GAAP, only goodwill arising as a consequence of an acquisition can be recognized as an asset and reported on the balance sheet.

For the following questions, circle the alternative that best answers the question:

LO 5 31. Which of the following assets is NOT depreciated or amortized over its life?
a) Land
b) Goodwill
c) Buildings
d) Plant and equipment

LO 5 32. Which of the following statements about the accumulated depreciation account is TRUE?
a) It is a long-term liability.
b) It provides a *contra* account to intangible assets.
c) It provides a *contra* account to tangible assets so that their net book value approximates their market value.
d) It represents the total depreciation charged over the life of the asset to which it relates, and reduces the book value of the asset.

Use the following information to answer questions 33 through 36:

On December 1, 1996, Company X bought from Company Y land with a warehouse on it for $800,000. Company Y showed the land and buildings on its balance sheet at $500,000. The fair market values of the land and building at the time of purchase were $700,000 and $300,000, respectively.

LO 3 33. How much of the purchase price should Company X allocate to land?
a) $700,000
b) $500,000
c) $300,000
d) $560,000

LO 3 34. What gain would Company X record in its accounts for the purchase of the land?
a) $140,000
b) $200,000
c) $100,000 loss
d) Zero

LO 8 35. What gain would Company Y show in its books for the sale of the land and building?
a) $200,000
b) $100,000
c) $500,000
d) $300,000

LO 5 36. Company X allocates the entire cost of the purchase to land. Normally it depreciates buildings over 20 years using the straight-line method with zero residual value and does not depreciate land. Because of its accounting treatment of the purchase, Company X's income for each of the next 20 years
a) will be overstated by $12,000.
b) will be understated by $12,000.
c) will be overstated by $15,000.
d) will be understated by $15,000.

LO 8 37. A machine with a cost of $100,000 and accumulated depreciation of $80,000 was sold at a loss of $6,000. The cash received from the sale was
a) $16,000.
b) $26,000.
c) $74,000.
d) $14,000.

LO 8 38. The net book value of equipment for Company Y was $150,000 on January 1 and $140,000 on December 31, 1996. During the year, depreciation expense for equipment was $20,000. Which of the following events is consistent with these facts?
a) Assets with a net book value of $10,000 were sold during the year; no assets were purchased.
b) Assets were purchased during the year for $30,000, and assets with a historic cost of $10,000 were sold during the year.
c) Assets with a net book value of $40,000 were sold during the year, and assets were purchased for $50,000.
d) Assets were purchased for $30,000 during the year; no assets were sold.

LO 8 39. On January 1, 1996, the balance in accumulated deprecation was $70,000. During the year, an asset with a historic cost of $20,000 was sold for $10,000 at a gain of $6,000. Depreciation expense on the remaining assets was charged on December 31 at $33,000. The balance on the accumulated depreciation account on December 31 was:

a) $103,000.
b) $ 87,000.
c) $ 83,000.
d) $ 93,000.

LO 6 40. A company uses straight-line depreciation for its buildings, assuming a thirty-year life and zero residual value. The CEO points out that the buildings last much longer than 30 years, often 60 years, and asks what impact depreciating buildings over 60 years rather than 30 years would have on earnings per share and debt-equity ratio. You reply that

a) earnings per share will increase, and debt-equity ratio will decrease.
b) both earnings per share, and debt-equity ratio will decrease.
c) both earnings per share and, debt-equity ratio will increase.
d) earnings per share will decrease, and debt-equity ratio will increase.

LO 9 41. Which of the following is not an intangible asset?

a) Patents
b) Improvements to a building the company already owns
c) Trademarks
d) Goodwill arising as a result of an acquisition

LO 8 42. A machine was bought for $120,000 and was depreciated using the straight-line method. It was expected to have a ten-year life and $20,000 residual value. After six years, the machine is made obsolete by a new technological development, and the company decides to keep the machine for two more years and then to sell it for scrap for $2,000. At the end of two years, the company carries out its plan and sells the machine for $2,000. The accounting treatment of this situation is:

a) No change in depreciation expense for Years 1 through 6. Depreciation expense for Years 7 and 8 is $10,000 per year, and in addition, the company recognizes a loss on sale in Year 8 of $38,000.
b) No change in depreciation expense for Years 1 through 6. Depreciation expense for Years 7 and 8 is $10,000 per year, and in addition, the company recognizes a loss on sale in Year 8 of $18,000.
c) No change in depreciation expense for Years 1 through 6. Depreciation expense for Years 7 and 8 is $29,000 per year, and no additional loss on sale will be recognized in Year 8.
d) The company restates its income for Years 1 through 6 to change the depreciation expense on the machine to $$11,800 each year. Depreciation expense for Years 7 and 8 is also $11,800 per year, and no additional loss on sale will be recognized in Year 8.

LO 5 43. A company uses the double declining-balance method of depreciation. It purchases an asset for $40,000, which is expected to have a ten-year life and $4,000 residual value. Which of the following statements is true?

a) The depreciation rate to be applied each year is 10%.
b) The depreciation charge in the last year is calculated to bring the net book value to $4,000.
c) By the end of three years, 60% of the original cost has been written off.
d) Depreciation in the first year is 20% of $36,000.

LO 9 44. Which of the following statements is true?

a) Goodwill, both as a result of an acquisition and internally generated, is the only intangible asset to appear on the balance sheet.
b) The interest expense incurred when money is borrowed to buy an asset may be capitalized as part of the asset's cost.
c) Accelerated methods are most appropriate when an asset's usefulness declines most in the later years of its life.
d) If an expenditure increases an asset's productivity or life, its cost may be added to the cost of the asset and depreciated.

LO 9 45. Which of the following sets of ratios can be used to gain insights into a company's management of its fixed assets?

a) Current ratio, quick ratio
b) Inventory turnover ratio, accounts receivable turnover
c) Debt to equity ratio, times interest earned
d) Average age, asset turnover

Answer each of the following problems:

LO 5,6 46. Company A is preparing its financial statements for the year ended December 31, 1997. The following information is available about Company A's long-term assets.

Asset	Purchase date	Purchase price	Estimated life at date of purchase	Depreciation basis	Residual value	Improvements or Changes in estimate
A	7/1/95	$100,000	6 years	Straight-line	$10,000	
B	1/1/96	60,000	3 years	Straight-line	0	On 1/1/97 expenditure of $20,000 was undertaken that increased the asset's life by 3 years
C	1/1/96	150,000	10 years	Double declining-balance	0	
D	1/1/96	150,000	5 years	Double declining-balance	0	

In addition, on January 1, 1997, Company B was acquired for a total purchase price of $200,000. The net market value of the individual assets was $100,000 at the time of the acquisition. Company A writes off goodwill over 40 years.

Required

1. Complete the following table:

Asset	Depreciation or amortization expense for 1997	Acquisition cost on 12/31/97	Accumulated depreciation on 12/31/97	Net book value on 12/31/97
A				
B				
C				
D				
E				
Goodwill				

2. **Asset A was sold for $50,000 on January 1, 1996. Calculate the gain or loss on sale, and show the journal entry recording the sale.**

LO 5 47. Jenny Corporation purchased a molding machine for $100,000 on January 1, 1996. The company uses straight-line depreciation for financial reporting and an accelerated method for tax purposes. The machine has a four-year life and zero residual value. The accelerated method results in 50%, 30%, 10%, and 10% respectively being written off over Years 1 through 4. The tax rate is 40%.

Required

1. Complete the following table:

Year	1	2	3	4	Total
Book depreciation					
Tax depreciation					
Difference					
Increase (decrease) in tax paid under accelerated method					

2. Explain why many companies choose accelerated methods of depreciation for tax purposes even although the net effect over the life of the vehicle is zero.

Critical Thinking Problem

LO 11 48. The statement of cash flows for the Disney Company is provided below:

CONSOLIDATED STATEMENT OF CASH FLO WS
(In millions)

Year ended September 30	**1995**	**1994**	**1993**
Cash Provided by Operations Before Income			
Taxes	$4,067.5	$3,127.7	$2,453.9
Income taxes paid	-557.4	-320.4	-308.7
	3,510.1	2,807.3	2,145.2
Investing Activities			
Film and television costs	-1,886.0	-1,433.9	-1,264.6
Investments in theme parks, resorts and other			
Property	-896.5	-1,026.1	-813.9
Euro Disney investment	144.8	-971.1	-140.1
Purchases of investments	-1,033.2	-952.7	-1,313.5
Proceeds from sales of investments	1,460.3	1,494.1	841
Other	-77.8	3.0	31.4
	-2,288.4	-2,886.7	-2,659.7
Financing Activities			
Borrowings	786.1	1,866.4	1,256.0
Reduction of borrowings	-771.9	-1,315.3	-1,119.2
Repurchases of common stock	-348.7	-570.7	-31.6
Dividends	-180.0	-153.2	-128.6
Other	182.4	76.1	136.1
	-332.1	-96.7	112.7
Increase (Decrease) in Cash and Cash			
Equivalents	889.6	-176.1	-401.8
Cash and Cash Equivalents, Beginning of Year	86.9	363	764.8
Cash and Cash Equivalents, End of Year	$1,076.5	$186.9	$363.0

Required

1. How much cash was used in the making of films in 1995, 1994, and 1993? How much cash was invested in theme parks in those three years? What other major purchases did Disney make during those years?

2. How much cash did Disney receive from selling investments during these three years? Can you tell whether they made a gain or a loss from the information provided?

3. Explain what you can tell from the cash flow statement about Disney's investment in Euro Disney over the three years. Why do you think Disney separated information about Euro Disney from information about its other investments?

Solutions

Fill in the Blanks

1. average life
2. average age
3. average accumulated expenditures
4. asset turnover
5. operating, investing
6. acquisition cost
7. depreciation
8. straight-line
9. goodwill
10. amortization
11. $1,000
12. $2,400
13. $2,160
14. $250
15. loss, $840

True/False

		COMMENT/EXPLANATION
16.	False	Under U.S. GAAP, research and development expenditures are expensed when incurred.
17.	False	Under U.S. GAAP, long-lived assets remain at historic cost.
18.	True	
19.	False	Land is not amortized over its life.
20.	True	
21.	False	Costs of installation may be capitalized.
22.	False	Depreciation is a method of cost allocation, not of valuation.
23.	True	
24.	True	
25.	False	Replacement of an engine could extend the vehicle's life and may therefore be regarded as capital expenditure.
26.	True	
27.	True	
28.	True	
29.	False	The loss on the sale of the asset is $5,000.
30.	True	

Multiple Choice

31. a
32. d
33. d
34. d
35. d
36. a
37. d
38. c
39. b
40. a
41. b
42. c
43. b
44. d
45. d

Problem 46

1.

Asset	Depreciation or amortization expense for 1997	Acquisition cost on 12/31/97	Accumulated depreciation on 31/12/97	Net book value on 31/12/97
A	15,000	100,000	37,500	62,500
B	12,000*	80,000	32,000	48,000
C	24,000 (20% x 120,000)	150,000	54,000	96,000
D	36,000 (40% x 90,000)	150,000	96,000	54,000
Goodwill	2,500	100,000	2,500	97,500

* Depreciation for 1997 is calculated as follows:

Original cost	$60,000
Depreciation in 1996	20,000
Net book value 1/1/97	40,000
Improvement	20,000
Total	60,000
Number of years of life	5 years
Depreciation per year	$12,000

2. Loss on sale = $50,000 - $62,500 = $12,500

	Debit	Credit
Cash	50,000	
Accumulated depreciation	37,500	
Loss on sale	12,500	
Asset A		100,000
Sale of asset at a loss		

Problem 47

1.

Year	1	2	3	4	Total
Book depreciation	25,000	25,000	25,000	25,000	100,000
Tax depreciation	50,000	30,000	10,000	10,000	100,000
Difference	25,000	5,000	(15,000)	(15,000)	0
Increase (decrease) in tax paid under accelerated method	(10,000)	(2,000)	6,000	6,000	0

2. Many companies choose accelerated methods of depreciation for tax purposes even though the net effect over the life of the vehicle is zero because money has a time value. The company can use cash to provide a return - for example by investing in CDs - until it is needed.

Critical Thinking Problem 48

1. The amounts invested are as indicated below:

	1996	1995	1994
Film and television costs	$ 1,886.0	$ 1,433.9	$ 1,264.6
Investments in theme parks, resorts, and other property	$ 896.5	$ 1,026.1	$ 813.9
Purchases of investments	$ 1,033.2	$ 952.7	$ 1,313.5

It is clear that Disney's biggest investment continues to be in the making of films and television programs. This is probably understandable, since most of its other businesses to a large extent derive from their films.

2. The proceeds from the sale of investments is as shown below. It is not possible to tell whether or not Disney made a profit on these transactions.

	1996	1995	1994
Proceeds from sales of investments	$ 1,460.3	$ 1,494.1	$ 841.0

3. The cash flow statement tells us that for the first two of the three years, the cash flow from Euro Disney was negative, but in the third year it became positive. Disney probably wanted to highlight the improved performance of Euro Disney, since it was one of the most troubled and least profitable investments the company had ever undertaken.

	1996	1995	1994
Euro Disney investment	$ 144.8	$ (971.1)	$ (140.1)

Chapter 9

Current Liabilities, Contingent Liabilities, and the Time Value of Money

Liabilities are the debts and obligations of an enterprise. This chapter begins a detailed examination of liabilities and how they are identified, measured, and recorded. Your overall objective for this chapter is to understand the nature of current liabilities and the measurement issues associated with them.

Learning Objectives

- **LO 1** Identify the components of the current liability category of the balance sheet.
- **LO 2** Examine how accruals affect the current liability category.
- **LO 3** Understand how changes in current liabilities affect the statement of cash flows.
- **LO 4** Determine when contingent liabilities should be presented on the balance sheet or disclosed in footnotes and how to calculate their amounts.
- **LO 5** Explain the difference between simple and compound interest.
- **LO 6** Calculate amounts using the future value and present value concepts.
- **LO 7** Apply the compound interest concepts to some common accounting situations.
- **LO 8** Understand the deductions and expense for payroll accounting.
- **LO 9** Determine when compensated absences must be accrued as a liability.

Key Textbook Exhibits

Exhibit 9-1 illustrates the way that McDonald's presents its current liabilities section of the balance sheet. You should note the types of accounts presented and the order in which they are presented.

Table 9-1 gives **future value factors** for different interest rates and periods. Note how the factors increase with both the interest rate and the number of periods. This is consistent with the idea that the longer you leave your money invested, and the higher the interest rate, the more money you will have at the end.

Table 9-2 gives **present value factors** for different interest rates and periods. Note that the higher the interest rate and number of periods, the lower the present value factor. Intuitively, the longer you have to wait for a payment and the higher the interest you can earn, the less value the payment will have to you now.

Review of Key Concepts

LO 1 **Current liabilities** is one of the two categories of liabilities presented in the balance sheet. Current liabilities are usually identified as those obligations that the firm must pay within one year or within the normal operating cycle. A liability that is expected to be paid more than a year from the balance sheet date is normally classified as a **long-term liability.**

LO 1 Current liabilities on the balance sheet are usually shown in the order they have to be paid, starting with the liability that is expected to be paid first and ending with the liability that is expected to be paid last. They are also shown at face value, ignoring the time value of money.

LO 1 Users of the company's financial statements, particularly potential suppliers and creditors, are concerned about the amount and nature of current liabilities. Current liabilities provide an invaluable insight into the short-term obligations of the company. The ability to meet these obligations is indicated by the relationship between current assets and current liabilities. A useful summary measure of the ability to meet short-term obligations through normal operations is the **current ratio.** Some users prefer to use the **quick ratio** as a measure of liquidity, since it represents the ability to immediately satisfy current liabilities.

$$\text{Current ratio} = \frac{\text{Current Assets}}{\text{Current Liabilities}}$$

$$\text{Quick ratio} = \frac{\text{Current Assets - Inventory}}{\text{Current Liabilities}}$$

LO 1 The three most common current liability accounts appearing on the balance sheet are **accounts payable, notes payable,** and **taxes payable.**

- **Accounts payable** arise when inventory, goods, or services are bought on credit as part of the normal operations of the business. The amount recorded is normally the gross amount of the invoice, ignoring any prompt payment discount. Invoice terms can be stated as 3/15, net 30. In other words, a 3% discount is available if payment occurs within 15 days; otherwise the full amount must be paid within 30 days.
- **Notes payable** are formal contracts requiring the company to pay both a sum of money, and interest on that money by a specified time in the future. They often arise from acquiring a cash loan from a bank or creditor, although they can arise through dealings with a supplier. Notes that are payable within a year of the balance sheet date are classified as current liabilities. The note can be accounted for in two ways depending on whether interest is paid on the note's due date or is paid in advance. To illustrate, assume that Zeta Corporation receives a six-month loan from its bank on January 1, Year 1. The face amount of the loan is $5,000 that must be repaid on July 1, Year 1. Interest on the note is 10% per annum.

First, assume that interest is paid on the note's due date. The journal entry recording the issue of the note is:

		Debit	Credit
1/1/Year 1	Cash	5,000	
	Note payable		5,000

The journal entry recording the repayment of the note with interest is:

	Debit	Credit
7/1/Year 1 Note payable	5,000	
Interest expense	250	
Cash		5,250

Now assume that interest on the note is deducted in advance, and the cash received from the bank on January 1, Year 1, is $4,750, which equals the face value of the note ($5,000) minus the interest on the note ($250). The journal entry on January 1, Year 1 is:

	Debit	Credit
1/1/Year 1 Cash	4,750	
Discount on note payable	250	
Note payable		5,000

When the note is repaid on July 1, two adjustments must be made. First, the repayment of the note must be recorded:

	Debit	Credit
7/1/Year 1 Note payable	5,000	
Cash		5,000

In addition, the discount on the note is transferred to interest expense over the life of the note. In summary, the journal entry is:

	Debit	Credit
Interest expense	250	
Discount on note payable		250

Test Your Understanding!

Question: Which type of note has the higher effective interest rate and why?

Answer: When the interest is paid at the end of the loan period, the borrower has the use of the total amount borrowed throughout the period of the loan ($5,000 in the case of Zeta). When the interest is paid at the beginning of the loan period, the borrower only has the use of the loan amount minus interest for the period of the loan ($4,750 for Zeta). The interest rate effectively paid is therefore higher in the second case than the first.

LO 2 **Taxes payable** represent obligations of the company to pay taxes of various types. There is often a delay between realizing the earnings on which the tax is to be paid and actually paying the cash sum due. Taxes must therefore be accrued and recorded as an expense when they are incurred, not when they are paid. In analyzing the performance of a company, the effect of tax changes should be separated from changes in operating performance.

LO 3 The change in the balance of each current liability is reflected in the statement of cash flows, usually in the operating activities category. If a current liability has decreased (increased), then cash has been used to pay the liability (or has been released by the increase of the liability). Where a current liability is not part of the normal operations of the company (for example, notes payable), then the change in that item will be found in the appropriate category of the cash flow statement.

LO 4 **Contingent liabilities** are liabilities that are not certain to be realized. Examples include potential damages under lawsuits and obligations under warranties and guarantees. The accounting treatment of contingent liabilities depends on the accountant's judgment as to the likelihood of the potential liability. If the liability is judged to be probable and if the amount can be reasonably estimated, then the liability should be accrued and recorded. If the liability is judged to be not probable but reasonably possible, then the liability should be disclosed in the footnotes to the financial statements but not reported in the balance sheet. Unlike contingent liabilities, **contingent assets** are not recorded until the gain actually occurs. This is consistent with the doctrine of conservatism.

LO 5 Interest payments can be calculated in one of two main ways:

- In a **simple interest** calculation, interest is earned only on the principal or capital sum.
- In a **compound interest** calculation, interest is earned both on the principal and on any interest previously earned. With compound interest, the more frequently interest is calculated, the more often interest is charged, and therefore the higher the effective interest rate. **Note** that in calculating future and present values, we assume compound interest.

Test Your Understanding!

Question: Suppose you are offered two loans: you pay simple interest on one and compound interest on the other. The capital sum, interest rate, and length of the loan are equal under both loans. Which loan would you prefer?

Answer: You would prefer the simple interest loan, since the amount of interest paid under compounding is substantially higher because you pay interest on both the principal and on any interest earned.

LO 6 The **future value** of a sum of money refers to how much the sum will amount to in the future, if we can invest at a specified rate of interest. In calculating future value, we need to specify

1. the sum invested (p)
2. the interest rate (i)
3. the number of periods compounding (n)

The formula to calculate future value is:

$$FV = p(1+i)^n$$

To illustrate, suppose that you invest $5,000 in a savings account that pays 4% annually. The total amount you will have in your account at the end of five years is

$$FV = 5{,}000\,(1+0.04)^5$$
$$= \$6{,}083$$

LO 6 In the same way that we can calculate the future value, we can calculate the **present value** of a sum of money at a specified time in the future. The present value of a sum of money is how much we need to invest now to have that sum in the future. Again, we need to specify three things:

1. the amount in the future (payment)
2. the interest rate (i)
3. the number of periods (n)

The formula to calculate present value is

$$PV = \text{payment}\,(1 + i)^{-n}$$

To illustrate, suppose that you wish to have $10,000 savings in ten years time in an account that pays 8% interest each year. How much do you have to put in the account now to have $10,000 in ten years?

$$PV = 10{,}000\,(1 + 0.08)^{-10}$$
$$= \$4{,}632$$

LO 6,7 An **annuity** is a series of equal payments made at regular intervals. Since many business contracts involve this type of payment scheme, shortcuts in handling future and present values of annuities have been derived. In calculating future and present values of annuities, it is possible, but time-consuming and tedious, to calculate individually the future or present value of each payment. To shorten this process, tables have been developed that give future value and present value factors for annuities of different lengths and at different interest rates. Tables 9-3 and 9-4 give future value and present value annuity factors. Annuities are particularly helpful when using compound interest concepts to solve for other unknowns, such as the effective interest rate on a series of payments.

Test Your Understanding!

Question: Suppose you wish to invest $1,000 four times a year for three years in a savings scheme, with the first payment being made in three months' time. The interest rate is 8% compounded four times a year. Which factor should you use in calculating the future value of this set of payments?

Answer: The number of periods is 12 (four times per year for three years); the interest rate per quarter year is 8%/4 = 2%, and the relevant factor from Table 9-3 is therefore 13.412. The future value of this series of payments is therefore $1,000 x 13.412 or $13,412.

LO 8,9 The appendix introduces the calculations and accounting entries necessary when payroll is recorded. When preparing the amount to be paid to each employee, the gross wages (including any overtime payment) is first calculated. Net pay is calculated from this by deducting

1. Income tax,
2. FICA (Federal Insurance Contributions Act or, more commonly, social securities tax), and
3. Voluntary deductions (health insurance, pension contributions, union dues, etc.).

Taxes on employers must also be calculated and charged as part of wage expense, and include

1. FICA (the employer normally has to pay an additional amount equal to that deducted from the employee) and
2. Unemployment tax.

Compensated absences are absences from employment for which it is expected that employees will be paid. As a result of a FASB ruling, most employers are required to record a liability and an expense for vacation days when earned, but sick days are not recorded until employees are actually absent. Compensated absences are another example of the use of the matching principle, since they are an attempt to match revenues with the costs of generating those revenues.

Review of Key Terms

Accounts payable	Amounts owed for the purchase of inventory, goods, or services acquired in the normal course of business.
Accrued liability	A liability that has been incurred but has not been paid by the date of the balance sheet.
Annuity	A series of equally spaced payments of equal amount.
Compensated absences	Absences from employment, such as sick days and vacation days, for which it is expected that employees will be paid.
Compound interest	Interest that is calculated on the principal plus interest already earned.
Contingent asset	A sum of money or asset that the company may receive that depends on an existing condition where the outcome of the condition is not known with certainty.
Contingent liability	A liability that involves an existing condition where the outcome of the condition is not known with certainty and is dependent on some future event.
Current liability	An amount of money owed by the enterprise that will be paid within one year, or during the next operating cycle.
Current maturities of long-term debt	The portion of long-term liability that will be paid within one year of the balance sheet date.
Discount on notes payable	A *contra* liability account that represents interest deducted in advance on a loan or a note.
Estimated liability	A contingent liability that is accrued and recorded on the balance sheet.
Future value of a single sum	The amount that will be accumulated in the future from a single sum that is invested now and that accrues interest until the future time.
Future value of an annuity	The amount that will be accumulated in the future when a series of payments is invested and accrues interest until that time.
Gross wages	The amount of an employee's wages before deductions.

Net pay	The amount of an employee's paycheck after deductions.
Notes payable	Amounts owed that are represented by a formal contractual agreement and usually involve the payment of interest.
Present value of a single sum	The amount of money now that is equivalent to the single sum to be received in the future.
Present value of an annuity	The amount needed now to be equivalent to a series of equally spaced payments in the future.
Simple interest	Interest that is calculated on the principal amount only.
Time value of money	The concept that indicates that people prefer a sum of money paid immediately to the same sum paid in the future.

Practice Test Questions and Problems

Complete each of the following statements:

LO 1 1. _______________ are distinguished from long-term liabilities because they are normally due to be paid within one year of the balance sheet date.

LO 4 2. A liability under a warranty agreement is an example of a _______________ liability.

LO 6 3. The higher the interest rate, the _____________ is the present value of a sum of money received in the future.

LO 5 4. Interest that is calculated on both the capital sum and any previously accumulated interest is called _____________ interest.

LO 6 5. The idea that a sum of money received now is worth more than the same sum received in the future is called the _____________ of money.

LO 9 6. FASB calls absences from employment for which it is expected that employees will be paid (such as sick days and vacation days) _______________.

LO 1 7. Amounts owed for the purchase of goods or services during the normal operations of the business appears in the balance sheet under the heading _______________.

LO 6 8. A series of equal payments at regular intervals is called an _______________.

LO 2 9. Obligations to pay taxes of various types appear in the balance sheet as _______________.

LO 8 10. To find an employee's __________________, it is necessary to deduct taxes, FICA, and any voluntary deductions from his or her ___________________.

LO 2 11. An __________________ is a liability that has been incurred but has not been paid by the date of the balance sheet.

LO 2 12. ____________________ is a contra liability account that represents interest deducted in advance on a loan or a note.

LO 1 13. The portion of long-term liability that will be paid within one year of the balance sheet date is called the ____________________.

LO 6 14. If an account pays an annual rate of 12% compounded quarterly, the interest received per quarter is ____________________.

LO 5 15. In a ____________________ calculation, interest is earned only on the principal or capital sum. In a ____________________ calculation, interest is earned both on the principal and on any interest previously earned.

Indicate whether each of the following statements is true or false:

LO 4 16. If a contingent liability is both probable and measurable, it should be disclosed in the footnotes to the accounts rather than reported in the balance sheet.

LO 6 17. If the interest rate were zero, then the present value of an annuity would equal the sum of the individual payments.

LO 2 18. The effective interest on a note payable is lower if the interest is deducted in advance than if it is paid at the same time as the capital is repaid.

LO 4 19. A contingent asset should always be reported in the balance sheet.

LO 6 20. The more often interest is compounded, the lower the effective interest rate.

LO 3 21. The current ratio is found by dividing the company's cash by its current liabilities.

LO 3 22. If a company increases its current liabilities by buying a piece of machinery for a short-term note payable, its quick ratio will increase.

LO 2 23. An invoice with terms 3/10, net 30 means that a 3% discount can be taken up to and including thirty days after invoice date.

LO 2 24. The time value of money is ignored when valuing current liabilities for the balance sheet.

LO 2 25. Current liabilities are presented in the balance sheet according to the date the liability was incurred.

LO 6 26. We wish to have \$110 in one year's time and can invest in an account that provides an annual interest rate of 10% compounded quarterly. We therefore need to invest a minimum of \$100 now.

LO 9 27. The amount to be paid to each employee is found by deducting the taxes paid by the employer, such as unemployment taxes and employer's portion of FICA, from the gross wages the employee earns.

LO 6 28. If we invest \$1,000 now in an account that pays a nominal 12% each year compounded annually, we will have the same as if we invested in an account that pays 12% each year, compounded quarterly.

LO 5 29. If we use simple interest, interest is earned only on the principal sum and not on interim interest earned.

LO 9 30. As a result of a FASB ruling, sick days to which employees are entitled must be recorded as a liability and an expense even although they were not used by the employee.

For the following questions, circle the alternative that best answers the question:

LO 1 31. For users of financial statements, the current liability classification in the balance sheet is important because it is closely tied to the concept of
a) materiality.
b) liquidity.
c) Profitability.
d) leverage.

LO 3 32. Alpha Company has current assets of $100,000 and current liabilities of $40,000. How much inventory could it purchase on account and achieve its minimum desired current ratio of 2:1?
a) $10,000
b) $20,000
c) $40,000
d) It cannot purchase any inventory on account and achieve its minimum desired current ratio.

LO 3 33. Beta Company has current assets of $80,000 and current liabilities of $60,000. How much of its short-term notes payable could it pay in cash and achieve its minimum desired current ratio of 2:1?
a) $10,000
b) $20,000
c) $40,000
d) It cannot repay any of its short-term notes payable and achieve its minimum desired current ratio.

LO 1 34. In the liabilities section of the balance sheet,
a) only current liabilities are adjusted for the time value of money.
b) only long-term liabilities are adjusted for the time value of money.
c) both current liabilities and long-term liabilities are stated at their face value.
d) both current liabilities and long-term liabilities are stated at their present value.

LO 2 35. An invoice received from a supplier for $5,000 on January 1, with terms 3/15, net 30 means that the company should pay
a) $5,000 between January 4 and January 16.
b) $4,850 before the end of January.
c) $4,250 before January 4.
d) either $4,850 before January 16 or $5,000 before the end of the month.

LO 3 36. In the statement of cash flows, an increase in short-term notes payable would be shown as

a) an increase in cash in the operating activities category.
b) a decrease in cash in the operating activities category.
c) an increase in cash in the financing category.
d) a decrease in cash in the financing category.
e) an increase in cash in the investing category.
f) a decrease in cash in the investing category.

LO 3 37. In the statement of cash flows, a decrease in accounts payable would be shown as

a) an increase in cash in the operating activities category.
b) a decrease in cash in the operating activities category.
c) an increase in cash in the financing category.
d) a decrease in cash in the financing category.
e) an increase in cash in the investing category.
f) a decrease in cash in the investing category.

LO 4 38. Omega Company is involved in two unrelated lawsuits, one as the plaintiff and one as the defendant. As a result of these two lawsuits, the company has therefore both a contingent asset and a contingent liability. How should Omega record these on its balance sheet?

a) Omega should record both the contingent liability and the contingent asset separately on the balance sheet.
b) Omega should record both the contingent liability and the contingent asset on the balance sheet by offsetting the liability against the asset.
c) Omega must record the contingent asset if the realization of the asset is probable and the amount can be reasonably estimated, but must not record the contingent liability on the balance sheet.
d) Omega must not record the contingent asset, but must record the contingent liability on the balance sheet, if the liability is probable and the amount can be reasonably estimated.

LO 4 39. You are due to receive a fixed $100,000 in three years from a rich uncle. If interest rates increase,

a) the present value of the $100,000 decreases.
b) the present value of the $100,000 increases.
c) the present value of the $100,000 is not affected by a change in interest rate.

LO 4 40. You are due to receive a fixed $100,000 in three years from a rich uncle. If interest rates increase,

a) the future value of the $100,000 decreases.
b) the future value of the $100,000 increases.
c) the future value of the $100,000 is not affected by a change in interest rate.

Use the following information to answer questions 41 through 43:
You have $1,000 to invest and have been offered the following interest rates:
Option I - Nominal rate of 10%, compounded twice a year,
Option II - Nominal rate of 12%, compounded annually, or
Option III - Nominal rate of 8%, compounded four times a year.

LO 6 41. You decide to choose Option I. How much will you have in your account at the end of five years?
a) $1,629
b) $12,578
c) $1,762
d) $1,611

LO 6 42. You decide to choose Option II. How much will you have in your account at the end of five years?
a) $6,353
b) $1,486
c) $1,791
d) $1,762

LO 6 43. You decide to choose Option III. How much will you have in your account at the end of five years?
a) $16,351
b) $1,486
c) $6,353
d) $1,469

LO 6 44. You are required to pay $5,000 for college fees for each of the next four years, and a friendly uncle has offered to give you enough money now to cover these future payments. How much must he give you now, if you can invest at 10% per year, compounded annually?
a) $40,555
b) $20,000
c) $15,850
d) $13,660

LO 6 45. You are required to pay $5,000 for college fees for each of the next four years, and a not-so-friendly uncle has offered to give $14,275 towards your college fees. What is the annual interest rate that you would need to earn to allow you to invest the money and meet the four payments?
a) 10%
b) 18%
c) 12%
d) 15%

Answer each of the following problems:

LO 4,6 46. The Clydesdale Company is a retailer of domestic appliances. As a sales promotion, the company offers to buy-back in eight years, at the original price, any washing machine purchased from it. Assume that you are interested in buying a washing machine that costs $300 and that the interest rate is 15%. You can obtain the same washing machine for $280 from a discount warehouse.

Required

1. What is the present value of the offer by Clydesdale, assuming you are certain to take up its buy-back offer in eight years?

2. How low could the probability of your taking up the offer be, before the discount warehouse price for the washing machine is competitive with Clydesdale's offer?

3. Clydesdale estimates that only 2% of people buying washing machines will take up the buy-back in eight years. If it sells 100,000 washing machines under this promotion, how should it record its liability under these buy-back agreements?

LO 1,2 47. Show the effect on the financial statements of the following transactions for Psi Company:

a) Inventory is purchased on account for $1,000 on June 10, 1996.

b) The terms of the purchase are 4/5, net 30. The inventory is paid for on June 12, 1996.

c) A twelve-month note is issued by Psi to East Fargo Bank on July 1, 1996. The face value of the note is $3,000, and interest (of 8% per annum) is payable at the time the note is issued.

d) On December 31, 1996, the interest on the note is accrued for reporting in the balance sheet.

e) A six-month note payable is issued by Psi to a supplier for inventory on October 1, 1996. The face amount of the note is $1,000 and interest (of 10% per annum) is payable at the same time as the principal is repaid on March 31, 1997.

f) On December 31, 1996, the interest on the note is accrued for reporting in the balance sheet.

g) The portion of long-term debt that becomes current on December 31, 1996, is $2,000.

h) Repayment is made on the current portion of long-term debt on January 31, 1997.

i) Psi estimates its liabilities under warranties for the coming year to be $10,000. No provision has yet been made for this in the balance sheet on December 31, 1996.

j) During 1997, repair costs for Psi under warranties amount to $9,500, all of which were paid in cash.

LO 2 48. JJ Corporation manufactures and sells computer peripherals. The company recently introduced a new laser printer which sells for $1000 and comes with a three-year parts and labor warrantee. The company offers this unusually long guarantee because it expects that, due to their revolutionary design, these printers will be substantially more reliable than previous models. The company expects only 1% of the printers to be returned for repair in each year of the three-year warranty period, and that labor and parts replacement will cost an average of $20 for each machine. During 1996, the first year that the printer was sold, 500 printers were sold.

Required

1. Show the impact on the financial statements of JJ Corporation's liability under the warranty agreement for the new printers at the end of 1996.

2. During 1997, the number of new printers returned for repair was 50 and actual repair costs averaged $100 per machine. Show the impact on the financial statements of the costs of repair under warranty, assuming all expenses were paid in cash.

3. Because of the higher than expected repair costs under warranty, the company investigated the new printers and discovered that a key microchip was subject to failure. These chips were replaced in all new printers sold during 1997, but it was not possible to retrofit the printers sold in 1996. The company estimates that an additional 100 of the printers sold during 1996 will require repairs at an average cost of $100. How should the contingent liability under the remaining warranty agreement for the first batch of 500 new printers be shown in the balance sheet on 12/31/97?

Critical Thinking Problem

LO 1,3 49. The accounts payable balance for Ben & Jerry's Corporation on December 31, 1997 is $1,300,000. It is expected that half of these accounts payable will be paid within thirty days of the balance sheet date, and the remainder will be paid within sixty days of the balance sheet date. Annual short-term interest rates at the balance sheet date are approximately 12%.

Required

1. What is the present value of the payments that Ben & Jerry's will make to its creditors over the next two months? You may assume that two payments are made: the first, one month from the balance sheet date, and the second, two months from the balance sheet date.

2. Do you think that the difference between the present value and the actual cash payments is significant?

Solutions

Fill in the Blanks

1. current liabilities
2. contingent liability
3. lower
4. compound
5. time value
6. compensated absences
7. accounts payable
8. annuity
9. taxes payable
10. net pay, gross wages
11. accrued liability
12. discount on notes payable
13. current maturities of long-term debt
14. 3%
15. simple interest, compound interest

True/False

		COMMENT/EXPLANATION
16.	False	If a contingent liability is both probable and measurable, it is reported in the balance sheet.
17.	True	
18.	False	If interest is deducted in advance on a note payable, less money is available during the period of the loan, and therefore the effective interest rate is higher.
19.	False	A contingent asset should not be reported on the balance sheet until it is realized.
20.	False	The more often compounding takes place, the higher the interest rate that is effectively paid or charged.
21.	False	The current ratio is the current assets divided by the current liabilities; the quick ratio is the cash or cash equivalents divided by the current liabilities.
22.	False	The transaction has no effect on cash, but increases current liabilities. The quick ratio (equal to cash divided by current liabilities) therefore decreases.
23.	False	3/10, net 30 means that a 3% discount can be taken up to 10 days from the invoice date and the net amount must be paid within 30 days of the invoice date.
24.	True	Only long-term liabilities are adjusted for the time value of money in the balance sheet.
25.	False	Current liabilities are presented in the balance sheet according to the date the liability is likely to be paid.
26.	False	Quarterly compounding would require an investment of less than $100 now.
27.	False	Employee's expenses are deducted to get net pay, not employer's.
28.	False	The more often interest is compounded in a period, the higher is the effective interest rate, even although the nominal rate does not change.
29.	True	
30.	False	Only vacation days need be accounted for.

Multiple Choice

31. b
32. b
33. c
34. b
35. d
36. c
37. b
38. d
39. a
40. c
41. a
42. d
43. b
44. c
45. d

Explanation of Question 32

Let \$x be the amount of inventory the company purchases on account. Then the current assets of \$100,000 increase by the amount of the inventory to 100,000 + x, and the current liabilities of \$40,000 increase by the new accounts payable to 40,000 + x.

Current ratio is current assets divided by current liabilities

i.e. (100,000 + x) / (40,000 + x).

This ratio must be greater than or equal to two.

We solve (100,000 + x) / (40,000 + x) >= 2 for x.

Therefore, x = 20,000.

Explanation of Question 33

Let \$x be the amount of cash the company uses to redeem notes payable. Then the current assets of \$80,000 decrease by the amount of cash to 80,000 - x, and the current liabilities of \$60,000 decrease by the retired notes payable to 60,000 - x.

Current ratio is current assets divided by current liabilities

i.e. (80,000 - x) / (60,000 - x).

This ratio must be greater than or equal to two.

We solve (80,000 - x) / (60,000 - x) >= 2 for x.

Therefore x = 40,000.

Problem 46

1. Original cost of machine $300

   Present value factor (8 years, 15%) 0.32690

   Present value of future payment $98.07

   The offer to buy-back the washing machine is worth $98 if you are certain to take up the offer. The discount warehouse offers a discount of ($300 - $280) = $20.

2. Your probability of taking up the offer could go as low as ($20/$98) = 20% before the discount warehouse price is competitive with Clydesdale's offer.

3. Whether Clydesdale reports the liability on the balance sheet or discloses it in the notes to the accounts depends on how much confidence it has in their estimated take up rate of 2%. Given that it is unlikely to have had experience with this type of offer, it would appear unlikely that its estimate is other than a guestimate. The argument would therefore be strong for disclosing the liability in the notes. If however, the company has some evidence for, and confidence in, the 2% estimate, it would record the liability at the present value of the likely cash flow in year eight. In this case, the liability would be long-term.

   i.e. 2% of 100,000 machines at $300 times the present value interest factor for eight years at 15% (0.32690)

   i.e. 2% x 100,000 x $300 x 0.32690 = $196,140.

Problem 47

		Debit	Credit
a) 6/10/96	Inventory	1,000	
	Accounts payable		1,000
	Purchase of inventory on account		

		Debit	Credit
b) 6/12/96	Accounts payable	1,000	
	Discount on payables		40
	Cash		960
	Payment for inventory		

		Debit	Credit
c) 7/1/96	Cash	2,760	
	Discount on notes payable	240	
	Note payable		3,000
	Issue of note for cash		

		Debit	Credit
d) 12/31/96	Interest expense	120	
	Discount on notes payable		120
	Interest expense on note		

		Debit	Credit
e)10/1/96	Inventory	1,000	
	Note payable		1,000
	Issue of note for purchase of inventory		

		Debit	Credit
f) 12/31/96	Interest expense	25	
	Interest payable		25
	Interest accrued on note payable		

		Debit	Credit
g) 12/31/96	Long-term debt	2,000	
	Current portion of long-term debt		2,000
	Adjusting entry for current portion of long-term debt		

		Debit	Credit
h) 1/31/97	Current portion of long-term debt	2,000	
	Cash		2,000
	Payment of current portion of long-term debt		

		Debit	Credit
i) 12/31/96	Warranty expense	10,000	
	Liability under warranty		10,000
	Provision for liability under warranty contracts		

		Debit	Credit
j) 12/31/97	Liability under warranty	9,500	
	Cash		9,500
	Cash expenses for repairs under warranty		

Problem 48

1. In 1996, the company estimates 1% of the 500 printers will be returned for repair at a cost of $20 each. The total contingent liability for these printers is $100. The effect of recognizing this liability on the financial statements is

		Debit	Credit
12/31/96	Warranty expense	100	
	Liability under warranty		100
	Provision for liability under warranty contracts		

2. Total repair costs in 1997 were 50 x $100 or $5,000. The journal entry to record the repair expenses is

		Debit	Credit
12/31/97	Liability under warranty	100	
	Warranty expense	4,900	
	Cash		5,000
	Cash expenses for repairs under warranty		

3. At the end of 1997, the company reevaluates its likely warranty expense as 100 printers at $100 per printer i.e. $10,000. The company should increase its contingent liability by this amount. The appropriate journal entry is

		Debit	Credit
12/31/97	Warranty expense	10,000	
	Liability under warranty		10,000
	Provision for liability under warranty contracts		

Critical Thinking Problem 49

1. The interest rate per month is the annual interest rate divided by 12 or 1%. The relevant present value factors are, therefore, 0.9901 for one month and 0.9803 for two months. The present value of the two payments is

   ($650,000 x 0.9901) + ($650,000 x 0.9803) = $1,280,760

2. The difference between the present value and the accounts payable balance is $19,240 or about 1.5%. Because this difference is not material, the accounts payable balance would not be adjusted for the time value of money.

Chapter 10

Long-Term Liabilities

This chapter explores the long-term liabilities section of the balance sheet. The first part of the chapter considers accounting for bonds, and the second part discusses other long-term liabilities such as leases and pensions. Your overall objective is to understand the financial and accounting issues associated with long-term liabilities so that you can interpret financial reports containing these items.

Learning Objectives

LO 1 Identify the components of the long-term liability category of the balance sheet.

LO 2 Define the important characteristics of bonds payable.

LO 3 Determine the issue price of a bond using compound interest techniques.

LO 4 Understand the effect on the balance sheet of issuance of bonds.

LO 5 Find the amortization of premium or discount on bonds payable using effective interest amortization.

LO 6 Find the gain or loss that occurs on retirement of bonds.

LO 7 Determine whether a lease agreement must be reported as a liability on the balance sheet.

LO 8 Explain deferred taxes and calculate the amount of deferred tax liability.

LO 9 Understand the meaning of pension obligation and the effect of pensions on the long-term liability category of the balance sheet.

LO 10 Explain the effects that transactions involving long-term liabilities have on the statement of cash flows.

Key Textbook Exhibits

Exhibit 10-4 illustrates the effective interest method of amortizing bond discount. Notice how the cash interest and the interest expense differ and how the effective interest is constant over the life of the bond.

Exhibit 10-7 illustrates the amortization of leases using the effective interest method. Note how it parallels the amortization of bond discount in Exhibit 10-3.

Review of Key Concepts

LO 1 All obligations of the company that will not be satisfied within one year are classified as long-term liabilities. Although many different items fall into this category, we concentrate on bonds or notes, pension obligations, leases, and deferred taxes.

LO 2 Bonds are securities that are traded on stock markets and that represent a liability of the company to repay long-term borrowing. Bonds must have the following items defined and specified on the bond certificate:

- **Due date or maturity date:** the point in time when the bond must be repaid.
- **Face value or par value:** the amount of money the firm must repay on the maturity date, typically $1,000.
- **Face rate or nominal rate:** the interest rate paid each interest period. The amount of interest is calculated by applying the face rate to the face value of the bond.
- **Collateral:** the assets that back the bonds and that can be claimed by the bondholders if the company defaults. Examples include the company's land, buildings, and inventory.

LO 3 Since bonds are traded on securities markets, the price that the company can sell its bonds for will depend on the return provided by other similarly risky investments. For example, if companies with similar risk are offering bond interest of 10% (**the market rate of interest**), and Company A is selling bonds offering interest of 12%, the demand for Company A's bonds will be considerable and their price will rise relative to other bonds. Similarly, if Company B is selling bonds offering 8%, which is less than the market rate of interest of 10%, Company B's bond prices will be lower than those of other comparable bonds. Using discounted cash flow techniques, we can value the bonds and confirm these relationships. For example, suppose that the bonds of both Company A and Company B mature in three years' time. The cash flows from a $1,000 bond are:

Present Value	Cash Flow - Year 1 Interest	Cash Flow - Year 2 Interest	Cash Flow - Year 3 Capital and interest
Company A	120	120	1,120
Company B	80	80	1,080

Assuming that Company A and Company B are equally risky, it is clear that Company A's bonds should have a higher value, since the cash flows are higher at each date. To find the present values of the two bonds, we must discount at the market rate of interest because we wish to compare the bonds with what the market is offering. Discounting at the market rate of interest, the present values of the bonds are:

Company A	=	120 x 0.91 + 120 x 0.83 + 1,120 x 0.75
	=	109 + 99 + 841
	=	1050
Company B	=	80 x 0.91 + 80 x 0.83 + 1,080 x 0.75
	=	73 + 66 + 811
	=	950

Confirming our intuition, Company A could sell its $1,000 for $1,050, at a **premium** and Company B could sell its $1,000 bond for $950, at a **discount**.

LO 4 When bonds are issued at face value, the accounting treatment is straightforward. The asset category (cash) and the liability category (bonds payable) of the balance sheet are both increased by the amount of cash received. When the bond is issued at a premium or a discount, the cash received is either greater or less than the amount that will be paid at the maturity of the bond. We will use the above examples of Company A and Company B to illustrate the different accounting treatments.

Issue at a premium

When Company A issues a $1,000 bond for $1,050, the difference between the face value (the company's liability under the bond) and the market value of the bond is called a **premium on bonds payable**. The premium on bonds payable is shown as an addition to bonds payable in the balance sheet. The effect of the issue on the financial statements is

	Debit	Credit
Cash	1,050	
Bonds payable		1,000
Premium on bonds payable		50

Issue at a discount

When Company B issues a $1,000 bond for $950, the difference between the face value of the bond and the market value is called a **discount on bonds payable**. The discount on bonds payable is shown as a *contra* to bonds payable in the balance sheet.

	Debit	Credit
Cash	950	
Discount on bonds payable	50	
Bonds payable		1,000

LO 5 When bonds are issued at a discount or premium, the discount or premium account must be written off over the life of the bonds. Each year, the interest expense of the bond is increased or decreased by the amount written off the discount or premium accounts. The effective interest paid on the bond is different from the nominal interest paid. Transferring an amount from the discount or premium account to interest expense is called amortization. The effective interest method is commonly used to calculate the appropriate amortization of the discount or premium.

The effective interest rate of a bond is defined as the annual interest expense over the carrying value, where carrying value is the face value, plus the unamortized premium or less the unamortized discount. Since the amount owed under the bond is constant over all periods, the effective interest rate of the bond should also be constant over all periods. The effective interest rate method amortizes the discount or premium by an amount that ensures that the effective interest rate is constant. To illustrate for Company A:

	Cash Interest (a)	Interest Expense (b)	Premium Amortized (c) = (a) - (b)	Carrying Value (d)	Effective Interest Rate (e) = (b) / (d)
Rate	12%	10%		1,000 + 50 = 1,050	
Year 1	120	10% of 1,050 = 105	120 - 105 = 15	1050 - 15 = 1,035	105/1,050 = 10%
Year 2	120	10% of 1,035 =103.50	120 - 103.50 = 16.5	1035 - 16.5 = 1,018.5	103.5/1,035 = 10%
Year 3	120	10% of 1,018.5 = 101.85	120 - 101.85 = 18.15	1018.5 - 18.15 = 1,000.35	101.85/1,018.5 =10%

The effective interest rate method results in a reduction of the carrying value of the bonds to their face value while ensuring that the effective interest on the bonds is constant. Note that again we are progressively reducing the interest expense each year by a proportion of the premium that was received at the beginning.

Test Your Understanding!

Question: Can you repeat the effective interest rate calculations for Company B? What are the interest expense and carrying values each year? What is the effect on interest expense of reducing the discount account each year?

Answer: Interest expense is $95 for Year 1, $96.50 for Year 2, and $98.25 for Year 3. The carrying value is $965 at the end of Year 1, $982.50 at the end of Year 2, and $999.75 at the end of Year 3. The effect of reducing the discount over the life of the bonds is to increase the interest expense each year.

LO 6 When bonds are retired early, they are normally repaid at more than their face value. The amount repaid may be higher or lower than the carrying value, and the company may therefore sustain a loss or realize a gain on the redemption of the bonds. The gain or loss on redemption is reported in the income statement as an extraordinary item.

LO 7 A lease is a contract in which the lessee is granted the right to use an asset in exchange for making payments to its owner, the lessor. In accounting for leases, the fundamental issue that must be resolved is whether the lease is a rental agreement or effectively a purchase. If the lease is simply an agreement to rent the asset, and the rights and responsibilities of ownership do not pass to the lessee, then the lease is accounted for as an operating lease. If the lease effectively transfers ownership rights to the lessee, then the lease is accounted for as a capital lease.

Under U.S. GAAP, capital leases must meet one or more of four criteria involving transfer or ownership at the end of lease period, bargain purchase option, the percentage of the asset life that the lease spans, and the present value of the lease payments in relation to the market value of the asset. If a lease satisfies the criteria for capital leases, it is deemed to effectively transfer ownership rights to the lessee. The lessee records the present value of the lease payments as an asset (leased assets) and as a liability (obligations under leases) at the inception of the lease. The asset is depreciated like any other long-term asset over the life of the lease. The obligation under leases is progressively reduced over the life of the lease using the effective interest rate method. Note that the balance in leased assets and the obligations under leases are unlikely to have equal balances during the life of the lease, since depreciation will not match the amortization of the obligation.

The effective interest rate method of amortizing a lease obligation results in the lease payment being analyzed into two components: interest for the year and reduction of lease obligation.

Operating leases are accounted for by the lessee by recording the cash payment under the lease each year. No liability or asset is recorded for these leases. However, FASB requires a footnote disclosing the amount of future lease obligations under operating leases.

LO 8 The calculation of net income for reporting often differs from the net income calculated for tax purposes. Permanent differences arise when an item is included for tax purposes but never included for book purposes. For example, tax-exempt bonds are included in reported income but not in taxable income. Temporary differences occur when there is a timing difference between when an item affects book and tax calculations. For example, depreciation charges are often based on straight-line methods for financial reporting and on accelerated methods for tax purposes. The total depreciation charged over the life of the asset is the same, but the depreciation charges for tax are greater in the early years. The deferred tax account, which appears as a long-term liability in the balance sheet, is used to reconcile temporary differences between book accounting and tax reporting.

To illustrate accounting for deferred tax, assume that Company C buys an asset for $60,000 in Year 1 and uses straight-line depreciation with zero terminal value and a four-year life. Under the Modified Accelerated Cost Recovery System allowed by the IRS, the amounts that can be written off for years 1 through 4 are 33.33%, 44.45%, 14.81%, and 7.41%, respectively. The following table illustrates the calculation of deferred taxes for this asset:

Year	Tax Depreciation	Book Depreciation	Difference	Tax Impact @ 40% Impact on Deferred Tax Account	Deferred Tax Account Balance
1	20,000	15,000	5,000	2,000 increase	2,000
2	26,670	15,000	11,670	4,668 increase	6,668
3	8,885	15,000	-6,115	-2,446 decrease	4,222
4	4,445	15,000	-10,555	-4,222 decrease	0
Total	**60,000**	**60,000**	**0**	**0**	

In the early years of the asset's life, the tax depreciation is greater than the book depreciation resulting in a deferred tax liability. The amount increases both the deferred tax account and the tax expense for the year. In the later years, the book depreciation is greater than the tax depreciation. The difference reduces both the balance in the deferred tax account and the tax expense in the income statement. The above illustrates the temporary nature of this type of deferred tax, since the tax impact is zero over the life of the asset.

LO 9 In accounting for pensions, two accounting issues must be resolved. pension expense on the income statement must reflect the accrued pension cost over the period, not just the cash paid to the pension fund (funding payment). The difference between the two is transferred to the accrued pension cost account.

The accrued pension cost appears either as an asset or a liability in the balance sheet and represents the accumulated difference between pension expense and total funding payments. In addition to accrued pension cost shown in the balance sheet, the company must provide additional footnote information. The accumulated benefit obligation (ABO) is a measure of the obligation to employees if they were to retire at their current salary;

the projected benefit obligation (PBO) calculates the pension obligation on the assumption of future salary increases. These are both compared to the value of the assets in the pension plan to indicate whether or not the plan is underfunded.

Three ratios are useful in assessing the company's reliance on debt finance and its ability to service that debt:

$$\text{Debt-to-Equity Ratio} = \frac{\text{Total Liabilities}}{\text{Total Stockholders' Equity}}$$

$$\text{Times Interest Earned} = \frac{\text{Income Before Interest and Taxes}}{\text{Interest Expense}}$$

$$\text{Debt Service Coverage} = \frac{\text{Cash Flow from Operations Before Interest and Taxes}}{\text{Interest and Principal Payments}}$$

LO 10 Changes in long-term liabilities are reflected in the financing section of the statement of cash flows.

Review of Key Terms

Accrued pension cost — An account that represents the difference between the amount of pension recorded as an expense and the amount of the funding payment made to the pension fund.

Accumulated benefit obligation — A measure of the amount owed to employees for pensions if the employees retired at their existing salary levels.

Bond issue price — The total of the present value of the cash flows produced by a bond. It is calculated as the present value of the annuity of interest payments plus the present value of the principal.

Callable bonds — Bonds that may be redeemed or retired before their specified due date.

Capital lease — A lease that meets one or more of the four FASB criteria and is recorded as an asset by the lessee.

Carrying value — The face value of a bond plus the amount of unamortized premium or minus the amount of unamortized discount.

Debenture bonds — Bonds that are backed by the general creditworthiness of the issuer and are not backed by specific collateral.

Deferred tax — The account used to reconcile the difference between the amount recorded as income tax expense and the amount that is payable as income tax.

Discount on bonds — The excess of the face value of bonds over the issue price. It occurs when the market rate on the bonds exceeds the face rate.

Effective interest method of amortization — The process of transferring a portion of premium or discount to interest expense. This method transfers an amount resulting in a constant effective interest rate.

Face rate of interest — The interest stated on the bond certificate. It is also called the *nominal* or *coupon rate*.

Face value — The principal amount of the bond as stated on the bond certificate.

Funding payment — A payment made by the employer to the pension fund or its trustee.

Gain or loss on redemption	The difference between the carrying value and the redemption price at the time bonds are redeemed. This amount is recorded as an income statement account.
Long term liability	An obligation that will not be satisfied within one year.
Market rate of interest	The interest rate that bondholders could obtain by investing in other bonds that are similar to the issuing firm's bonds.
Operating lease	A lease that does not meet any of the four FASB criteria and is not recorded by the lessee.
Pension	An obligation to pay retired employees as compensation for service performed while employed.
Permanent difference	A difference between the accounting for tax purposes and the accounting for financial reporting purposes. This type of difference occurs when an item affects one set of calculations but never affects the other set.
Premium on bonds	The excess of the issue price over the face value of bonds. It occurs when the face rate on the bonds exceeds the market rate.
Projected benefit obligation	A measure of the amount owed to employees for pensions that incorporates an estimate of the future salary increases that employees will receive.
Serial bonds	Bonds that do not all have the same due date. A portion of the bonds come due each time period.
Temporary difference	A difference between the accounting for tax purposes and the accounting for financial reporting purposes. This type of difference affects both book and tax calculations but not in the same time period.

Practice Test Questions and Problems

Complete each of the following statements:

LO 9 1. The__________________________ benefit obligation is a measure of the amount of pension benefits payable to employees if they were to retire at their current salary levels.

LO 9 2. A pension plan is __________________________ if the plan assets exceed the obligations under the plan.

LO 10 3. Changes in the deferred tax account appear in the __________________________ section of the statement of cash flows.

LO 2 4. __________________________ is the assets that back bonds and that can be used by bondholders to satisfy interest and capital payments if the bond issue defaults.

LO 2 5. __________________________ bonds are bonds that may be retired before their due date by the issuer; __________________________ bonds can be retired before their due date by the bond holder.

LO 3 6. The ________________________ equals the present value of the future cash flows from the bond, discounted at the market rate of interest.

LO 4 7. Bonds are issued at a ________________________ if the issue price exceeds the face value.

LO 5 8. The ________________________ of a bond is found by deducting amortized discount or adding unamortized premium to the face value of the bond.

LO 9 9. Amortizing bond discount or premium using the ________________________ method ensures that interest expense equals a constant percentage of carrying value over the life of the bond.

LO 9 10. The ________________________ ratio is a measure of how adequately the cash flow from operations covers interest and principal repayments on a bond.

LO 8 11. ________________________ is the difference between the accounting for tax purposes and the accounting for financial reporting purposes. This type of difference occurs when an item affects one set of calculations but never affects the other set.

LO 8 12. The account used to reconcile the difference between the amount recorded as income tax expense and the amount that is payable as income tax is called the ________________________.

LO 6 13. ________________________ is the difference between the carrying value and the redemption price at the time bonds are redeemed. This amount is recorded as an income statement account.

LO 9 14. ________________________ is an account that represents the difference between the amount of pension recorded as an expense and the amount of the funding payment made to the pension fund.

LO 9 15. ________________________ is a measure of the amount owed to employees for pensions that incorporates an estimate of the future salary increases that employees will receive.

Indicate whether each of the following statements is true or false:

LO 7 16. A company has a debt covenant requiring that the ratio of debt to equity not exceed 0.5:1; the ratio is currently 0.4:1. The company would probably prefer to acquire property under an operating lease rather than a capital lease.

LO 4 17. If the market rate of interest is less than the face rate of bonds, then the bonds must be issued at a discount.

LO 2 18. Convertible bonds allow the company to convert the bonds into equity if it wishes.

LO 2 19. Serial bonds are often preferred by growing companies because the companies do not need to repay the principal all at one time but rather can spread the payment of principal over a period.

LO 3 20. A bond that did not pay interest, but only repaid the principal at some future date, would have a present value equal to the principal.

LO 5 21. The effective-interest method of bond amortization results in the effective interest rate on the bond being constant over the entire life of the bond.

LO 6 22. If bonds are retired early, the company must pay more than the principal and it therefore incurs a loss on redemption.

LO 7 23. To determine whether a lease is a capital lease, ascertain whether the lease is effectively an installment sale rather than a rental.

LO 8 24. Deferred tax liability arises because of both permanent and temporary differences between income reported for financial purposes and that reported for tax purposes.

LO 9 25. The accrued pension cost is a liability that represents the amount by which a pension fund's assets are exceeded by the potential claims on those assets.

LO 8 26. Alpha Corporation uses straight-line depreciation. The balance in Alpha's deferred tax account reflects all the temporary differences between accounting methods chosen for tax and book purposes.

LO 8 27. Alpha Corporation uses straight-line depreciation. The amount in Alpha's income statement for "tax expense" is the cash paid in taxes for the year.

LO 8 28. Alpha Corporation uses straight-line depreciation. A credit balance on the deferred tax account indicates that Alpha has underpaid its taxes for the current year.

LO 9 29. The cash a company pays as a funding payment to its pension scheme is not the same as pension expense.

LO 3 30. The market rate of interest is the interest rate that bondholders could obtain by investing in other bonds that are similar to the issuing firm's bonds.

For the following questions, circle the alternative that best answers the question:

LO 4 31. If a bond covenant specifies that the ratio of long-term debt to stockholders' equity must not exceed 0.75:1 and the ratio is currently standing at 0.70:1, which of the following actions will result in a risk that the bond covenant is violated?

a) Pay a cash dividend to stockholders
b) Issue stock for cash
c) Issue stock to employees for service rendered
d) Retire callable bonds

LO 3 32. If a bond is issued at a premium, then the interest expense each year
a) is greater than the cash payment for interest.
b) is less than the cash payment for interest.
c) equals the cash payment for interest.
d) cannot be determined without details of the bond issue.

Use the following information to answer questions 23 through 25:
On January 1, 1997, Omega Corporation issued a three-year, $1,000 bond with a nominal interest rate of 9%. At the time, the market rate of interest was 9%. Omega uses the effective interest rate method to account for the premium or discount on bonds.

LO 4 33. The company's issue price for the bond would be
a) $1,000.
b) $1,300.
c) $1,025.
d) $700.

LO 4 34. The present value of the bond is
a) $1,000.
b) $1,300.
c) $1,025.
d) $700.

LO 4 35. The total interest expense recognized over the life of the bond is
a) $300.
b) $275.
c) $25.
d) $270.

LO 4 36. At the end of 1997, the carrying value of the bond was
a) $1,000.
b) $1,300.
c) $1,025.
d) $700.

LO 4 37. The effective annual interest rate on the bond is
a) 9%.
b) more than 9%.
c) less than 9%.

Use the following information to answer questions 38 through 41:
On January 1, 1994, Company T leased equipment under a five-year lease with payments of $10,000 on each December 31 of the lease period. The present value of the lease payments is $37,908, using a discount rate of 10%.
Assume the equipment is depreciated straight-line over 5 years with zero salvage value.

LO 7 38. If the lease is considered a capital lease, depreciation expense and interest expense for 1994 are
a) $3,791 and $7,582.
b) $7,582 and $0.
c) $7,582 and $3,791.
d) $7,582 and $10,000.

LO 7 39. If the lease is considered a capital lease, the balance sheet value of the leased asset and the lease obligation on January 1, 1994 are
a) $50,000.
b) $0.
c) $37,908.
d) $10,000.

LO 7 40. If the lease is considered an operating lease, which of the following expenses are recognized in the 1994 income statement?
a) Depreciation $7,582 and interest $3,791
b) Depreciation $10,000 and interest $10,000
c) Depreciation $10,000 and interest $0
d) Rental under lease $10,000

LO 7 41. If the lease is considered an operating lease the amount shown on the December 31, 1994 balance sheet for leased assets is
a) $50,000.
b) $40,000.
c) $10,000.
d) $0.

LO 9 42. The accrued pension cost is
a) the amount of benefits payable to employees under the pension scheme if they were to retire at their current salaries.
b) the amount of benefits payable to employees under the pension scheme if it is assumed that they earn future salary increases.
c) the cash payment made each year into the pension fund.
d) the difference between pension expense and the cash payment into the pension fund.

LO 3 43. A company issues bonds on January 1, 1997, and they are publicly traded. Which of the following factors does not affect the market price of the bond on July 30, 1998?
a) Current market interest rate
b) Nominal interest rate of bond
c) Original issue price of bond
d) Maturity date of bond

LO 3 44. Bonds are issued on January 1, 1998, at an issue price of $1232. They have a ten-year life, $1,000 face value, and a nominal interest rate of 8%. The market rate of interest at the time of the bond issue is

a) more than 8%.
b) less than 8%.
c) 8%.

LO 9 45. Companies P and Q are identical in all respects except that P has long-term liabilities of $1 million, on which it pays 10% interest, and stockholders' equity of $1 million, whereas Q has no long-term liabilities and stockholders' equity of $2 million. Which of the following statements is true?

a) P's quick ratio is higher than Q's.
b) P's debt/equity ratio is higher than Q's.
c) P's debt service coverage is higher than Q's.
d) P's current ratio is higher than Q's.

Answer each of the following problems:

LO 3 46. On January 1, 1994, Alpha Company issued bonds with a face value of $100,000, a period to maturity of five years, and a nominal interest rate of 10% payable annually on December 31.

Required

1. Without doing any calculations, indicate whether the company could issue the bonds at, above, or below face value in each of the following circumstances:
   a) The market rate of interest is 10%.
   b) The market rate of interest is 14%.
   c) The market rate of interest is 6%.

2. Support your intuition in the question above by calculating the present value of the bond for each of a), b), and c).

LO 2,3 47. Beta Company issues bonds with a face value of $50,000, a three-year period to maturity, and a nominal interest rate of 10%. Interest is paid annually in arrear, and the market rate of interest at the time of the issue is 9%.

Required

1. Ignoring any issue costs, calculate the proceeds of the bond issue.

2. Show the effect of the bond issue on the accounting equation.

3. Complete the following table using the effective interest rate method of bond amortization:

Date	Cash Interest	Premium Amortized	Interest Expense	Unamortized Premium	Carrying Value	Interest Expense as % of Carrying Value
1/1/Year 1						
12/31/Year 1						
12/31/Year 2						
12/31/Year 3						

LO 7,9 48 The following information has been extracted from the financial statement and notes of Computers R Us for the year ended January 30, 1995:

Summary Balance Sheet on January 30, 1995

Current assets		$2,384,508
Property and equipment		2,803,550
Other assets		134,794
Total assets		$5,322,852
Current liabilities	$1,587,649	
Deferred income taxes		175,430
Long-term debt		660,488
Obligations under capital leases		10,264
Stockholders' equity		2,889,021
Total liabilities and stockholders' equity		$5,322,852

Minimum rental payments for operating leases are provided in the notes as follows:

1996	$ 160,287
1997	159,088
1998	159,233
1999	158,151
2000	157,299
2001 and later	2,285,913

Required

1. Assuming a 10% discount rate and that all payments for 2001 and later are actually made in 2001, calculate the present value of the payments under operating leases.

2. Assume now that the operating leases were capital leases and that the present value of the leases would be included as both an asset and a liability in the balance sheet. Restate the summary balance sheet on that assumption.

3. Calculate the debt-to-equity ratio for both the original and restated summary balance sheets.

4. Use your calculations to explain why many companies prefer to record the assets that they lease from another company as operating rather than capital leases.

Critical Thinking Problem

LO 9 49. The footnotes to the financial statements of Company A for the year ended December 31, 1997, provide the following information about the company's pension plan:

Accumulated benefit obligation	$445 million
Projected benefit obligation	$560 million
Plan assets at fair value	$780 million

Required

1. Explain the difference between accumulated benefit obligation and projected benefit obligation.

2. Does either the projected benefit obligation or the accumulated benefit obligation allow for additional obligations because of projected additional years of service of existing employees?

3. If you were an employee of Company A, would you feel confident that the company would be able to pay your pension when you retired?

Solutions

Fill in the Blanks

1. accumulated
2. overfunded
3. operating
4. collateral
5. callable, redeemable
6. bond issue price
7. premium
8. carrying value
9. effective interest
10. debt service coverage
11. permanent difference
12. deferred tax
13. gain or loss on redemption
14. accrued pension cost
15. projected benefit obligation

True/False

		COMMENT/EXPLANATION
16.	True	
17.	False	The bonds would be issued at a premium, since they are returning a higher interest rate then comparable bonds.
18.	False	Convertible bonds allow the investor to convert the bonds into equity.
19.	True	
20.	False	The present value of a sum of money in the future is worth less than if the sum were to be received now.
21.	True	
22.	False	Whether a gain or loss is recognized on early redemption depends on *both* the price at which the company redeems the bonds (redemption price) and the carrying value of the bond. If the carrying value is above the redemption price, a gain will be recognized.
23.	True	
24.	False	Deferred tax liability results only when there are temporary differences between income reported for financial and tax purposes.
25.	False	The Accrued Pension Cost appears either as an asset or a liability in the balance sheet and represents the accumulated difference between pension expense and total funding payments.
26.	True	
27.	False	Tax expense is the amount the company would have paid if tax accounting and book accounting were identical.
28.	False	A credit balance indicates a temporary difference between tax and book accounting.
29.	True	
30.	True	

Multiple Choice

31.	a	39.	d
32.	b	40.	d
33.	a	41.	d
34.	a	42.	d
35.	a	43.	c
36.	a	44.	b
37.	c	45.	b
38.	c		

Problem 46

1.

a) at face value
b) below face value
c) above face value

2.

Year	Cash Payment	Discount Factor	Present Value	Discount Factor	Present Value	Discount Factor	Present Value
		10%		14%		6%	
1	$10,000	0.91	$9,091	0.88	$8,772	0.94	$9,434
2	$10,000	0.83	$8,264	0.77	$7,695	0.89	$8,900
3	$10,000	0.75	$7,513	0.67	$6,750	0.84	$8,396
4	$10,000	0.68	$6,830	0.59	$5,921	0.79	$7,921
5	$110,000	0.62	$68,301	0.52	$57,131	0.75	$82,198
	Proceeds from issue	**a)**	**$100,000**	**b)**	**$86,268**	**c)**	**$116,849**

Problem 47

1.

	Interest rate	9%	
Year	Cash Flow	Discount Factor	Present Value
1	5,000	0.92	$4,587
2	5,000	0.84	$4,208
3	55,000	0.77	$42,470
	Issue price		$51,266
	Premium		$1,266

2.

	Debit	Credit
Cash	51,266	
Bonds payable		50,000
Premium on bonds payable		1,266
Issue of bonds at a premium		

3.

Date	Cash Interest	Premium Amortized	Interest Expense	Unamortized Premium	Carrying Value	Interest Expense as % of Carrying Value
1/1/Year 1					51,266	
12/31/Year 1	5,000	386	4,614	880	50,880	9.00%
12/31/Year 2	5,000	421	4,579	845	50,459	9.00%
12/31/Year 3	5,000	459	4,541	807	50,000	9.00%

Problem 48

1.

	Discount rate	10%	
	Lease Payments	*Discount Factor*	*Present value*
1996	$160,287	0.91	$145,715
1997	$159,088	0.83	$131,478
1998	$159,233	0.75	$119,634
1999	$158,151	0.68	$108,019
2000	$157,299	0.62	$97,670
2001 and later	$2,285,913	0.56	$1,290,338
		Total	$1,892,855

2. and 3.

Summary Balance Sheet on January 30, 1995

	Unadjusted Balances	*Effect of Capitalizing leases*	*Adjusted Balances*
Current assets	$2,384,508		$2,384,508
Property and equipment	2,803,550	+$1,892,855	4,696,405
Other assets	134,794		134,794
Total assets	$5,322,852		$7,215,707
Current liabilities	$1,587,649		$1,587,649
Deferred income taxes	175,430		175,430
Long term debt	660,488		660,488
Obligations under capital leases	10,264	+$1,892,855	1,903,119
Stockholders equity	2,889,021		2,889,021
Total liabilities and stockholders' equity	$5,322,852		$7,215,707
Debt-to-equity ratio	1.00		1.49

4. It is apparent from the above table that capitalizing the leases significantly impacts the debt-to-equity ratio of Computers R Us. If you were asked to lend the company money or wanted to buy its bonds, the adjusted debt-to-equity ratio would be more relevant. Clearly, the company has long-term commitments under leases that do not appear in the balance sheet and yet are likely to impact significantly the availability of cash to pay interest and dividends. The capitalization of leases in this case provides significant insights into the company's capital structure.

Critical Thinking Problem 49

1. The accumulated benefit obligation (ABO) is a measure of the obligation to employees if they were to retire at their current salary; the projected benefit obligation (PBO) calculates the pension obligation on the assumption of future salary increases.
2. Neither the ABO nor the PBO allow for possible additional years of service by existing employees and therefore neither represents a true economic measure of pension obligation.
3. Since the plan assets currently exceed both the ABO and the PBO, an employee could be reasonably confident about receiving his or her pension. However, the company must continue to make the necessary funding payments to the pension fund for this situation to continue.

Chapter 11

Stockholders' Equity

This chapter examines the second main source of financing for a corporation: stock and the transactions associated with it. You have two overall aims in this chapter. First, you should understand the different components of stockholders' equity. Second, you should be able to account for stock transactions, including the issue and repurchase of stock and the various forms of dividend transactions.

Learning Objectives

LO 1	Identify the components of the stockholders' equity category of the balance sheet and the accounts found in each component.
LO 2	Understand the characteristics of common and preferred stock and the differences between the classes of stock.
LO 3	Determine the impact when stock is issued for cash or for other consideration.
LO 4	Describe the financial statement impact of stock treated as treasury stock.
LO 5	Compute the amount of cash dividends when a firm has issued both preferred and common stock.
LO 6	Understand the difference between cash and stock dividends and the effect of stock dividends.
LO 7	Determine the difference between stock dividends and stock splits.
LO 8	Understand how investors use ratios to evaluate owners' equity.
LO 9	Explain the effect that transactions involving stockholders' equity have on the statement of cash flows.
LO 10	Describe the important differences between the sole proprietorship and partnership forms of organization versus the corporate form.

Key Textbook Exhibit

Exhibit 11-1 illustrates the relative advantages and disadvantages of stock versus debt financing.

Review of Key Concepts

LO 1 The stockholders' equity category of the balance sheet represents the stockholders' interest in the corporation and contains two principal components: **contributed capital and retained earnings**. Contributed capital represents the consideration, normally cash, that the corporation has received for the issue of stock. In determining contributed capital, several key parameters must be defined.

- **Number of shares.** Three separate numbers must be identified. **Authorized shares** represent the maximum number of shares that the corporation may issue. This is determined when the company is incorporated and is usually set high enough to allow for the future growth. **Issued shares** represent the number of shares that have been sold or transferred to stockholders. **Outstanding shares** are shares that are actually in the hands of stockholders. The difference between numbers of shares issued and outstanding derives from shares that the company has itself repurchased as treasury stock.
- **Par value and additional paid-in capital. Par value** causes many students confusion but simply represents the arbitrary face value of the stock set by the corporation. Since corporations can face legal obstacles if they attempt to issue stock at a price below par value, the par value is usually set low. However, par value does not influence the price at which the company can sell its stock. When a company sells its stock at a price above par value, the difference between par value and issue price is **called additional paid-in capital**. This appears as a credit balance in the stockholders' equity section of the balance sheet.

As its name suggests, the **retained earnings** balance is the total earnings of the company since its inception, minus any dividends (including stock dividends) that the company has paid. Note that a large balance on the retained earnings account does not indicate that the same amount of cash is available to pay dividends.

Test Your Understanding!

Question: Suppose Company A wishes to issue common stock. Is the amount of money Company A can raise influenced by whether the par value per share is 10 cents or 50 cents?

Answer: No! Company A simply issues a larger number of shares if the par value is 10 cents rather than 50 cents, but the same amount of money is raised in both cases.

LO 2 There are two principle types of stock: **preferred stock** and **common stock.** The difference between the two types of stock typically relates to dividend payments. For preferred stock, dividends are a fixed and stated percentage of the stock's par value; in addition, dividends on preferred stock must be paid before dividends are paid on common stock. Preferred stock can be **cumulative** (any dividend unpaid in previous years must be paid before any dividend on common shares is paid), **participating** (preferred stockholders may share in further distributions after preferred and common dividend have been paid), **convertible** (can be converted to common shares by the shareholder), or **callable** (can be retired by the company after they have been issued). Since the dividend on preferred stock is more stable and predictable than that on a share of common stock, preferred stock is arguably more like a bond than common stock. For that reason, in analyzing company accounts, many analysts regard preferred stock as debt rather than equity.

LO 3 Stock can be issued for cash, for noncash consideration, and on a subscription basis.

- When stock is issued for **cash**, it is often issued for more than its par value. For example, suppose Corporation A issues 100,000 common shares with a par value per share of 10 cents, for 25 cents each. The total cash received is $25,000, but the par value of the shares issued is $10,000. The difference between the total cash and the par value is reported in a special account called **Additional Paid-In Capital**, which appears as part of stockholders' equity.
- When **noncash consideration** is received in return for the issue of stock, the key problem is determining the value of the transaction. The general rule is that the transaction should be recorded at fair market value. Market value can be found from either the value of the consideration given (stock) or the value of the consideration received (assets). Suppose, for example, that instead of cash, Corporation A had received a manufacturing plant and machinery in exchange for its 100,000 preferred shares. The shares are not traded on the market. Although the par value of the stock will remain at $10,000, the additional paid-in capital will depend on the value of the plant and machinery. How easy it is to value the plant and machinery depends on how active the market for that type of plant and machinery is. In some cases, it will not be possible to identify a market price and some surrogate will have to be used, such as an appraisal by an independent valuer.

LO 4 Companies repurchase their own shares for many reasons: to prevent a takeover, to increase the stock's market price, to provide stock that can be used for employee stock bonuses. When stock is repurchased it may or may not be canceled or **retired**. Stock that is repurchased but not retired is called **treasury stock**.

Treasury stock appears as a *contra* in the stockholders' equity section of the balance sheet and can be recorded using either the par value method or the cost method. To illustrate the more commonly used cost method, suppose Corporation B repurchases 10,000 shares of stock for 50 cents per share. When the stock is repurchased, the journal entry recording the repurchase is

	Debit	Credit
Treasury stock	5,000	
Cash		5,000

The treasury stock balance of $5,000 appears as a *contra* to the stockholder's equity in the balance sheet. If the company subsequently reissues the stock, the accounting treatment depends on whether or not it is reissued at above or below the repurchase cost. If the stock is reissued above the repurchase price, the additional consideration is recorded in additional paid-in capital. If the stock is reissued at less than the repurchase price, the difference between the sales price and the repurchase price is deducted from additional paid-in capital or from retained earnings if no additional paid-in capital is available.

When treasury stock is retired, the relevant balances in both the treasury stock account and the additional paid-in capital account must be eliminated. When the total of the related par value and additional paid-in capital is less than the consideration paid for the retired stock, the difference reduces the retained earnings account. When the original issue price is higher than the repurchase price of the stock, the difference is reported in the paid-in capital from stock retirement account.

Test Your Understanding!

Question: Initially, Company A and Company B have the identical number of authorized, issued, and outstanding shares. Both repurchase identical numbers of their own shares. Company A retires its repurchased stock, but Company B holds the stock as treasury stock. Does the issued stock of both companies remain the same?

Answer: No! Company A's issued shares will be lower than Company B's.

LO 5 When companies declare a cash dividend, a liability called **dividend payable** is created by reducing retained earnings on the day that the dividend is declared. When the dividend is actually paid, the dividend payable account is eliminated, and cash account is reduced by the amount of the dividend.

The allocation of dividend to preferred and common stockholders depends on the terms of the preferred stock. Holders of **noncumulative preferred shares** are entitled only to the current year's preferred dividend, even if there are unpaid arrears of preferred dividend from previous years. Before any dividend is paid to the common stockholders, holders of **cumulative preferred shares** must be paid any arrears of dividend in addition to the current year's dividend. In addition to arrears and current year's dividends, holders **of cumulative and participating preferred shares** may be paid additional dividends if the dividend on the common stock reaches a stated percentage.

LO 6 **Stock dividends** occur when companies issue additional shares of stock to existing stockholders. They provide an alternative to the traditional cash dividend. The principle advantages of stock dividends are that

- they preserve the company's cash,
- they can reduce the stock price making the stock more accessible to a wider range of investors, and
- they can have tax benefits to recipients, since they do not represent taxable income.

Normally, stock dividends involve reducing the retained earnings account by the amount of the stock dividend. Note that stock dividends do not affect the assets, liabilities, or total amount of stockholders' equity. Rather, they simply increase the number of shares of stock. Relatively small stock dividends are recorded at the market value of the stock on the declaration day. As with cash dividends, the value of the stocks issued in excess of par increases additional paid-in capital. With larger stock dividends, the stock dividend is recorded at par rather than at market value. When the dividend is declared, a stockholders' equity account, called common stock dividend distributable, is created. When the distribution actually takes place, that account is closed to the common stock account.

LO 7 **Stock splits** occur when the company reduces its par value per share. Companies carry out stock splits for reasons similar to those for stock dividends. In a stock split, the stock's market price is reduced, making it more marketable. Stock splits, however, require no accounting entries, since the total par value of the shares outstanding does not change.

LO 8 In analyzing stockholders' equity in a corporation, two different measures are useful: **book value per share** and **market value per share**. Book value per share of common stock represents the rights that each share of common stock has in the net assets of the company. In this calculation, the rights of the preferred stockholders must be deducted. The market value per share is the price at which the share is currently trading on the stock exchange. Note that the book value per share is different from the market value per share. Since book value is based on the historic cost of assets, of the two measures, market value per share gives the better indication of the future financial performance of the company.

LO 9 The cash inflow from the sale of stock and the cash outflow from stock repurchases appear in the financing section of the statement of cash flows. Similarly, since dividends represent a cost of financing the business, dividend payments also appear as a cash outflow in the financing section of the cash flow statement. Note that dividends appear on the statement of cash flows when they have been paid as opposed to when they are declared.

LO 10 The following table summarizes the main differences between the three forms of organization:

	Sole Proprietorship	Partnership	Corporation
Ease of transfer of ownership	Difficult: Owner must find a buyer to buy the whole business, and, when ownership is transferred, the original entity ceases to exist.	Difficult: When one partner leaves, the partnership is dissolved and a new one must be formed.	Easy: Usually shares are traded on a Stock Exchange and the sale of stock is a simple transaction. The corporation as an entity continues in existence even although its shares change hands.
Personal liability of owners	Owner has unlimited liability for business debts.	Partners have unlimited liability for business debts.	Stockholders' liability is limited to the value of their stock.
Ease of raising additional capital	Limited by resources of owner.	Limited by resources of partners.	Corporations can relatively easily raise additional capital by selling more stock.
Separation of ownership and entity	Separate accounting entity.	Separate accounting entity.	Separate legal, tax, and accounting entity

Review of Key Terms

Additional paid-in capital The amount received for the issuance of stock in excess of the par value of the stock.

Authorized shares The maximum number of shares a corporation may issue as indicated in the corporate charter.

Book value per share Total stockholders' equity divided by the number of shares of common stock outstanding.

Callable stock Allows the issuing firm to eliminate a class of stock by paying the stockholders a fixed amount.

Convertible stock Allows preferred stock to be returned to the corporation in exchange for common stock.

Cumulative feature The holders of this stock have a right to dividends in arrears before the current year dividend is distributed.

Dividend payout ratio The annual dividend amount divided by the annual net income.

Issued shares The number of shares sold or distributed to stockholders.

Market value per share The selling price of the stock as indicated by the most recent stock transactions.

Outstanding shares The number of shares issued less the number of shares held as treasury stock.

Par value An arbitrary amount stated on the face of the stock certificate that represents the legal capital of the firm.

Participating feature Stock that has a provision allowing the stockholders to share in the distribution of an abnormally large dividend on a percentage basis.

Retained earnings Net income that has been made by the corporation but not paid out as dividends.

Retirement of stock Repurchases by a corporation of its own stock with no intention to reissue at a later date.

Stock dividend Declaration and issue of additional shares of its own stock by a corporation to existing stockholders.

Stock split Creation of additional shares of stock and reduction of the par value of the stock.

Treasury stock Stock issued by the firm and then repurchased but not retired.

Practice Test Questions and Problems

Complete each of the following statements:

LO 8 1. ______________________ represents the rights that each share of common stock has in the net assets of the company.

LO 9 2. Dividend payments appear as a cash ______________________ in the ______________________ section of the cash flow statement.

LO 7 3. In a ______________________, the number of shares outstanding is increased and the par value per share is decreased.

LO 7 4. In a ______________________, retained earnings are used to distribute additional stock to shareholders.

LO 2 5. Preferred stock that confers the right to receive arrears of dividends is called ______________________.

LO 3 6. In a ______________________, an investor agrees to buy a specified number of shares at a specified price but to pay for them at some future date.

LO 1 7. ______________________ represents the total number of shares the company has sold, including those it has subsequently repurchased but not retired.

LO 8 8. The ______________________ is the price at which the stock is currently selling.

LO 6 9. The ______________________ is calculated as the annual dividend divided by annual net income.

LO 4 10. ______________________ is stock that has been repurchased by the firm but not retired.

Use the following information to answer questions 11 through 15:
The following information has been extracted from the Santa Maria Corporation's financial statements for the year ended December 31, 1997.

	December 31, 1997	December 31, 1996
Common stock: issued and outstanding, 10 cents par value	$ 200,000	$ 150,000
Additional paid in capital	100,000	50,000
Preferred stock: 5%, $10 par value	10,000	10,000
Retained earnings	800,000	700,000
Total dividend paid and payable on both common and preferred stock	50,000	20,000

LO 3 11. During 1997, the company issued ______________ shares of common stock, with a par value of ______________, at an issue price of ______________.

LO 3 12. Total proceeds from the issue of common stock were ______________.

LO 5 13. The total dividend paid and payable on preferred stock during 1997 was ______________.

LO 5 14. The total dividend paid and payable on common stock during 1997 was ______________.

LO 5 15. Net income for 1997 was ______________.

Indicate whether each of the following statements is true or false:

LO 1 16. When a company has repurchased but not yet retired its own stock, the number of issued and outstanding shares will differ.

LO 1 17. Par value is the price at which stock was originally issued.

LO 2 18. Preferred stockholders have the right to receive their dividends before any dividend is paid on common stock.

LO 1 19. Additional paid-in capital is the difference between par value and the stock's current market value.

LO 1 20. As long as a company's net earnings are positive, its retained earnings balance will increase.

LO 4 21. The difference between the authorized and issued shares is identified as treasury stock on the balance sheet.

LO 8 22. The book value per share is the minimum price at which the company's shares should trade on the stock market.

LO 2 23. The Acme Corporation had net earnings of $15,000 in Year 5. The company has 10,000 10% cumulative, preferred shares with a par value of $20 per share. The dividend payable to the preferred stockholders is $15,000 for Year 5.

LO 2 24. Cumulative preferred stock confers the right to share in earnings after a stated level of common stock has been paid.

LO 9 25. When dividends are declared, they are reported both in the Income Statement and as a cash flow in the Statement of Cash Flows.

LO 6 26. Both stock and cash dividends reduce stockholders' equity.

LO 7 27. Stock splits require no accounting entries, and they reduce market and par value per share.

LO 8 28. Market value per share gives a better insight into the likely future financial performance of the company than book value per share.

LO 4 29. When a company repurchases its stock, its authorized share capital is reduced.

LO 2 30. A company that has been in business for several years wishes to raise $1 million by issuing common stock. The par value of its common stock is 10 cents per share, so it will issue 10 million shares to raise the required amount.

For each of the following questions, circle the alternative that best answers the question:

Use the following information to answer questions 31 through 34:
Corporation A has 1 million authorized common shares of par value $0.10. It has 250,000 issued shares and 10,000 shares in treasury. Answer each question independently.

LO 1 31. The number of outstanding shares of Corporation A is
a) 1 million
b) 250,000
c) 240,000
d) 990,000

LO 6 32. If the company declares a 20% stock dividend, the number of outstanding shares after the stock dividend is
a) 351,000
b) 288,000
c) 12 million
d) Cannot say unless the details of the treasury stock purchase are known.

LO 7 33. If the company has a 3-for-1 stock split, the number of outstanding shares after the stock split is
a) 2,970,000
b) 720,000
c) 3 million
d) 750,000

LO 1 34. The par value of 10 cents is which of the following?
a) The minimum price at which the stock can trade
b) The maximum dividend that can be paid on the stock
c) An arbitrary value that represents the face value of the stock
d) The maximum price at which the stock can be issued

Use the following information to answer questions 35 through 40:
The following appears in the stockholders' equity section of Corporation B's balance sheet at the beginning of year 3:

Preferred Stock		
10,000, 10% nonparticipating, cumulative shares		
$10 par value shares	100,000	
Additional paid-in capital	50,000	
		150,000
Common Stock		
Authorized 10 million shares, 10 cents par value		
Issued 5 million shares	500,000	
Additional paid-in capital	300,000	
		800,000
Retained earnings		250,000
Total stockholders' equity before treasury stock		1,200,000
Less treasury stock: 100,000 shares at cost		(130,000)
Total stockholders' equity		$1,070,000

Corporation B has paid *no* dividends for the last two years because of a temporary downturn in business. For year 3, the company has net earnings of $450,000 and the company's board of directors intends to pay $400,000 as total dividend.

LO 5 35. For year 3, dividends per share for preferred stockholders will be
a) $1
b) $10
c) $3
d) $30

LO 5 36. For year 3, the total dividend available to common stockholders is
a) $400,000
b) $450,000
c) $420,000
d) $370,000

LO 1 37. The common stock was initially sold for an average of
a) 13 cents per share
b) 10 cents per share
c) 16 cents per share
d) 8 cents per share

LO 5 38. After the dividends for year 3 have been paid, the balance on the retained earnings account will be
a) $250,000
b) $300,000
c) $200,000
d) Cannot tell from available information

LO 7 39. Company B makes a 2-for-1 stock split at the end of year 3 after the dividends have been paid. The number of shares outstanding after the split is
a) 20 million
b) 10 million
c) 99 million
d) 98 million

LO 7 40. Company B makes a 2-for-1 stock split at the end of year 3, after the dividends have been paid. The book value per common share *after* the split is
a) 11.4 cents
b) 10.9 cents
c) 9.9 cents
d) 9.7 cents

LO 4 41. Alpha Inc. has 3,000 shares in treasury for which it paid $8,000, and which have a total par value of $3,000. The shares were originally issued for $5,000. Which of the following statements is true?
a) The treasury stock appears on the balance sheet as marketable securities.
b) If Alpha reissues the stock at $10,000, it must deduct $2,000 from additional paid-in capital.
c) If Alpha retires the stock, it reduced retained earnings by $3,000.
d) Alpha may only reissue the stock to its employees for the payment of stock bonuses.

LO 10 42. Which of the following statements is true?
a) The corporate form of enterprise provides more financial protection for its owners than either sole proprietorships or partnerships.
b) Transfer of ownership is equally easy with sole proprietorships, partnerships, and corporations.
c) Corporations are more restricted in their ability to raise capital than partnerships or sole proprietorships because they must sell their stock through a stock exchange.
d) Corporations, partnerships, and sole proprietorships are all legally separate entities from their owners.

Use the following information to answer questions 43 through 45:
Jura Juice Company has three partners: Grumpy, Sneezy, and Happy. The partnership agreement provides for the following distribution to partners:

	Grumpy	**Sneezy**	**Happy**
Annual salary	$50,000	$50,000	$100,000
Interest on invested capital before distribution of profits for the year.	?	?	?
Distribution of remaining income	25%	25%	50%
Capital balance on December 31, 1997			
- before distribution for year	$500,000	$600,000	$1,000,000
- after distribution for year	$610,000	$720,000	$1,230,000

All partners receive the same rate of interest on their invested capital. Happy's share of remaining income was $80,000 for the year.

LO 9 43. Sneezy receives total interest and salary for the year to December 31, 1997, of $53,000. The interest paid on invested capital is
a) 10%.
b) 5%.
c) 7.5%.
d) 12.5%.

LO 9 44. The remaining income (after salaries and interest on capital) that was distributed to all three partners for 1997 was

e) $460,000.
f) $160,000.
g) $80,000.
h) $200,000.

LO 9 45. The total income that was distributed to partners for 1997 was

a) $160,000.
b) $200,000.
c) $460,000.
d) $80,000.

Answer each of the following problems:

LO 1,4 46. The stockholders' equity section of the February 1, 1997, balance sheet of Alphanumeric Corporation appears as follows:

Additional paid-in capital - preferred	$ 45,000
Non cumulative preferred stock, $10 par value, ? shares issued	25,000
Additional paid-in capital - common	384,803
Retained earnings	2,092,329
Common stock, 10 cents par value, 550,000 shares authorized, 297,940 shares issued	29,794
Treasury stock - common, 8641 shares at cost	127,717

Required

1. Calculate the number of shares of preferred stock issued.

2. Calculate the number of shares of common stock outstanding.

3. Calculate the average per-share sales price of the preferred stock when issued.

4. Calculate the average per-share sales price of the common stock when issued.

5. Calculate the cost of the treasury stock per share.

6. Prepare in good form the stockholders' equity section of Alphanumeric's balance sheet.

LO 2,4 47. The following list of accounts appears in Omega Corporation's trial balance on August 31, 1995. All of the accounts have their normal balances. Omega is authorized to issue 2,000,000 shares of common stock and 4,000 shares of preferred stock. The preferred stock is cumulative, nonparticipating. The treasury stock represents 5,000 shares at cost.

Common stock, 50 cents par	$ 200,000
Additional paid-in capital - common	50,000
Preferred stock, $5 par, 3%	20,000
Retained earnings	430,000
Treasury stock (common)	10,000
Dividends paid (for first quarter)	$15,000
Dividends payable (for second quarter)	12,000

Required

1. Prepare the owners' equity section of the balance sheet for Omega.

2. Explain why some of the listed accounts do not appear in the owners' equity section.

LO 3,4 48. Horatio Company undertook the following transactions in its first year of operations:

a) Authorized share capital is 2 million common shares, 50 cents par value.
b) Issued 200,000 common shares at $2 each.
c) Issued 20,000 common shares in return for machinery and a building. The machinery has a market value of $5,000, but the value of the building is indeterminate. At the time of the stock issue, the market value of the common stock was $2.50.
d) Reported net earnings for the year of $420,000.
e) Declared a 3-for-1 stock split. After the split, the stock price was $4 per share.
f) Declared and paid a dividend of $0.10 per share.

Required

1. Complete the following table, indicating the effect of each transaction on the accounting equation.

	Assets	= Liabilities	+ Stockholders' Equity
a)			
b)			
c)			
d)			
e)			
f)			

2. Prepare the owners' equity section of the balance sheet.

3. Calculate the dividend yield, earnings per share, and dividend payout ratio after the split has taken place.

Critical Thinking Problem

LO 7 49. Tiree Corporation declared a 100% stock dividend on January 1, Year 1. At that time, the company had issued 200,000 common shares of stock with a par value of $1 per share. Prior to the stock dividend, the market price of the company's stock was $10.

Required

1. How many shares did the company issue in its stock dividend?

2. Show the effect of the stock dividend on the financial statements when it was declared.

3. Assuming nothing else changed, what would be the stock price immediately after the stock dividend was paid.

4. Mr. Mull owns 100 shares of Tiree's common stock. He is concerned that although he has more stock in the corporation after the stock dividend, each share is worth less than before the dividend and that overall he is worse off after he has received the dividend. Is he correct? Why?

5. In the light of your answer to Mr. Mull, can you think of why Tiree would choose to make a stock dividend?

Solutions

Fill in the Blanks

1.	book value per share of common stock	9.	dividend payout ratio
2.	outflow, financing	10.	treasury stock
3.	stock split	11.	500,000, 10 cents, 20 cents
4.	stock dividend	12.	$100,000
5.	cumulative	13.	$500
6.	subscription agreement	14.	$49,500
7.	issued stock	15.	$150,000
8.	market value per share		

True/False

		COMMENT/EXPLANATION
16.	True	
17.	False	Par value is the arbitrary face value of the stock.
18.	True	
19.	False	Additional paid-in capital is the difference between par value and the stock's original issue price.
20.	False	Retained earnings is increased by net income and decreased by cash dividends and net losses. Even if the company has positive net earnings, if dividends are greater than net earnings retained earnings can decline.
21.	False	Treasury stock is stock that the company has repurchased.
22.	False	Since the stock market price reflects future cash flow from the stock, it may be lower than book value per share, which reflects the historic cost of the company's assets.
23.	False	Since the preferred stock is cumulative, the preferred stockholders are entitled to their full $20,000 dividend for Year 5. If Acme cannot meet its obligation to the preferred stockholders in Year 5, in future years, it must pay the arrears of dividend on preferred stock before paying any dividends to common stockholders.
24.	False	Cumulative preferred stock means that any preferred dividend unpaid in previous years must be paid before any dividend on common shares is paid; participating preferred stock means that preferred stockholders may share in further distributions after preferred and common dividends have been paid.
25.	False	Dividends are reported in the statement of cash flows only when they have been paid.
26.	False	Only cash dividends reduce stockholders' equity.
27.	True	
28.	True	
29.	False	The company's authorized share capital is unaffected by stock transactions.
30.	False	The number of shares the company will issue is determined by the market price of the share, not their par value.

Multiple Choice

31.	c	39.	d
32.	b	40.	d
33.	b	41.	c
34.	c	42.	a
35.	c	43.	b
36.	d	44.	b
37.	c	45.	c
38.	b		

Problem 46

1. $25000/$10 = 2,500 shares
2. 297,940 - 8,641 = 289,299
3. $(45,000 + 25,000)/2,500 = $28
4. $(384,803 + 29,794)/297,940 = $1.39
5. $127,717/8,641 = $14.72
6.

Preferred Stock		
2,500, 5% nonparticipating, cumulative shares		
$10 par value shares	$ 25,000	
Additional paid-in capital	45,000	
		$ 70,000
Common Stock		
Authorized 550,000 shares, 10 cents par value		
Issued 297,940 shares	29,794	
Additional paid-in capital	384,803	
		414,597
Retained earnings		2,092,329
Total stockholders' equity before treasury stock		2,576,926
Less treasury stock: 8,641 shares at cost		(127,717)
Total stockholders' equity		$2,449,209

Problem 47

1. Preferred Stock

4,000, 3% nonparticipating, cumulative shares		
$5 par value shares		$ 20,000
Common Stock		
Authorized 2,000,000 shares, 50 cents par value		
Issued 400,000 shares	$ 200,000	
Additional paid-in capital	50,000	
		250,000
Retained earnings		430,000
Total stockholders' equity before treasury stock		700,000
Less treasury stock: 5,000 shares at cost		(10,000)
Total stockholders' equity		$690,000

2. Neither dividends paid nor payable appears in the owners' equity section, since these balances have already been deducted from retained earnings.

Problem 48

1.

	Assets	= Liabilities	+ Stockholders' Equity
a)	0	0	0
b)	+ 400,000	0	+ 400,000
c)	+ 60,000	0	+ 60,000
d)	+ 420,000	0	+ 420,000
e)	0	0	0
f)	(66,000)	0	(66,000)

2. Common Stock

Authorized 6 million shares, 16 cents par value	
Issued 660,000 shares	110,000
Additional paid-in capital	350,000
460,000	
Retained earnings	354,000
Total stockholders' equity	$814,000

3. Dividend yield = Dividend per share/ Market price per share
= 10 cents / $4
= 2.5%

Earnings per share = Net income/number of shares
= $420,000 / 660,000
= 64 cents

Dividend payout = Dividends per share/Earnings per share
= 20 cents / 64 cents
= 31%

Critical Thinking Problem 49

1. The company issued an additional 200,000 common shares, each with a par value of $1 and a market value of $10. After the stock dividend, the company has 400,000 issued shares with a par value of $1.

2.

	Debit	Credit
Retained earnings	2,000,000	
Common stock		200,000
Additional paid-in capital		1,800,000

3. The total market value of the company's stock before the stock dividend is
200,000 shares @ $10 per share = $2,000,000.
Since no other changes have taken place, the total market value of the company's stock must be unchanged after the stock dividend. Since the company now has 400,000 shares, the value of each share after the stock dividend is
$$\frac{\$2{,}000{,}000}{400{,}000 \text{ shares}} = \$5 \text{ per share.}$$

4. The value of Mr. Mull's 100 shares after the stock dividend is
100 x $10 = $1,000.
After the stock dividend, Mr. Mull has 200 shares, which have a value of
200 x $5 = $1,000.
The stock dividend has not increased Mr. Mull's wealth, and there has been no economic exchange between the company and Mr. Mull.

5. Stock dividends can be used as a substitute for cash dividends when a company is short of cash but, since we have seen in Part 4 that stock dividends do not transfer wealth from the company to the stockholder, this argument is weak. It can also be argued that stock dividends are a way of reducing the price of the stock and making it more marketable. However, stock dividends are usually smaller than the example in this problem and have a relatively small effect on stock price. It is also claimed that stock dividends provide a way of capitalizing retained earnings, but doing this can put constraints on future cash dividends. Overall, the arguments for making a stock dividend are fairly weak, and stock dividends are often interpreted as a sign of financial weakness.

Chapter 12

Analysis of Retained Earnings and Stockholders' Equity

This chapter continues the exploration of the income statement by considering the detailed treatment of several special items that are reported on the income statement. In addition, the retained earnings statement is discussed, and the components of stockholders' equity are reviewed. Your objectives are to understand the accounting issues associated with the special income statement items, the statement of retained earnings, and the statement of stockholders' equity.

Learning Objectives

LO 1 Understand a multi-step corporate income statement and its categories.

LO 2 Describe the appropriate presentation and disclosure of discontinued operations.

LO 3 Determine when items should be considered extraordinary, and develop the income statement presentation when such items are present.

LO 4 Analyze accounting changes, and determine the effect on the income statement.

LO 5 Use the earnings per share ratio as a measure of a company's profitability.

LO 6 Identify the proper way to present corrections of errors on the retained earnings statement.

LO 7 Understand the effect that appropriations and other restrictions have on retained earnings.

LO 8 Prepare a statement of stockholders' equity.

LO 9 Understand the meaning and importance of comprehensive income.

LO 10 Explain the effects that income statement events have on the statement of cash flows.

Key Textbook Exhibits

Exhibit 12-1 shows the multi-step income statement of Cisco Systems. Note how the statement explains the source of the net income in terms of both revenues and expenses. Such an analysis is invaluable in comparing a corporation's performance over several periods.

Exhibit 12-4 shows the connection between three of the financial statements: the income statement, the statement of retained earnings, and the balance sheet.

Exhibit 12-5 is Starbuck's Statement of Stockholders' Equity. Note the type of information contained in it and how much more complex it is than the statement of retained earnings.

Review of Key Concepts

LO 1 Since the purpose of an income statement is to provide information about the profitability of an entity's activities during the reporting period, many companies adopt a **multi-step income statement**. A multi-step income statement explains the source of the net income in terms of both revenues and expenses. Such an analysis is invaluable in comparing a corporation's performance over several periods. In addition to reporting net income, the multi-step income statement provides information about the types of revenues and expenses that have generated the reported income. A distinction is made between **income from operations**, and income and losses from other sources. In the latter category, **discontinued operations**, **extraordinary items**, and the **changes in accounting principles** are the most common sources of gains or losses.

LO 2 When major segments of a business are disposed of or sold, the economic effect should be reported separately in the income statement. For example, suppose Corporation X sold its retail division at the beginning of Year 5 for $900,000. At the time of sale, the division had a total book value of $1,200,000. At first, it appears that the company has made a loss on sale of $300,000 ($900,000 - $1,200,000) from the retail division during Year 5. However, if Corporation X has profits from other operations, it can deduct the losses from the discontinued operations against its taxable profits. If we assume that Corporation X's marginal tax rate is 40%, the company will deduct a total of $300,000 from its taxable income and reduce its tax bill by $120,000 (40% x $300,000) during Year 5 because of the **discontinued operations**. The net effect of the discontinued operations is therefore $180,000 ($300,000 - $120,000), since the tax effect reduces the effective loss.

LO 3 From an accounting perspective, an event is regarded as **extraordinary** if it is both unusual and infrequent. Clearly, significant judgment must be applied in determining what constitutes unusual and infrequent. Since extraordinary gains and losses must be reported separately from operating income, they provide an opportunity for the manipulation of reported earnings. As with the effects of discontinued operations, the effect of any loss or gain (net of any tax effect) should be reported in a separate category in the income statement.

LO 4 When a firm changes an accounting principle - for example the method of depreciation it uses - income from previous years will be affected. The cumulative effect of the change in accounting principle, net of any tax effect, should be reported as a separate item on the current year's income statement.

Test your understanding!

Question: Why is it only the previous years' effects of the accounting change are reported? How do we report the effect on the current year?

Answer: Only the effect on **previous years**' income should be reported, since the effect on current year's income will appear in the expenses or revenues for the current year.

LO 5 Earnings per share indicates the earnings that have been provided for each share of common stock, and is calculated from

$$\text{Earnings Per Share} = \frac{\text{Net Income - Preferred Dividends}}{\text{Weighted Average Number of Shares of Common Stock}}$$

Earnings per share indicates the earnings that have been earned for the common stockholder, so preferred dividends must be deducted from the numerator. The denominator is the weighted average number of common shares outstanding during the period. If there have been no changes in the number of shares outstanding during the period, then the denominator is simply the number of shares outstanding during the period. When, however, there have been changes in the number of outstanding shares during the period, because of stock issues or repurchases, then the denominator must be the weighted average of the shares outstanding. Note also that earnings per share and dividends per share are often unrelated. For example, many companies that have large earnings per share ratios do not pay dividends.

Test your understanding!

Question: Corporation Y has one million common shares outstanding at the beginning of Year 1; after 3 months another 200,000 shares are issued. What is Corporation Y's weighted average number of shares outstanding during the year?

Answer: The calculation is as follows:

(3/12) x 1,000,000 + (9/12) x 1,200,000 = 1,150,000

When calculating the earnings per share for Corporation Y, the number of shares used in the denominator would be 1,150,000.

LO 6,7 We dealt above with adjustments that must be reported on the current year's income statement: extraordinary items, changes in accounting principles and discontinued operations. There are also adjustments that are reflected in other components of stockholders' equity, and the text identifies three of them.

- **Prior period adjustments**, as their name suggests, affect only the income of previous periods. They may result from a correction of a theoretical or mechanical error in the preparation of an earlier year's income statement. Since the balance on the retained earnings account is the total of all previous periods' income, less any dividends, prior period adjustments must be made in the retained earnings account. The adjustment to the retained earnings account should again be net of taxation and should be presented as the first item after the beginning balance on the retained earnings statement.
- **Appropriations of retained earnings** are used to identify portions of retained earnings that are earmarked for certain purposes (such as a major expansion or acquisition) and that are therefore not available for distribution as dividends. Note, however, that such an appropriation does not generate the cash or other assets to carry out the expansion or acquisition; instead, it signals to shareholders and others that the company has plans that will require funds in the future.
- **Unrealized gains and losses on investments in securities** is an example of another class of adjustments to stockholders' equity. These adjustments are not recorded either in the income statement or in the statement of retained earnings, but as a separate component of stockholders' equity. An unrealized gain or loss on investments in securities arises when securities that the company owns have risen or dropped in value. Although the company has not yet realized a gain or loss, the change in value is deemed to be important information for users of accounts. For amplification of this point, see Chapter 13.

LO 8 A **statement of stockholders' equity** summarizes all the changes to all components of stockholders' equity during an accounting period. Where the only changes have been earnings and dividends, a statement of retained earnings provides all necessary information. For many corporations, however, the changes in stockholders' equity are more complex, and the statement of changes in stockholders' equity provides valuable summary information to the user.

LO 9 As we have seen above, although the great majority of transactions involving the company's profitability are reported through the income statement, items such as unrealized losses on securities are not. This latter class of transactions represents an easing of FASB's long-held belief that the income statement should be all-inclusive and report all transactions affecting the entity's profits. Recently, the term **comprehensive income** has been used to represent the increase in net assets resulting from *all* transactions during a period, other than investments by and distributions to owners. Comprehensive income includes both transactions reported in the income statement and those that are reported elsewhere in stockholders' equity. It is therefore a better measure than net income of the economic change in the company over the period. However, the idea of comprehensive income has yet to be operationalized.

LO 10 Extraordinary losses often appear as an addition to net income in statements of cash flow prepared using the indirect method. This does not mean that the loss has generated cash. Rather, as with depreciation, the loss has been deducted in arriving at net income. If the loss does not have a cash flow effect, as in an uninsured loss, it must be added back to net income to find cash flow from operations. Similarly, an extraordinary gain that does not have a cash flow effect will be deducted from net income in the cash flow statement. The treatment of the cumulative effects of accounting principles is identical to that for extraordinary items, since changes in accounting principles result in bookkeeping changes, not cash flows. Thus, a cumulative effect that was deducted from (added to) the income statement should be added to (deducted from) the operating category of the statement of cash flows.

Review of Key Terms

Appropriation of retained earnings	An account that indicates that a company has designated a portion of the balance of retained earnings for a specific purpose.
Change in accounting principle	An income statement item that occurs when a company changes from one accounting method to another.
Comprehensive income	The amount that reflects the total change in net assets from all sources except investment or withdrawals by the owners of the company.
Cumulative effect	The total effect of a change in accounting principle for all years prior to the current year.
Discontinued operations	A category on the income statement indicating that a major segment or division of the company has been, or will be, sold.
Earnings per share	A number that represents the rights of the common stockholders to the income of the company; it is calculated as net income minus preferred dividends, divided by the number of shares of common stock outstanding.
Extraordinary item	An item that is considered both unusual and infrequent and is presented in a separate category of the income statement.
Gross profit	The amount of net sales minus the amount of cost of sales.
Gross profit percentage	A ratio calculated as the gross profit divided by the net sales.
Income before income taxes	A subtotal on the income statement calculated as operating income plus other income items, such as interest, and minus other expense items.
Multi-step income statement	An income statement that presents revenues and expenses by category.
Operating income	A subtotal on the income statement calculated as gross profit minus operating expenses.
Prior period adjustment	A correction that is not recorded on the income statement but is presented as an adjustment to the balance of the retained earnings account.
Statement of stockholders' equity	A statement that indicates the differences between beginning and ending balances for all accounts in the stockholders' equity category.
Unrealized loss on investment in securities	An account in the stockholders' equity category that reflects that the investment in certain securities was reduced to market value.
Weighted average number of shares	The number of shares of stock weighted by the time period that the stock was outstanding.

Practice Test Questions and Problems

Complete each of the following statements:

Use the following information to answer questions 1 and 2.
In Year 2, Snyder Corporation, a retailer of mountain bikes, discontinued its division that provided financing for credit sales. The division's loss from operations in Year 2 was $20,000, the division's assets had a net book value of $100,000 and were sold for $60,000. Snyder's marginal tax rate was 40%.

LO 2 1. The amount reported as earnings associated with the discontinued division is ____________________.

LO 2 2. The amount reported as loss from the disposal of assets of the discontinued division is ____________________.

LO 2 3. When a company disposes of a major division or segment, it must report the net effect of the disposal as a ____________________ on the income statement.

LO 3 4. Northern Transport, a Chicago trucking company, lost two trucks in an earthquake in Los Angeles. Northern Transport should report the loss as an ________________ loss.

LO 1 5. The difference between gross profit and operating expenses is reported as ________________ on the multi-step income statement.

LO 2 6. Income before income taxes is found by deducting interest expense from, and adding interest income to, ____________________.

LO 4 7. The cumulative effect on a prior period's net income of a change from FIFO to weighted-average is reported on the income statement as the effect of a ____________________.

Use the following information to answer questions 8 through 10:
Williams Transport reported net income of $1,505,000 for the year ending December 31, Year 1. On July 1, Year 1, Williams issued an additional 100,000 shares, bringing its total shares issued to 300,000 shares. In addition, the company has 50,000 10% preferred shares with a par value of $1.

LO 5 8. Preference dividend for Year 1 is ____________________.

LO 5 9. The weighted average number of shares for Year 1 is ____________________.

LO 5 10. The earnings per share for Year 1 is ____________________.

LO 8 11. ____________________ is a statement that indicates the differences between beginning and ending balances for all accounts in the stockholders' equity category.

LO 5 12. ____________________ is a number that represents the rights of the common stockholders to the income of the company; it is calculated as net income minus preferred dividends, divided by the number of shares of common stock outstanding.

LO 7 13. ____________________ is an account in the stockholders' equity category that reflects that the investment in certain securities was reduced to market value.

LO 7 14. ____________________ is an account that indicates that a company has designated a portion of the balance of retained earnings for a specific purpose.

LO 9 15. The amount that reflects the total change in net assets from all sources except investment or withdrawals by the owners of the company is called ____________________.

Indicate whether each of the following statements is true or false:

LO 1 16. Of the various measures of income reported in a multi-step income statement, net income is the only one in which all aspects of the company's performance during the year are reflected.

LO 4 17. When a firm changes one of its accounting principles, the cumulative effect of the change up to the prior year must be reported in a separate category of the income statement.

LO 4 18. A company reporting an extraordinary loss will report more than one earnings per share figure.

LO 3 19. Under U.S. GAAP, all gains and losses on the redemption of bonds should be classified as extraordinary items on the income statement by the firm that issued the bonds.

LO 1 20. In a multi-step income statement, tax expense is deducted to find income from operations.

LO 9 21. Comprehensive income can always be found by comparing net assets at the beginning and end of the period.

LO 8 22. A statement of stockholders' equity explains changes in the beginning balances in the stockholders' equity section of the balance sheet.

LO 7 23. An appropriation of retained earnings limits the ability of the company to pay dividends.

LO 3 24. A loss resulting from a tornado would be accounted for as an extraordinary loss if it happened in California, but not if it occurred in Florida.

LO 3 25. Extraordinary losses must always be reported separately in the income statement.

Use the following information to answer questions 26 through 30:
On January 1, 1997, the Buellton Corporation has 200,000 shares of common stock issued and outstanding, and no preferred stock. On July 1, 1997, the company issues an additional 100,000 shares of common stock. For the year ended December 31, 1997, the company has earnings per share of $1.00, and the retained earnings balance at the end of the year, after payment of dividends, is $2,000,000: an increase of $60,000 from the balance on January 1, 1997. The debt-to-equity ratio remained unchanged over the year at 2:1, and the stockholders' equity section of the balance sheet contained only common stock, additional paid in capital, and retained earnings.

LO 5 26. The weighted average number of shares for Buellton used in the calculation of earnings per share is 250,000.

LO 5 27. Net income for the year is $250,000.

LO 5 28. Total dividends paid on common stock are $300,000.

LO 5 29. Dividend per share paid on common stock is $1.

LO 5 30. Total liabilities over the year did not change.

For each of the following questions, circle the alternative that best answers the question:

Use the following information to answer questions 31 to 33.
Corporation A loses equipment in an earthquake. The equipment is uninsured, and the carrying value of the lost equipment was $150,000. The company's tax rate is 40%.

LO 3 31. The effect of the loss from the earthquake would be found in which of the following headings in a multi-step income statement?
a) Operating revenues and expenses
b) Other revenues or expenses
c) Disposal of a business segment
d) Extraordinary gains or losses

LO 3 32. The net effect of the loss communicated on the multi-step income statement is
a) $150,000
b) $ 90,000
c) $ 60,000
d) None of the above

LO 3 33. Assume now that the machinery had been insured for $30,000 and that the insurance company pays that amount to Corporation B less the deductible of $5,000. The net effect of the loss now communicated on the income statement is
a) $ 50,000
b) $125,000
c) $ 75,000
d) None of the above

LO. 4 34. Company A, which has been in business for two years, switches in Year 3 to an accelerated depreciation method from straight line. Additional depreciation of $30,000 and $60,000 should be charged for Years 1 and 2, respectively, and accelerated depreciation of $120,000 should be charged for Year 3. The company's marginal rate of taxation is 40%. The cumulative effect of the change in accounting principle should be shown in the Year 3 income statement as

a) $ 90,000 increase in income
b) $ 54,000 increase in income
c) $210,000 increase in income
d) $126,000 decrease in income

LO 1 35. Which of the following would NOT appear as part of operating income in a multi-step income statement?

a) Revenues of a store that continues to operate
b) Income tax on current year's income
c) Selling expenses for the current year
d) The salaries of employees of a business segment that was sold in a previous year

LO 5 36. Company A has issued stock of 200,000 shares on January 1, Year 1. On November 1, Year 1, the company issues an additional 60,000 shares. In calculating the earnings per share for the year to December 31, Year 1, the denominator used is

a) 200,000
b) 260,000
c) 210,000
d) 10,000

LO 8 37. Which of the following would not be found in stockholders' equity?

a) Foreign currency translation adjustment
b) Dividend payable
c) Additional paid-in capital
d) Unrealized loss on investments in securities

LO 1 38. Which of the following would not appear in a multi-step income statement?

a) Cash dividends on preferred and common stock
b) Current year's net income
c) An extraordinary loss on the redemption of bonds
d) Cumulative effect of change in accounting principle

LO 5 39. The balances on retained earnings at the beginning and end of Year 1 were $85,000 and $125,000, respectively. The only other change in stockholders' equity was a 2-for-1 stock split at the beginning of the year. The number of issued shares before the split was 20,000. The earnings per share for Year 1 is

a) $1
b) $2
c) $3.13
d) Not enough information is provided to answer the question.

LO 1 40. In a multi-step income statement, a loss on the sale of machinery is found in
a) operating revenues and expenses.
b) other revenues and expenses.
c) extraordinary gains or losses.
d) disposal of a business segment.

LO 5 41. San Marcos Corporation has earnings per share of 10 cents for the year ended December 31, 1997. On January 1, 1997, the company had 100,000 shares of common stock issued and outstanding, and on March 31, 1997, the company issued an additional 60,000 shares. Net income for 1997 was
a) $14,500
b) $16,000
c) $11,500
d) $10,000

LO 5 42. Milngavie Inc. has earnings per share for the year ended March 31, 1998, of 10 cents. On April 1, 1997, the company issued 200,000 shares of common stock, and on March 31, 1998, it issued 290,000 shares of common stock. The company's net income for the year to March 31, 1998 is $23,000. The company issued the additional common stock on
a) July 31, 1997
b) November 30, 1997
c) January 1, 1998
d) June 30, 1997

LO 3 43. Alpha Company incurred an extraordinary loss, which it reported on its income statement at the after-tax amount of $63,000. The company's marginal tax rate is 30%. The total loss incurred was
a) $70,000
b) $90,000
c) $81,900
d) $44,100

LO 2 44. In a multi-step income statement, the sale of a manufacturing facility that results in eliminating a major business segment would be reported as
a) operating revenues and expenses.
b) other revenues or expenses.
c) disposal of a business segment.
d) extraordinary gain or loss.

LO 9 45. The calculation of comprehensive income includes
a) net income.
b) foreign currency translation adjustment.
c) unrealized gains or losses.
d) all of the above.

Answer each of the following problems:

LO 1 46. The following information has been extracted from the Hillhead Corporation's adjusted trial balance on December 31, Year 1.

$ in millions	**Debit**	**Credit**
Operating revenues		3,300
Operating expenses	2,000	
Loss on sale of equipment	400	
Gain on sale of business segment		1,200
Income from disposed segment		300
Loss on retirement of debt	300	
Increase in inventory value from change from LIFO to FIFO		800

Taxes on income from continuing operations are $380 for the year, and the effective income tax rate on other items is 40%. The loss on sale of equipment occurred as a result of a major refurbishment of the company's manufacturing facility. The loss is considered unusual but not infrequent.

Required
Prepare an income statement in a multi-step format.

LO 1 47. The following information is available for Daizychain Stores for the year ending December 31, Year 2:

Sales	$4,000,000
Cost of sales	1,700,000
Gross margin	2,300,000
Selling and administrative expenses	700,000
Interest expense	380,000
Income taxes	480,000

Although Daizychain's operations had traditionally been in both manufacturing and retailing, the information above relates only to its retailing activities since it closed its manufacturing division in Year 2. Daizychain's marginal tax rate is 40%, and the following additional information is available:

a) Daizychain's store in Isla Vista was burned to the ground after a freak gas explosion. The total loss amounts to $200,000, of which $150,000 is covered by insurance.
b) One of Daizychain's inventory items was made obsolete by the introduction of a new product, and the entire inventory of that product had to be scrapped. The loss associated with this amounted to $20,000.
c) In Year 2, Daizychain decided to cease all manufacturing operations and sold its manufacturing facilities. The loss associated with the sale of the facilities was $85,000, and the manufacturing division had made losses of $20,000 in Year 2 prior to the sale.
d) Daizychain changed its accounting method for depreciation, from straight line to accelerated. Prior periods' reported net income would have been increased by $200,000 if accelerated depreciation had been used.
e) On October 1, Year 2, Daizychain issued 40,000 additional shares of common stock, bringing its total shares outstanding at the end of the year to 230,000.

Required
Prepare a multi-step income statement for the year ended December 31, Year 2, including an appropriate analysis of earnings per share.

Critical Thinking Problem

LO 1,3 48. The consolidated income statements for the Walt Disney Company for the years 1993 through 1995 are reproduced below.

CONSOLIDATED STATEMENT OF INCOME

(In millions, except per share data) Year ended September 30	1995	1994	1993
Revenues			
Filmed entertainment	$6,001.5	$4,793.3	$3,673.4
Theme parks and resorts	3,959.8	3,463.6	3,440.7
Consumer products	2,150.8	1,798.2	1,415.1
	12,112.1	10,055.1	8,529.2
Costs and Expenses			
Filmed entertainment	4,927.1	3,937.2	3,051.2
Theme parks and resorts	3,099.0	2,779.5	2,693.8
Consumer products	1,640.3	1,372.7	1,059.7
	9,666.4	8,089.4	6,804.7
Operating Income			
Filmed entertainment	1,074.4	856.1	622.2
Theme parks and resorts	860.8	684.1	746.9
Consumer products	510.5	425.5	355.4
	2,445.7	1,965.7	1,724.5
Corporate Activities			
General and administrative expenses	183.6	162.2	164.2
Interest expense	178.3	119.9	157.7
Investment and interest income	-68	-129.9	-186.1
	293.9	152.2	135.8
Loss from Investment in Euro Disney	-35.1	-110.4	-514.7
Income Before Income Taxes and Cumulative Effect of Accounting Changes	2,116.7	1,703.1	1,074.0
Income taxes	736.6	592.7	402.7
Income Before Cumulative Effect of Accounting Changes	1,380.1	1,110.4	671.3
Cumulative Effect of Accounting Changes			
Pre-opening costs	--	--	-271.2
Postretirement benefits	--	--	-130.3
Income taxes	--	--	30
Net Income	$1,380.1	$1,110.4	$299.8
Amounts Per Common Share			
Earnings Before Cumulative Effect of Accounting Changes	$2.60	$2.04	$1.23
Preopening costs	--	--	-0.5
Postretirement benefits	--	--	-0.24
Income taxes	--	--	0.06
Earnings Per Share	$2.60	$2.04	$0.55

Required

1. What are the most significant changes between 1994 and 1993 that could explain the substantial increase in net income reported?

2. Would you classify the loss from EuroDisney as an extraordinary loss in 1993? Why or why not?

3. In assessing the likely future performance of the Walt Disney Company, which of the earnings per share figures presented would you find most relevant, and why?

Solutions

Fill in the Blanks

1. $12,000 loss
2. $24,000 loss
3. discontinued operation
4. extraordinary loss
5. operating income
6. operating income
7. change in accounting principle
8. $5,000
9. 250,000
10. $6
11. statement of stockholders' equity
12. earnings per share
13. unrealized loss on investment in securities
14. appropriation of retained earnings
15. comprehensive income

True/False

		COMMENT/EXPLANATION
16.	True	
17.	True	
18.	True	
19.	True	
20.	False	Income from operations is calculated before deduction of tax.
21.	False	Comprehensive income is used to represent the increase in net assets resulting from all transactions during a period, *other than* investments by and distributions to owners. If owners' equity changed because of distributions or investments, then the change in net assets over the period would not represent comprehensive income.
22.	True	
23.	True	
24.	True	
25.	True	
26.	True	
27.	True	
28.	False	Dividend is $240,000,calculated as the difference between net income ($300,000) and increase in retained earnings ($60,000).
29.	False	Dividend per share is $0.80.
30.	False	Since common stock, retained earnings, and possibly additional paid in capital all increased, and the debt-to-equity ratio remained constant, the debt must also have increased.

Multiple Choice

31.	d	39.	a
32.	b	40.	b
33.	c	41.	a
34.	b	42.	b
35.	d	43.	b
36.	c	44.	c
37.	b	45.	d
38.	a		

Problem 46

Hillhead Corporation
Income statement year ending December 31, Year 1

Operating revenues		$ 3,300
Operating expenses		(2,000)
Net operating income		1,300
Other income and expense		
Loss on sale of equipment		(400)
Income from continuing operations before tax		900
Income taxes		(380)
Income from continuing operations		520
Discontinued operations		
Gain on disposal of business segment ($300 less tax effect $120)	$ 720	
Operating income from disposed segment ($1,200 less tax effect of $480)	180	900
Income before extraordinary item		1,420
Extraordinary loss		
Loss on retirement of debt ($300 less tax effect of $120)		(180)
Income before cumulative effect		1,240
Cumulative effect		
Gain on change in inventory costing method ($800 less tax effect of $320)		480
Net income		$1,720

Problem 47

Daizychain Stores
Income statement year ending December 31, Year 2

Sales		$ 4,000,000
Less Cost of sales		(1,700,000)
Gross margin		2,300,000
Selling and administrative expense		(700,000)
Income from operations		1,600,000
Other income and expense		
Interest expense	$ (380,000)	
Loss on obsolete inventory	(20,000)	(400,000)
Income from continuing operations before tax		1,200,000
Income taxes		(480,000)
Income from continuing operations		720,000
Discontinued operations		
Loss on disposal of manufacturing division ($85,000 less tax effect $34,000)	(51,000)	
Operating loss of division ($20,000 less tax effect of $8,000)	(12,000)	(63,000)
Income before extraordinary item		657,000
Extraordinary loss		
Loss from explosion ($50,000 less tax effect of $20,000)		(30,000)
Income before cumulative effect		627,000
Cumulative effect		
Gain on change in depreciation method ($200,000 less tax effect of $80,000)		120,000
Net income		$ 747,000

Weighted average number of shares = (190,000 x 9/12) + (230,000 x 3/12) = 200,000

Earnings per share:

Income from continuing operations	$ 720,000/200,000	$ 3.60
Discontinued operations	(63,000)/200,000	(0.32)
Income before extraordinary item	657,000/200,000	3.28
Extraordinary loss - loss from explosion	(30,000)/200,000	(0.15)
Income before cumulative effect	627,000/200,000	3.13
Cumulative effect	120,000/200,000	0.60
Net income	$ 747,000/200,000	$ 3.73

Critical Thinking Problem 48

1. There are two main sources of the dramatic rise in profitability: the cumulative effect of accounting changes and the loss on EuroDisney in 1993. The accounting changes arise mainly from adjustments in the way in which preopening costs and postretirement benefits are accounted for. By far the biggest change, however, is due to the reduction in losses for EuroDisney.
2. The loss from EuroDisney should not be classified as an extraordinary item since it is a continuing part of Disney's operations. The segregation of the loss from EuroDisney is designed to ensure that these large losses do not distort the profitable results that Disney has experienced in its other activities.
3. Of the earnings per share figures, the one most likely to be useful in assessing future performance is the one calculated on the assumption that the new accounting method for preopening costs is applied retroactively. The EPS calculated before the accounting changes are included probably overstates likely future income, and the EPS calculated after the cumulative effect is accounted for probably understates it.

Chapter 13

Additional Reporting Issues: Intercompany Investments and Foreign Currency

This chapter focuses on some of the issues facing corporations as a result of the globalization of business. Your objective is to understand the nature of intercompany investment and the accounting issues associated with it. You should also gain insights into the reporting issues associated with international investment and operations.

Learning Objectives

- **LO 1** Explain the various reasons that one company might invest in another company.
- **LO 2** Understand the accounting and reporting requirements for held-to-maturity securities.
- **LO 3** Understand the accounting and reporting requirements for trading securities.
- **LO 4** Understand the accounting and reporting requirements for available-for-sale securities.
- **LO 5** Understand the accounting and reporting requirements for equity investees.
- **LO 6** Explain the different forms of business combinations and how to account for a merger using the purchase method.
- **LO 7** Explain when, why and how consolidated financial statements are prepared.
- **LO 8** Understand how to account for foreign currency transactions.
- **LO 9** Understand how to translate foreign financial statements into U.S. dollars.
- **LO 10** Describe the reporting requirements for segments of a business.

Key Textbook Exhibits

Exhibit 13-2 summarizes the accounting and reporting requirements for each of the three categories of investments, held-to-maturity, trading, and available-for-sale. Note the different values at which the three different types are reported, and how and where changes in fair value are reported.

Exhibit 13-3 summarizes the different types of business combinations. Note how the combination is achieved in each case and the form of the surviving entity.

Exhibits 13-11 and 13-12 illustrate the translation of a foreign balance sheet and income statement. Note how the rules identified in the paragraph above relating to foreign currency translation are applied.

Review of Key Concepts

LO 1 Companies invest in other companies for two reasons: to invest spare cash, or for strategic reasons. As with individuals, companies may invest cash that is not needed immediately in securities of other companies. Such investments have the sole purpose of providing a return until the cash is needed. On the other hand, companies may have strategic reasons for wishing to gain control or influence the companies they invest in. The accounting treatment of each type of investment is different. According to current accounting standards, the level of stockholding the company acquires determines that accounting treatment to use. The following table summarizes the current rules.

Stockholding In Investee Company	Influence of Investor Company on Investee Company	Accounting Treatment
Less than 20%	No significant influence	Depends on type of investment, see LO 2,3,4 below
Between 20% and 50%	Significant influence	Equity method, see page 260, LO 5 below
More than 50%	Control	Consolidation, see page 262, LO 7 below

The accounting method used for investments of less than 20% in the investee company depends on which of three categories the investment falls into. **Held-to-maturity securities** are *bonds* that the investor has both the intention and ability to hold to maturity. **Trading securities** are *stocks and bonds* bought to sell again in the near future. **Available-for-sale securities** are securities, *either stocks or bonds,* not classified as held-to-maturity or trading securities.

LO 2 The accounting treatment of **held-to-maturity securities** is similar to accounting for bond issues covered in Chapter 10 but, obviously, is carried out from the investor's, rather than the issuer's, perspective. Recall that when a bond issue is made at a price different from the face value of the bonds, the difference appears in either a premium or a discount account. This premium or discount is subsequently written off to the income statement over the life of the bonds. However, when bonds are purchased rather than sold no separate premium or discount account is opened for held-to-maturity securities. The total price paid for the bonds is recorded in an investment account.

For example, assume that Corporation X buys 1,000, 10% bonds with a face value of $1,000 for $1,050 per bond on January 1 Year 1 from Corporation A (see Chapter 10 for Corporation A's reporting). Also assume that Corporation X intends to keep the bonds until they mature on December 31, Year 5, and that interest on the bonds is paid annually in arrear. The journal entry to record the bond purchase is as follows:

	Debit	Credit
Investment in bonds	1,050,000	
Cash		1,050,000

As we discussed in Chapter 10, the premium or discount on the bond is written off over the life of the bond. In the case of Company X, the premium on the bonds is $50,000. When interest is received each year, the premium is written off by reducing the investment account by a proportion of the premium. For example, using the effective interest rate method, we see from Chapter 10 that $15 per bond of premium is amortized in the first year. When interest is received by Company X, the journal entry to record the interest is as follows:

	Debit	Credit
Cash	100,000	
Investment in bonds		15,000
Interest income		85,000

Test your understanding!

Question: Why are we reducing the amount of interest income that is being recognized? Aren't we understating the interest income?

Answer: When we paid a premium for the bonds, we paid more than the amount we would receive when they matured. By writing off the premium over the life of the bonds, we achieve two things. First, we reduce the amount in the investment account to the amount that we will be repaid on maturity. Second, we recognize that the interest we earn is less than it would have been if we had bought the bonds at face value.

LO 3 **Trading securities** are bought with the intention of selling them in the near future. They are therefore reported as current assets. When they are bought, trading securities are recorded at cost. At the end of the accounting period, if the market price has changed, the investment account is adjusted so that the balance on the account equals the new market price. Any gain or loss is recognized in the income statement. For example, if Company X buys stock in Company C for $200,000 and at the end of the accounting period the stock has a market value of $150,000, a loss of $50,000 will be recognized in the income statement. The investment account will be reduced by the same amount. This process is called **marking to market.**

LO 4 **Available-for-sale** securities encompass any investment in stocks or bonds that does not qualify as trading securities, and bonds that are not intended to be held to maturity. They may be reported as either long-term or short-term assets. As with trading securities, available-for-sale securities must also be marked to market. However, instead of the gain or loss being reported in the income statement, it is entered into an unrealized gain or loss account, which appears as part of stockholders' equity.

Test your understanding!

Question: Why is the difference between the book value and the current market price treated differently for trading securities and for available-for-sale securities?

Answer: The argument hinges on the fact that available-for-sale investments are expected to be held for longer than trading securities. Trading securities are expected to be sold within the next year; available-for-sale investments are not. For trading securities, the current market price provides a good indication of what the final sale price will be. Therefore the gain or loss on these securities can be reliably estimated and reported in the income statement. Since it is uncertain when available-for-sale securities will be sold, the current market price does not offer similar insights into the ultimate gain or loss on these securities. However, the current market price is an important piece of information, and the best guide to the current value of these investments. The current market price of available-for-sale securities should be reported in the balance sheet along with the unrealized gain or loss.

LO 5 When a company holds between 20% and 50% of another company's stock, the investor company is deemed to be capable of exerting significant influence over the investee company, or **affiliate**. The accounting treatment of this type of investment, called the **equity method,** requires that a proportion of the increase in retained earnings of the affiliate be reported on the income statement of the investor company.

To illustrate, suppose that Company Y pays $250,000 for 25% of the equity of Company Z on January 1, Year 1. At that time, Company Z's retained earnings are $250,000. The journal entry is as follows:

	Debit	Credit
Investment in Company Z	250,000	
Cash		250,000

During the next year, Company Z's reported income and dividends are $100,000 and $60,000, respectively. At the end of the year, Company Y increases the book value of its investment in Company Z, by its share of Company Z's reported income for the year. Company Z's income *before* the payment of dividends is $100,000, and Company Y's share is 25%, or $25,000.

	Debit	Credit
Investment in Company Z	25,000	
Equity income		25,000

At the end of the year, Company Y receives dividends from Company Z of $15,000 (25% of $60,000). Since Company Y has increased the book value of the investment by its share of the total earnings of Company Z, it must reduce the book value of the investment by the amount of the dividend.

	Debit	Credit
Cash	15,000	
Investment in Company Z		15,000

These adjustments ensure that the net increase in the investment account ($10,000 = $25,000 - $15,000) equals Company Y's share of the increase in Company Z's retained earnings over the period.

Test your understanding!

Question: Does the equity method amount to marking the investment to market?

Answer: No! The equity method reflects changes in the affiliate's retained earnings. Since security prices reflect information not only about past performance but also about the company's expected future performance, it is unlikely that the change in retained earnings will match the change in the affiliate's market price.

LO 6 A business combination takes place when one company (Company A) gains control of another (Company B). A business combination has both legal and accounting implications for the company involved.

From a legal perspective, there are three different forms of business combination that can take place. In a **statutory merger**, Company A acquires the net assets of Company B, with A surviving after the merger and B going out of existence. With a **statutory consolidation,** A and B combine net assets, with both companies ceasing to exist and a new corporation, say C, being created. In a **stock acquisition**, Company A acquires the stock of Company B, and both A and B continue to exist, but B is controlled by A. The following table summarizes the three types.

Legal Form	What Happens	After the Combination
Statutory merger	A acquires net assets of B.	A is the surviving entity. B goes out of existence.
Statutory consolidation	A and B combine net assets.	A and B go out of existence. New entity, C, is created.
Stock acquisition	A acquires stock of B.	A and B continue to exist.

LO 6 For any of the three legal forms of business combination, one of two different accounting methods, **purchase or pooling**, may be applied. Current accounting practice dictates the circumstances in which each of the methods may be used, with the purchase method being by far the most common.

To illustrate the use of the purchase method with a simple example, assume that Company A and Company B's summary balance sheets are as follows on January 1, Year 1.

	Company A	Company B
Current assets	$1,000,000	$200,000
Long-term assets	2,000,000	500,000
Total assets	$3,000,000	$700,000
Current liabilities	$1,500,000	$500,000
Shareholders' equity		
Capital stock, $1 par	1,000,000	150,000
Retained earnings	500,000	50,000
Total liabilities and stockholders' equity	$3,000,000	$700,000

Now assume that Company A buys all of Company B's stock for $200,000 cash. The cash balance in Company A's balance sheet decreases by $200,000, and a new account, Investment in Company B, is opened. There is no change in Company B's accounts, since only the holders of the stock have changed, not the amount of stock issued.

	Company A	Company B	Combined
Current assets	$ 800,000	$200,000	$1,000,000
Investment in Company B	200,000		
Long-term assets	2,000,000	500,000	2,500,000
Total assets	$3,000,000	$700,000	$3,500,000
Current liabilities	$1,500,000	$500,000	$2,000,000
Shareholders' equity			
Capital stock, $1 par	1,000,000	150,000	1,000,000
Retained earnings	500,000	50,000	500,000
Total liabilities and stockholders' equity	$3,000,000	$700,000	$3,500,000

Assume that a single balance sheet is drawn up, that reflects the total assets and liabilities under the control of Company A. Also assume that the book values of Company B reflect their fair values. In this case, the consolidation is relatively easy since the amount paid for Company B equals the book value of the net assets. The consolidated balance sheet above is found by replacing the balance in the Investment in Company B account with the individual assets and liabilities.

The example above illustrates the principle of consolidation: the investment account in the acquirer company is replaced with the individual assets and liabilities of the acquired. In practice however, it is extremely rare for the investment account to equal the book value of the acquired company's net assets. To illustrate the treatment when the two amounts differ, assume that the fair value of Company B's long-term assets is $650,000 and that Company A pays $400,000 for the investment in Company B. The fair value of Company B's net assets is ($200,000 + $650,000 - $500,000) = $350,000, which is still less than the amount that Company A paid. The difference between the amount paid for the net assets and the fair value of the net assets of the acquired company is called **goodwill.**

Test your understanding!

Question: Why would a company pay more than the fair value of the net assets to gain control of another company?

Answer: Additional benefits over and above the assets of the acquired company can be obtained in a merger or acquisition. For example, the acquirer may obtain access to new markets through the acquired company that will increase the parent company's profitability. Similarly, the acquired company may have competence in new production methods that can be used to improve the operating activities of the parent. The key point is that the acquirer expects its future cash flows to increase as a result of the acquisition. The increased cash flows may not be reflected in the fair value of the acquired company's net assets.

To prepare the balance sheet of the combined business, it is again necessary to replace the Investment in Company B balance in Company A's balance sheet with the individual assets and liabilities of Company B, but this time at fair value. Where the fair value of the net assets is less than the Investment in Company B balance, the difference appears as goodwill in the assets of the combined balance sheet.

	Company A after paying $400,000 for Company B)	Adjustments using Company B's net assets at fair value	Combined
Current assets	$ 600,000	$+200,000	$ 800,000
Investment in Company B	400,000	-400,000	
Goodwill		+50,000	50,000
Long-term assets	2,000,000	+650,000	2,650,000
Total assets	$3,000,000	$+500,000	$3,500,000
Current liabilities	1,500,000	$+500,000	$2,000,000
Shareholders' equity			
Capital stock, $1 par	1,000,000		1,000,000
Retained earnings	500,000		500,000
Total liabilities and stockholders' equity	$3,000,000	$+500,000	$3,500,000

LO 7 Although in both statutory mergers and statutory consolidations only one legal entity remains, stock acquisitions result in two separate legal entities. However, both are under the control of a single management, the parent company. In the case of stock acquisitions therefore, accounting practice requires that a single set of **consolidated accounts** be prepared as above to show the total assets and liabilities of the business combination. These accounts must be prepared both at the time the acquisition takes place and at the end of each accounting period. In addition to a balance sheet, a consolidated income

statement must be prepared to show the net income of the combined entity. When the parent company owns less than 100% (but more than 50%) of the subsidiary, a **minority interest** exists. Minority interests represent a claim on the net assets of the business combination. The proportion of the net assets of the subsidiary attributable to minority interests is shown between long-term liabilities and stockholders' equity on the consolidated balance sheet.

LO 8 An **exchange rate** measures the relative worth of two currencies. Since the currencies' relative worth depends on the relative strengths of the two countries' economies, exchange rates move over time. When that happens, companies that trade abroad can make a gain or a loss on their foreign operations. To illustrate, suppose Company X agrees to buy machinery from a United Kingdom company and to pay 100,000 pounds sterling on delivery. At the time the contract was signed, the exchange rate was $1.50 to the pound so Company X expected to pay $150,000 for the machinery. When the machine was delivered three months later, the exchange rate had moved to $1.40 to the pound and the machine cost the company $140,000, an exchange rate gain of $10,000. Clearly the reverse can happen and the company can also lose on foreign exchange transactions.

LO 9 When companies have foreign subsidiaries or affiliates, it is necessary to convert the affiliates' or subsidiaries' accounts to be consistent with the accounts of the U.S. parent company. The foreign accounts will differ in two ways. First, they will have been drawn up according to local accounting standards and must be converted to U.S. GAAP. Second, they will be stated in the local currency of the affiliate or subsidiary and will require to be translated to U.S. dollars. Since exchange rates move over time, the exchange rate to be used in translation must be determined. In deciding this, current U.S. practice first requires that the **functional currency** be identified. This is normally the currency in which the company does most of its business, but if that currency is in an economy that has very high rates of inflation, the American dollar is used. If the local currency is deemed to be the functional currency, all income statement items are translated at the average rate for the year, all assets and liabilities are translated at the rate at the end of the year (current rate), and stockholders' equity is translated at the exchange rate at the time the stock was issued (historic rate). A "plug" figure to balance the balance sheet is found and is reported as a separate balance in the stockholders' equity section as a **translation adjustment.**

LO 10 Although much of the discussion above has centered on the need for aggregated financial information, there are circumstances in which users would benefit from disaggregation of financial information. For example, a company may have significant foreign operations, or be operating in several different industries. In these cases, users can obtain a better understanding of the company's operations if financial information is provided about the individual countries or about the different industries. Current accounting practice requires that segment information be provided if certain criteria, relating to the significance of the different segments in the company's operations, are met. Four areas of disclosure are defined:

- Operations in different industries
- Operations in foreign countries
- Major customers
- Export sales

When a company has significant operations (as defined by the accounting standard) in more than one industry, the company must disclose in a footnote, revenues, operating profit or loss, carrying value of assets, depreciation, depletion and amortization, and capital expenditures for each industry segment. For significant geographic segments, only revenues, operating profit or loss, and the carrying value of assets need be disclosed by geographic area. When the company has a significant amount of export sales, the amount of these sales must be disclosed. In addition, the revenue from any customer to whom sales of more than 10% of the company's total sales are made must also be disclosed.

Review of Key Terms

Affiliate A company that has enough of its stock held by another company to give the other entity significant influence over it.

Amortized cost method A method of accounting for investments in bonds in which the investment account is adjusted periodically to recognize the amortization of premium or discount.

Available-for-sale securities Stocks and bonds that are not classified as either held-to-maturity or trading securities.

Conglomerate A combination of companies with operations in different industries.

Consolidated financial statements Statements that report on the parent corporation and any separate legal entities, called *subsidiaries.*

Equity method A method of accounting for investments in which income is recognized as a proportionate share of the income of the investee.

Exchange rate A measure of the relative worth of two different currencies.

Foreign currency transaction A transaction in which a company agrees to receive or make payment in a foreign currency.

Foreign currency translation The process of restating the financial statements of a company from one currency to another.

Functional currency The currency of the primary economic environment in which an entity operates.

Goodwill An intangible asset that represents the excess of the purchase price for a business over the fair value of the net assets acquired.

Held-to-maturity securities Investments in bonds of other companies in which the investor has the positive intent and the ability to hold the securities to maturity.

Horizontal combination A combination of businesses that are in competition with each other.

Minority interest The owners' equity of a subsidiary not attributable to the interest of the parent.

Parent An entity that controls another entity by ownership of a majority of the other company's common stock.

Pooling of interests method An accounting approach to recording a business combination that is sometimes used when shares of stock in the two companies are exchanged.

Purchase method An accounting approach for recording a business combination that is used when one company uses cash, other assets, or debt to acquire the other company.

Statutory consolidation A business combination in which a new entity is created to carry on the activities of the entities involved in the combination.

Statutory merger A business combination in which only one of the two entities survives.

Stock acquisition — A business combination in which one company acquires a majority of the common stock of the other company.

Subsidiary — A separate legal entity controlled by another entity.

Trading securities — Stocks and bonds of other companies bought and held for the purpose of selling them in the near term to generate profits on appreciation of their price.

Translation adjustment — The amount needed to balance the two sides of a balance sheet when financial statements are translated from one currency into another currency.

Vertical combination — A combination of a company with either a supplier or a customer.

Wholly owned subsidiary — A subsidiary in which the parent owns all of the common stock.

Practice Test Questions and Problems

Complete each of the following statements:

LO 6 1. If Company A and Company B combine in a ___________________, A acquires the net assets of B, and B ceases to exist.

LO 6 2. If Company A and Company B combine by a ___________________, both A and B continue to exist.

LO 6 3. A company with activities in widely varying industries is called a ___________________.

LO 5 4. Investments of between 20% and 50% in the common stock of another company must be accounted for under the ___________________.

LO 7 5. Consolidation of two companies' accounts involves reciprocal accounts of the two companies being deleted, or ___________________, and similar accounts in the balance sheet of the two companies being added together, or _______________.

LO 7 6. ___________________ is the portion of a subsidiary's stockholders' equity that is owned by stockholders other than the parent corporation.

LO 8 7. If a U.S. company has a receivable in a foreign currency, and the foreign currency ___________________ against the U.S. dollar, the U.S. company may receive more dollars for the receivable than it expected.

Use the following information to answer questions 8 through 10:

100% of the stock of Minor Corporation was acquired by Major Corporation on January 1, Year 1, for $600,000. On that date, Minor Corporation's net assets had a book value of $300,000 and a fair value of $500,000.

LO 7 8. Goodwill of ____________________ is recorded in the consolidated balance sheet immediately after the purchase.

LO 7 9. The net tangible assets of Minor Corporation are recorded at ____________________ in the consolidated balance sheet immediately after the purchase.

LO 7 10. After the purchase, Minor's books show net assets of ____________________.

LO 6 11. A combination of a company with either a supplier or a customer is known as a ____________________.

LO 6 12. A subsidiary in which the parent owns all of the common stock is known as a ____________________.

LO 9 13. ____________________ is the amount needed to balance the two sides of a balance sheet when financial statements are translated from one currency into another currency.

LO 7 14. ____________________ is an intangible asset that represents the excess of the purchase price for a business over the fair value of the net assets acquired.

LO 3 15. ____________________ are stocks and bonds of other companies bought and held for the purpose of selling them in the near term to generate profits on appreciation of their price.

Indicate whether each of the following statements is true or false:

LO 2 16. Since only bonds have a maturity date, only bonds can be held-to-maturity securities.

LO 7 17. The pooling method of consolidation may be used only where the stock of the acquired company is bought with cash.

LO 10 18. Segment information can be required in four areas: operations in foreign countries, operations in different industries, major customers, and export sales. The most comprehensive information is provided for operations in foreign countries.

LO 8 19. In translating foreign currency transactions, the functional currency is the currency of the primary economic environment in which the foreign entity operates.
It therefore may or may not be the local currency of the foreign country.

LO 6 20. A horizontal combination occurs when companies of similar size combine. A vertical combination involves companies of different sizes.

LO 7 21. Under the purchase method of consolidation, the assets of both the subsidiary and the parent are revalued to their fair values.

LO 7 22. Goodwill only occurs under the purchase method of consolidation.

LO 7 23. When consolidated accounts are prepared, the long-term assets of the subsidiary can be revalued to fair value only when the purchase method of consolidation is used.

LO 3 24. For both trading securities and available-for-sale securities, changes in fair value increase stockholders' equity.

LO 2 25. Bonds can be classified only as held-to-maturity securities and cannot be classified as available-for-sale or trading securities.

LO 3 26. For trading securities, changes in fair value are reported in the income statement. For available-for-sale securities, the change is reported directly in the balance sheet and is not reported in the income statement.

LO 3 27. Zeta Inc. owns stock in Delta Corporation and classifies the investment as trading securities. When Zeta sells the stock, it will report the sale as a cash flow from investing activities in the Statement of Cash Flows.

LO 5 28. When an investment is sold that was accounted for under the equity method, the gain or loss on sale is calculated as the difference between the sale proceeds and the original cost of the investment.

LO 5 29. Trading securities, available-for-sale securities, and investments accounted for under the equity method all appear on the balance sheet at fair value.

LO 6 30. Under GAAP, companies that merge can choose to account for the combined entity using either the purchase or the pooling method.

For each of the following questions, circle the alternative that best answers the question:

LO 4 31. Alpha Corporation owns stock in Zeta Corporation. Which of the following criteria must be satisfied if Alpha accounts for the investment as available-for-sale securities?:

a) Alpha's investment represents 25% of Zeta's outstanding stock.
b) Alpha owns 5% of Zeta's outstanding common stock and bought it with the intention of holding it for a short time and selling it at a profit.
c) Alpha owns 75% of Zeta's stock.
d) Alpha owns 3% of Zeta's stock and does not intend to sell it in the near future.

Use the following information to answer questions 32 through 35:
Alpha bought 5% of Delta's stock for $2 per share. At the balance sheet date, one month later, the Delta stock is selling for $2.60 per share and has paid a dividend per share of $0.30.

LO 4 32. If Alpha accounts for Delta stock as available-for-sale, the stock will be reported in the balance sheet at

a) $2.60 per share.
b) $2 per share.
c) $2.30 per share.
d) $2.90 per share.

LO 4 33. If Alpha accounts for Delta stock as available-for-sale, the entry in the income statement will be
a) unrealized gain of $0.90 per share.
b) unrealized gain of $0.60 per share and dividend income of $0.30 per share..
c) unrealized gain of $2.60 per share.
d) dividend income of $0.30 per share.

LO 3 34. If Alpha accounts for Delta stock as trading securities, the stock will be reported in the balance sheet at
a) $2.60 per share.
b) $2 per share.
c) $2.30 per share.
d) $2.90 per share.

LO 3 35. If Alpha accounts for Delta stock as trading securities, the entry in the income statement will be
a) unrealized gain of $0.90 per share.
b) unrealized gain of $0.60 per share and dividend income of $0.30 per share.
c) unrealized gain of $2.60 per share.
d) dividend income of $0.30 per share.

LO 7 36. Aber Company owns 90% of the common stock of Breughal Corporation. Which of the following statements is true?
a) Aber's investment in Breughal is accounted for under the pooling method by adding 90% of Breughal's net income each year to the original cost of the stock.
b) Aber's investment in Breughal is marked to market each year, but the change in the stock price is recorded in an unrealized gain or loss account in stockholders' equity rather than the income statement.
c) The 10% of Breughal's stock that is not owned by Aber is called minority interest and appears in the consolidated balance sheet.
d) The income statements and balance sheet of the two companies are combined using only 90% of Breughal's assets and liabilities.

LO 9 37. Gamma Corporation has a wholly owned British subsidiary. The British pound is the functional currency for translating the subsidiary's financial statements. Which of the following statements is false?
a) The original contributed capital of the U.K. subsidiary is translated at the Pound/$ exchange rate when the stock was first issued.
b) Assets and liabilities of the U.K. subsidiary are translated using the Pound/$ exchange rate at the end of the period.
c) All income statement items are translated at the average Pound/$ exchange rate over the period.
d) The translation adjustment is found by comparing the net income of the U.K. subsidiary translated at both the year-end exchange rate and the average exchange rate.

LO 10 38. Disclosure of segment information is NOT required to be disclosed for which of the following areas?
a) Operations in different industries
b) Operations in different states
c) Operations in foreign countries
d) Major customers

LO 10 39. Which of the following does not need to be reported about significant industry segments?
a) Revenues
b) Operating profit or loss
c) Taxes paid
d) Capital expenditures

LO 10 40. Which of the following does not need to be reported about significant foreign segments?
a) Capital expenditures
b) Revenues
c) Operating profits and losses
d) Carrying value of assets

LO 1 41. A company purchases 25% of the stock of the supplier of a key component in its manufacturing process. Which of the following is the most likely reason for the acquisition?
a) To obtain a return on idle cash
b) To control the activities of the supplier
c) To influence significantly the activities of the supplier
d) None of the above

LO 7 42. Zeta owns 80% of the stock of Alpha. Which of the following methods should Zeta use to account for its investment in Alpha?
a) Equity method
b) Fair value method
c) Consolidation
d) Amortized cost method

Use the following information to answer questions 43 and 44:

Arran Corporation buys a 25% stake in Jura Inc. on January 1, 1997, for $2,000,000. The investment is accounted for using the equity method. During the year to December 31, 1997, Jura reports total income of $1,600,000, and on December 31, 1997, Arran's balance sheet shows its investment in Jura at $2,300,000.

LO 5 43. For the year to December 31, 1997, Arran's income statement reports its income from the equity investment in Jura as
a) $300,000
b) $400,000
c) $100,000
d) $500,000

LO 5 44. Jura's total dividend paid for the year ended December 31, 1997 was
a) $1.2 million
b) $300,000
c) $400,000
d) None of the above

LO 6 45. Alpha and Beta agree to merge and form a new company Gamma. Alpha and Beta will cease to exist when the new company is formed. This type of business combination is called:

a) a statutory merger.
b) a consolidation.
c) a statutory consolidation.
d) a horizontal combination.

Answer each of the following problems:

LO 6 46. Giant Corporation paid $300,000 on January 1, Year 1 to acquire all the assets and assume all the liabilities of Pettit Company. After the purchase, Pettit will cease to exist. Pettit's summary balance sheet is as follows:

Pettit Company
Balance sheet on January 1, Year 1

Current assets	$ 30,000	Liabilities	$400,000
Plant and Equipment	470,000	Contributed capital	100,000
Land	30,000	Retained earnings	30,000
	$530,000		$530,000

Giant determines that the book values of Pettit's liabilities and current assets approximate their fair values. However, the fair value of the land is found to be $400,000, and the fair value of the plant and equipment is $200,000.

Required

1. Explain what type of business combination this is.

2. Compute the amount of goodwill that Giant should record in connection with the combination.

3. Show the journal entry recording the combination in Giant's ledger.

4. What would be the impact on the earnings reported by Giant after the merger if Giant did not value the assets at fair value but retained the original book values?

LO 5,9 47. Sam Company owns 40% of the ordinary shares (common stock) of Bulldog PLC, a UK retail group. Sam accounts for the investment using the equity method and on Sam's balance sheet on December 31,Year 2, the investment in Bulldog appeared at $150,000. Bulldog's summary income statement for the year ended December 31,Year 3, was as follows:

Bulldog PLC - Income statement
Year ending December 31, Year 3 (UK pounds)

Sales	£ 360,000
Cost of sales	(220,000)
Interest expense	(20,000)
Net earnings	£ 120,000

On May 1, Year 3, Bulldog declared and paid dividends totaling £20,000. On November 1, Year 3, it declared and paid dividends totaling £40,000. The British pound is used as the functional currency, and the following exchange rates are available:

Date	Exchange rate ($/£)
January 1,Year 3	$2.00 / £
May 1, Year 3	$1.80 / £
January 1,Year 3	$1.60 / £
December 1,Year 3	$1.60 / £
Average for Year 3	$1.75 / £

Required

1. Translate Bulldog's income statement from British pounds to U.S. dollars. Why is this necessary?

2. What amount should Sam recognize in its income statement as earnings from Bulldog for Year 3?

3. At what amount should Sam report the investment in Bulldog in its balance sheet dated December 31, Year 3? Remember to translate the dividends received at the exchange rate when they were paid.

LO 5 48. On January 1, Year 1, Glasgow Inc. bought 100,000 common shares of Edinburgh Corporation for $3.2 million cash. This investment represented 40% of Edinburgh's outstanding common stock. Glasgow intended to hold the stock indefinitely and to account for the investment using the equity method. During Year 1, Edinburgh earned net income of $250,000 and paid a dividend of $1 per share on December 31. During Year 2, Edinburgh made a net loss of $100,000 and paid a dividend of 50 cents per share on December 31.

Required

1. Show the journal entries in Glasgow's ledger during Years 1 and 2.

2. At what amounts would the investment in Edinburgh be shown in Glasgow's December 31, Year 1, and December 31, Year 2 balance sheets?

Critical Thinking Problem

LO 10 49. The following geographic segmental information has been extracted from the accounts of the Disney Corporation for the fiscal year ended September 30, 1995:

Geographic Segments			
Domestic Revenues			
United States	$9,311.00	$7,697.60	$6,710.80
United States export	547.8	458	399.8
International Revenues			
Europe	1,552.10	1,344.80	984.6
Rest of world	701.2	554.7	434
	---------	---------	---------
	$12,112.10	$10,055.10	$8,529.20
	=========	=========	=========
Operating Income			
United States	$1,745.80	$1,392.70	$1,591.70
Europe	464.1	405	121.8
Rest of world	323.2	226	82.5
Unallocated expenses	-87.4	-58	-71.5
	---------	---------	---------
	$2,445.70	$1,965.70	$1,724.50
	=========	=========	=========
Identifiable Assets			
United States	$13,437.50	$11,306.10	$11,084.50
Europe	1,060.20	1,237.80	519.7
Rest of world	108.1	282.4	146.9
	---------	---------	---------
	$14,605.80	$12,826.30	$11,751.10
	=========	=========	=========

Required

1. Which geographic segment appears more profitable, in relation both to its sales and its assets employed?

2. Would you support a proposal that Disney close down its international activities and concentrate on its domestic market?

Solutions

Fill in the Blanks

1. statutory merger
2. stock acquisition
3. conglomerate
4. equity
5. elimination, aggregation
6. minority interest
7. strengthens
8. $100,000
9. $500,000
10. $300,000
11. vertical analysis
12. wholly owned subsidiary
13. translation adjustment
14. goodwill
15. trading securities

True/False

		COMMENT/EXPLANATION
16.	True	
17.	False	The pooling method is sometimes used to record a business combination when shares of stock in the two companies are exchanged.
18.	False	The most comprehensive segment information is required for industry segments.
19.	True	
20.	False	A horizontal combination involves a combination with either a supplier or a customer. A vertical combination involves businesses that are in competition with each other.
21.	False	Under the purchase method, only the assets of the subsidiary are revalued to their fair values.
22.	True	
23.	True	
24.	True	
25.	False	Held-to-maturity securities are bonds that the investor has both the intention and ability to hold to maturity. Trading securities are stocks and bonds that are bought and held for the purpose of selling them in the near future. Available-for-sale securities are securities, either stocks or bonds, not classified as held-to-maturity or trading securities. Bonds can therefore be classified as any of the three types of security.
26.	True	
27.	False	It will be classified under operating activities.
28.	False	Gain or loss is the difference between book value and sale proceeds.
29.	False	Securities accounted for under the equity method do not appear at fair value but are adjusted for the proportionate increase in the affiliate's retained earnings.
30.	False	Strict criteria have to be met before the pooling method can be used.

Multiple Choice

31.	d	39.	c
32.	a	40.	a
33.	d	41.	c
34.	a	42.	c
35.	b	43.	b
36.	c	44.	c
37.	d	45.	c
38.	b		

Problem 46

1. Since only one company survives, the business combination is a statutory merger.

2.

Assets	$530,000
Plus revaluation of land	370,000
Less revaluation of plant, etc.	(270,000)
Less liabilities	(400,000)
Value of net assets	$230,000

Goodwill = $300,000 - $230,000 = $70,0000

3.

	Debit	Credit
Current assets	30,000	
Plant etc.	200,000	
Land	400,000	
Goodwill	70,000	
Cash		300,000
Liabilities		400,000

4. As a result of recording Pettit's assets and liabilities at fair value, depreciation will be charged on the lower, revalued amount for plant and equipment. Additional depreciation will be charged on goodwill, but typically, goodwill is written off over a longer time period than plant and equipment (40 years). The amount of goodwill in this case is substantially lower than the amount by which the plant and machinery were revalued. The depreciation charges after revaluation will therefore be substantially lower than before the merger; this will result in higher reported earnings from the assets of Pettit.

Problem 47

1.

	Pounds	Dollar/Pound exchange rate	Dollar
Sales	360,000	1.75	630,000
Cost of sales	(220,000)	1.75	(385,000)
Interest expense	(20,000)	1.75	(35,000)
Net earnings	120,000	1.75	210,000

The translation must be made to allow Sam to account for the investment in Bulldog using the equity method.

2. Amount reported in Sam's income statement = 40% x $210,000
= $84,000

3.

Opening balance in investment account	$150,000
Plus income for year	84,000
Less dividend - May (40%x 20,000 x 1.8)	(14,400)
Less dividend - November (40% x 40,000 x 1.6)	(25,600)
Closing balance in investment account	$194,000

Problem 48

1. Effect of initial purchase

	Debit	Credit
Investment in equity securities	3,200,000	
Cash		3,200,000

Effect of Edinburgh's earnings, Year 1

	Debit	Credit
Investment in equity securities	100,000	
Equity income		100,000

Effect of Edinburgh's dividend, Year 1

	Debit	Credit
Cash	100,000	
Investment in equity securities		100,000

Effect of Edinburgh's loss, Year 2

	Debit	Credit
Loss on equity investment	40,000	
Investment in equity securities		40,000

Effect of Edinburgh's dividend, Year 2

	Debit	Credit
Cash	50,000	
Investment in equity securities		50,000

2.

Original cost	$3,200,000
Plus Share of net income, Year 1	100,000
Less Dividend received, Year 1	- 100,000
Balance on investment account, Dec. 31, Year 1	**$3,200,000**
Less Share of net loss Year 2	- 40,000
Less Dividend received, Year 2	- 50,000
Balance on investment account, Dec. 31, Year 2	**$3,110,000**

Critical Thinking Problem 49

1. The table below shows how revenues and profits in different parts of the world have changed over the three years, and how profits in these different areas relate to the revenues and assets employed. We can see that revenues in Europe and the rest of the world have enjoyed considerable growth during the three years, and that the growth in profits has also been strong, especially in the last year reported.

   When profits are related to revenues and assets employed, again we can see that all geographic segments are performing well, with the rest of the world other than the U.S. and Europe being particularly buoyant.

2. It would not make sense for Disney to close down its international operations on the basis of these numbers. The "rest of the world" is particularly profitable for very little investment, presumably because the Disney movies are shown overseas and provide the advertising necessary for selling Disney's other products. Further, the international activities show healthy growth in both revenues and profits, and there is no reason to suppose that these markets have yet become saturated, so further growth is possible.

	1995	**1994**	**1993**	
% Change on Previous Year				
Revenues	21.0%	14.7%	-	U.S.
	15.4%	36.6%	-	Europe
	26.4%	27.8%	-	Rest of World
Profits	25.4%	-12.5%	-	U.S.
	43.0%	173.9%	-	Europe
	50.7%	-18.9%	-	Rest of World
Profits as % of				
Revenues	18.7%	18.1%	23.7%	U.S.
	29.9%	30.1%	12.4%	Europe
	46.1%	40.7%	19.0%	Rest of World
Assets Employed	13.0%	12.3%	14.4%	U.S.
	43.8%	32.7%	23.4%	Europe
	299.0%	80.0%	56.2%	Rest of World

Chapter 14

The Statement of Cash Flows

The Statement of Cash Flows is the last major financial statement to be considered in detail. In previous chapters you have looked at the impact of different elements of the income statement and balance sheet on the cash flow statement. This chapter considers the cash flow statement in detail and identifies a way in which the statement can be prepared. Your objective in this chapter is to understand the components and presentation of the cash flow statement and how the statement can be derived from information contained in the balance sheet and income statement.

Learning Objectives

LO 1 Explain the purpose of a statement of cash flows.

LO 2 Explain what cash equivalents are and how they are treated on the statement of cash flows.

LO 3 Describe operating, investing, and financing activities and give examples of each.

LO 4 Describe the difference between the direct and indirect methods of computing cash flows from operations.

LO 5 Use T accounts to prepare the statement of cash flows, using the direct method to determine cash flows from operating activities.

LO 6 Use T accounts to prepare a statement of cash flows, using the indirect method to determine cash flows from operations.

LO 7 Use a worksheet to prepare a statement of cash flows, using the indirect method to determine cash flows from operating activities.

Key Textbook Exhibits

Exhibit 14-5 illustrates the format of the statement of cash flows. Note the classification of cash flows into investing operating and financing activities.

Exhibit 14-6 classifies various activities according to whether they would appear as financing, operating, or investing activities and describes their effect on cash flow.

Exhibit 14-19 illustrates the use of a worksheet to prepare the statement of cash flows.

Review of Key Concepts

LO 1 The **Statement of Cash Flows** provides valuable information to supplement the information provided in the income statement and balance sheet. The cash flow statement not only reports the change in the entity's cash balance over the period but it also explains it. Current accounting practice requires that cash flows be classified according to whether they relate to **operating, investing, or financing activities** of the entity.

LO 2 The cash flow statement must report not only changes in the actual cash balances but also changes in cash equivalents. A cash equivalent is any item that can be readily converted into a known amount of cash and have a maturity to the investor of three months or less.

Test your understanding!

Question: Assume that on November 1, Year 5, Company X accepts a note receivable that is due to mature on December 31, Year 5. Is the note a cash equivalent?

Answer: Yes! The note is readily convertible to a known amount of cash, and it has a maturity to the investor (Company X) of less than three months.

LO 3 Cash flows must be classified according to whether they are operating, investing, or financing activities.

- **Operating activities** are those activities necessary to acquire, produce, and sell products and services. Examples include a house builder buying timber, a bank processing loan applications, and an insurance company paying sales commissions to its sales force.
- **Investing activities** are those activities that relate to the acquisition and disposal of long-term assets. Examples include the purchase of plant and equipment, and the sale of stocks or bonds held as investments.
- **Financing activities** are those activities resulting in changes in the debt or equity of the company. Examples include the issue of stocks or bonds, the repayment of bonds, and the repurchase of the company's own stock.

LO 4 When reporting cash flows from operations, either the **direct** or the **indirect** method can be used. With the direct method, the cash flows from individual operating activities are reported on the statement of cash flows. With the indirect method, the net income figure from the income statement is adjusted to a cash rather than an accrual basis. To illustrate the two methods, assume that Company Z begins operations on January 1, Year 1, and on that day, the owner provides cash of $100,000 to the business in return for 100,000 $1 shares. The company's balance sheet and income statement at the end of Year 1 are as follows:

Income statement for year ended December 31, Year 1	
Sales	$1,500,000
Expenses	900,000
Net income before tax	600,000
Taxes	200,000
Net income	$400,000

Balance Sheet on December 31, Year 1

Cash	$ 50,000	Accounts payable	$ 70,000
Accounts receivable	100,000	**Stockholders' Equity**	
Land	420,000	Outstanding stock at par	100,000
		Retained earnings	400,000
	$570,000		$570,000

Test your understanding!

Question: Net income, which is all derived from operating activities, is shown as $400,000. Can we conclude that we have also generated cash of $400,000 from operations?

Answer: No! Since we have both accounts receivable and accounts payable on the balance sheet, we must have made both credit sales and credit purchases; therefore our cash flows from operations is unlikely to equal our net income. As we illustrate below, the changes in accounts receivable and accounts payable are used to find the cash flows from operations in both the direct and indirect methods.

Direct method

Since we have an accounts receivable balance, not all our sales were for cash. We find the cash from customers by subtracting accounts receivable from total sales, i.e., $1,500,000 - $100,000 = $1,400,000. Similarly, since we have an accounts payable balance, not all our expenses were paid in cash. We find the cash outflow for purchases by subtracting accounts payable from expenses, i.e., $900,000 - $70,000 = $830,000. Since there is no tax payable on the balance sheet, the tax expense must equal the cash paid. These calculations allow us to prepare the following statement of cash flow using the direct method.

Statement of Cash Flow - Direct Method

Cash flows from operating activities	
Cash collected from customers	$1,400,000
Less cash payments for operating expenses	- 830,000
Less cash payments for taxes	- 200,000
Net cash inflow from operating activities	$370,000
Cash flows from investing activities	
Purchase of land	- 420,000
Cash flows from financing activities	
Issuance of capital stock	100,000
Net increase in cash	50,000
Cash balance at beginning of period	0
Cash balance at end of period	$50,000

Indirect method

In this method, we reconcile the net income from operations to the amount of cash provided by operations. The net income of $400,000 was derived from sales of $1,500,000. However, not all customers paid cash, and the cash collected from sales was $100,000 less than $1,500,000. We must therefore subtract $100,000 from net income to adjust for non-cash sales. Similarly, expenses of $900,000 were not all paid in cash and the accounts payable balance of $70,000 represents expenses that have not yet used cash. We must therefore add back $70,000 to net income. As before, tax paid and tax expense are identical. The statement of cash flows using the indirect method therefore is as follows:

Statement of Cash Flow - Indirect Method	
Cash flows from operating activities	
Net income	$400,000
Increase in accounts receivable	- 100,000
Increase in accounts payable	70,000
Net cash inflow from operating activities	$370,000
Cash flows from investing activities	
Purchase of land	- 420,000
Cash flows from financing activities	
Issuance of capital stock	100,000
Net increase in cash	50,000
Cash balance at beginning of period	0
Cash balance at end of period	$50,000

Note that the calculation of cash flows from operating activities is different in the two methods, but both methods result in identical figures for cash flows from operations. Also note that apart from the derivation of cash flows from operating activities, the cash flow statements produced under the two methods are identical.

LO 4 When a company enters into a significant noncash transaction, accounting standards require that it be reported either in a separate schedule or in a footnote to the cash flow statement. For example, if a stockholder was issued a large block of shares in return for giving the company a valuable such as land, this transaction would not appear in the statement of cash flows since cash was not exchanged. However, the company is required to report the transaction in a footnote or in a separate schedule.

LO 5 A standard procedure for preparing a statement of cash flows can be developed for both the indirect and direct methods. For the direct method, the following four steps are taken:

1. Set up three master T accounts to record cash flows from each of operating, investing, and financing activities. Cash inflows will be recorded on the debit (or left) side of these accounts; cash outflows on the credit (or right) side of the account.
2. Determine the cash flows from operating activities.
3. Determine the cash flows from investing activities.
4. Determine the cash flows from financing activities.

To illustrate this method, assume that at the end of Year 2, Company Z's income statement and balance sheet are as follows:

Income statement for year ended December 31, Year 2	
Sales	2,000,000
Expenses	- 1,260,000
	740,000
Gain on sale of land	60,000
Net income before tax	800,000
Taxes	- 300,000
Net income	$500,000

Balance Sheet on December 31, Year 2

Cash	$ 100,000	Accounts payable	$ 90,000
Accounts receivable	80,000	**Stockholders' Equity**	
Equipment (at cost)	200,000	Outstanding stock at par	150,000
Land	400,000	Retained earnings	540,000
	$780,000		$780,000

The following information is available for Year 2:

a) Land that had originally cost $20,000 was sold for $80,000.
b) Stock was issued for cash.
c) A cash dividend was declared and paid.

Step 1 Set up three master T accounts to record cash flows from each of operating, investing, and financing activities. Note that these accounts are initially empty.

Cash Flows from Operating Activities

Cash receipts from customers	2,020,000	1,240,000	Cash payments to suppliers
		300,000	Tax paid

Cash Flows from Investing Activities

Sale of land	80,000	200,000	Purchase of equipment

Cash Flows from Financing Activities

Stock issue	50,000	360,000	Dividend paid

Step 2 Determine the cash flows from operating activities.
We analyze each item on the income statement and its related balance sheet account balance to find the cash flow associated with it.

a) Sales revenue and accounts receivable are clearly related. We reconstruct the T account for accounts receivable to find the cash received from customers:

Accounts Receivable

Jan.1,Year 2	100,000		
Sales	2,000,000	?	Cash collections
Dec. 31, Year 2	80,000		

To balance the account, cash received from customers must be ($100,000 + $2,000,000 - $80,000) = $2,020,000. This is posted to the debit side of the cash flows from operating activities account.

b) Expenses and accounts payable are also related. The T account for accounts payable is as follows:

Accounts Payable

		70,000	Jan. 1,Year 2
Cash payments	?	1,260,000	Expenses
		90,000	Dec. 31, Year 2

To balance the account, cash paid to suppliers must be ($70,000 + $1,260,000 - $90,000) = $1,240,000. This again appears in the cash flows from operating activities account, but this time on the credit side, since it is a cash outflow.

c) The cash received from the sale of land is reported in the cash flows from investing activities section of the cash flow statement. We therefore ignore the gain when finding the cash flows from operating activities.

d) The last item on the income statement is tax expense. There is no tax payable on either balance sheet, so we can conclude that the tax expense was equal to the cash outflow for taxes. $300,000 appears in cash flows from operating activities.

Step 3 Determine the cash flows from investing activities.
We next find the cash flows from investing activities. There are two main types: cash outflows from the purchase of long-term assets and cash inflows from the sale of long-term assets.

a) Equipment with a book value of $200,000 appears for the first time in Year 2's balance sheet and must have been purchased in Year 2. Since it appears at cost, we can conclude that the company paid $200,000 for it. The T account for equipment appears as follows:

Equipment		
Jan. 1, Year 2	0	
Cash payment	?	
Dec. 31, Year 2	200,000	

The cash outflow of $200,000 is recorded in the cash flows from investing activities account.

b) We are told that land with an original cost of $20,000 was sold for $80,000 during the year.

Land			
Jan. 1,Year 2	420,000		
Acquisitions	?	20,000	Disposals
Dec. 31, Year 2	400,000		

From the T account, we see that no acquisitions of land have taken place, and we can reconstruct the journal entry recording the sale of land:

	Debit	Credit
Cash	80,000	
Land - original cost		20,000
Gain on sale		60,000
To record sale of land.		

The cash inflow from the sale is $80,000 and is recorded in the cash flows from investing activities account.

Step 4 Determine the cash flows from financing activities.
The cash flows from financing activities are found by considering the changes in long-term liability and stockholders' equity accounts.

a) By comparing the balance sheets at the beginning and end of Year 2, we see that capital stock has increased. Reconstructing the capital stock account:

Capital Stock		
	100,000	Jan. 1,Year 2
	?	Issue of stock
	150,000	Dec. 31,Year 2

We can deduce that the company has issued stock for cash of $50,000. This is recorded as a cash inflow in the cash flows from financing activities account.

b) We are told that the company has paid a cash dividend, but we are not told how much was distributed. We also note that no statement of retained earnings is presented and that the dividend has not been deducted from the net income in the income statement. Reconstruct the retained earnings account:

Retained Earnings			
		400,000	Jan. 1,Year 2
Dividend	?	500,000	Net income, Year 2
		540,000	Dec. 31,Year 2

We can see that the dividend paid must have been ($400,000 + $500,000 - $540,000) = $360,000. This appears as a cash outflow in the cash flows from financing activities account.
The cash flow statement is now prepared from the master T accounts above.

Statement of cash flows for year ended December 31, Year 2

Cash flows from operating activities	
Cash receipts from customers	$ 2,020,000
Less cash payments to suppliers	(1,240,000)
Taxes paid	(300,000)
Net cash flows from operations	$480,000
Cash flows from investing activities	
Sale of land	80,000
Less purchase of equipment	(200,000)
Net cash flows from investing activities	$(120,000)
Cash flows from financing activities	
Stock issue	50,000
Dividend paid	(360,000)
Net cash flows from financing activities	$ (310,000)
Net cash inflow	50,000
Opening cash balance	50,000
Closing cash balance	$100,000

Although the above example is relatively straightforward, it illustrates the principles involved in the preparing the statement. A more sophisticated example appears in the text and in the first problem in this chapter of the study guide.

LO 6 We can adapt the above method to find the cash flows from operating activities using the indirect method. Using the example of Company Z above, the procedure starts with the net income reported for Year 2 of $500,000 and adjusts for cash flow differences.

a) Accounts receivable decreased over Year 2 by $20,000. In other words, the company received more cash than its net sales figure would suggest. The net income figure understates the cash inflow from sales, and the $20,000 reduction in accounts receivable must be added to net income to find cash flows from operations.

b) Accounts payable increased by $20,000 over Year 2. This implies that the cash paid to creditors was less than the expenses figure in the income statement would suggest. The net income figure overstates the cash outflow for expenses, understating the cash flows from operations. The $20,000 increase in accounts payable must be added to net income to find cash flows from operations.

c) As before, the gain on the sale of land of $60,000 is reported in cash flows from investing activities and must be deducted from net income to find cash flows from operations.

The cash flows from operations under the indirect method is as follows:

Cash flows from operating activities	
Net income	$500,000
Plus Reduction in accounts receivable	20,000
Increase in accounts payable	20,000
Less Gain on sale	(60,000)
Net cash flows from operations	$(480,000)

Many students find the indirect method counter-intuitive and have difficulty with the direction of the adjustments. In practice, the vast majority of firms use the indirect method so you need to understand it. To help you, the following table is reproduced from the text. It provides a list of the most common adjustments to net income under the indirect method. However, by far the most effective way to deal with this type of problem is to get as much practice as you can. You should work through the problems in this study guide, as well as the problems in the text.

Additions to net income	**Deductions from net income**
Decrease in accounts receivable	Increase in accounts receivable
Decrease in inventory	Increase in inventory
Decrease in prepayments	Increase in prepayments
Increase in accounts payable	Decrease in accounts payable
Increase in accrued liabilities	Decrease in accrued liabilities
Losses on sales of long-term assets	Gains on sales of long-term assets
Losses on retirements of bonds	Gains on retirements of bonds
Depreciation, amortization, and depletion	

Test your understanding!

Question: One of the most common adjustments to net income under the indirect method is adding back depreciation expense. Does this mean that depreciation represents a source of cash? Could we generate more cash flow if we depreciated assets over a shorter period?

Answer: No! Depreciation is added back to net income because it is an expense that does not result in a cash outflow.

LO 6 Cash flow statements provide crucial information to users. A measure that provides further insight into the company's cash flow position is **cash flow adequacy**, which measures the cash available to meet future debt obligations after providing for taxes, interest costs, and capital expenditures and is calculated as follows:

$$\text{Cash Flow Adequacy} = \frac{\text{Cash Flow from Operating Activities - Capital Expenditures}}{\text{Average Amount of Debt Maturing over the Next Five Years}}$$

LO 7 A worksheet can also be used to derive the cash flow statement. The following is an illustration of the use of the worksheet method for the Company Z example.

	Balances			**Cash Outflows & Inflows**		
Accounts	**Dec. 31, Year 2**	**Jan. 1, Year 2**	**Changes***	**Operating**	**Investing**	**Financing**
Cash	100,000	50,000	50,000			
Accounts receivable	80,000	100,000	[5] (20,000)	[5] 20,000		
Land	400,000	420,000	[2] (20,000)		[2] 80,000	
Equipment	200,000	0	[1] 200,000		[1] (200,000)	
Accounts payable	90,000	70,000	[3] (20,000)	[3] 20,000		
Outstanding stock	150,000	100,000	[4] (50,000)			[4] 50,000
Retained earnings	540,000	400,000	[6] 360,000 [7] (500,000)	[2] (60,000) [7] 500,000		[6] (360,000)
Totals			0	**480,000**	**(120,000)**	**310,000**

Comments

1. $200,000 cash was spent on equipment. The amount appears as a reduction in cash from investing.
2. Land with an original cost of $20,000 was sold for $80,000. The gain is deducted from the operating cash flows since it is included in net income.

3. & 5. Changes in accounts payable and accounts receivable both result in increases in the operating cash flows.

4. Stock is issued for cash. $50,000 appears in the cash flows from financing activities column.
6. Cash dividends are deducted in the financing column.
7. Net income of $500,000 appears as an inflow in the cash flows from operations column.

Review of Key Terms

Cash equivalent An item readily convertible to a known amount of cash and with an original maturity to the investor of three months or less.

Direct method The approach to preparing the operating activities section of the statement of cash flows in which cash receipts and cash payments are reported.

Financing activities Activities concerned with the raising and repayment of funds in the form of debt and equity.

Indirect method The approach to preparing the operating activities section of the statement of cash flows in which net income is reconciled to net cash flows from operations.

Investing activities Activities concerned with the acquisition and disposal of long-term assets.

Operating activities Activities concerned with the acquisition and sale of products and services.

Statement of cash flows The financial statement that summarizes an entity's cash receipts and cash payments during the period from operating, investing, and financing activities.

Practice Test Questions and Problems

Complete each of the following statements:

LO 3 1. Purchases of machinery are reported in the ____________________ section of the statement of cash flows.

LO 3 2. Interest paid on bonds appears in the cash flows from the ____________________ section of the statement of cash flows.

LO 3 3. ____________________ activities are concerned with changes in long-term liabilities and contributed capital.

LO 4 4. The ____________________ method of presenting cash flows from operations requires the conversion of income statement items from an accrual basis to a cash basis.

LO 5 5. Zeta Company's opening and closing accounts receivable balances for Year 1 were $30,000 and ____________________. Zeta's credit sales were $10,000 more than the cash it received from its customers in that year.

LO 2 6. ____________________ include all assets that are readily convertible to a known amount of cash and have a maturity to the company of three months or less.

Use the following information to answer questions 7 through 15.

Beano Corporation **Summary balance sheet**	**Year ended** **Dec. 31, Year 2**	**Year ended** **Dec. 31, Year 1**
Cash	$10,000	$ 8,000
Accounts receivable	5,000	6,000
Inventory	4,000	8,000
Prepaid insurance	3,000	4,000
Plant and equipment	20,000	17,000
Accumulated depreciation	- 8,000	- 6,000
Total assets	$34,000	$37,000
Accounts payable	$11,000	$10,000
Long-term notes payable	5,000	4,000
Common stock	14,000	14,000
Retained earnings	4,000	9,000
Total liabilities and stockholders' equity	$34,000	$37,000

Plant with original cost of $4,000 was sold during the year for its net book value of $2,000. Net income for Year 2 was $7,000. The company uses the indirect method to report cash flows from operations.

LO 5 7. Depreciation expense for Year 2 was ________________.

LO 5 8. Dividends paid during Year 2 were ________________.

LO 5 9. Cash flows from investing activities during Year 2 was ________________.

LO 5 10. Cash flows from financing activities during Year 2 was ________________.

LO 6 11. If the company uses the indirect method for reporting cash flows from operations, the change in accounts receivable balance is ________________ net income to find cash flows from operations.

LO 6 12. If the company uses the indirect method for reporting cash flows from operations, the change in prepaid insurance balance is ________________ net income to find cash flows from operations.

LO 6 13. If the company uses the indirect method for reporting cash flows from operations, the change in accounts payable balance is ________________ net income to find cash flows from operations.

LO 5 14. If total sales for the year are $43,000, and the company uses the direct method for reporting cash flows from operations, cash received from customers was ______________.

LO 5 15. If cost of sales for the year is $30,000 and the company uses the direct method for reporting cash flows from operations, cash paid to suppliers was ______________.

Indicate whether each of the following statements is true or false:

LO 6 16. Since depreciation expense is added back to net earnings to find cash flows from operations when the indirect method is used, accelerated depreciation methods result in greater cash flows.

LO 2 17. Cash flow statements should report only changes to cash balances held in checking and savings accounts.

LO 3 18. A stock split is reported under cash flows from financing activities in the statement of cash flows.

LO 4 19. The only difference between the direct and indirect methods is how cash flows from operations is reported.

LO 2 20. A three-month note receivable with two months to maturity at the balance sheet date would NOT be classified as cash for the purposes of the cash flow statement.

LO 5 21. An increase in salaries payable would indicate that cash paid for salaries was greater than salaries expense for the period.

LO 5 22. An increase in inventory indicates that accounts payable have increased over the period.

LO 6 23. The loss on disposal of plant must be added back to net income under the indirect method.

LO 3 24. Dividends paid are reported in the statement of cash flows as part of the cash flows from financing activities.

LO 3 25. The conversion of convertible bonds payable to common stock is reported as part of cash flows from financing activities.

LO 2 26. The purchase of a 30-day T-Bill for cash would appear as a use of cash in the investing section of the statement of cash flows.

LO 3 27. Cash flows are categorized into three categories: investing, operating, and financing in the statement of cash flows.

LO 3 28. Negative cash flows from investing activities indicates that the company has purchased new assets.

LO 4 29. Although FASB prefers the direct method for reporting cash from operations, the vast majority of companies use the indirect method.

LO 6 30. If the indirect method is used, the company need not reconcile net income and cash flows from operations.

For each of the following questions, circle the alternative that best answers the question:

LO 6 31. Which of the following is NOT added to net earnings to find cash flows from operations under the indirect method?
a) A loss on the sale of a building
b) Interest expense
c) Depreciation expense
d) An increase in wages payable

LO 6 32. Which of the following is consistent with a firm reporting both positive cash flows from operations and a net loss?
a) An increase in accounts receivable
b) A decrease in accounts payable
c) An increase in inventory
d) A loss on the sale of machinery

Use the following information to answer questions 33 through 36:
The following balances appeared on Beta Company's balance sheets on December 31, Year 1, and December 31, Year 2. As reported on the income statement, sales for the year were $100,000, rent expense was $50,000, and cost of sales was $40,000. All sales and purchases were on credit.

	Year ended Dec. 31, Year 2	*Year ended Dec. 31, Year 1*
Accounts receivable	$20,000	$16,000
Accounts payable	25,000	20,000
Prepaid rent	10,000	15,000
Inventory	28,000	25,000

LO 5 33. Cash paid for rent during Year 2 was
a) $40,000
b) $45,000
c) $50,000
d) $55,000

LO 5 34. Cash received from customers during Year 2 was
a) $100,000
b) $80,000
c) $96,000
d) $84,000

LO 5 35. Purchases of goods for resale during Year 2 were
a) $43,000
b) $37,000
c) $65,000
d) $40,000

LO 5 36. Cash paid to creditors during Year 2 was
a) $20,000
b) $35,000
c) $45,000
d) $38,000

LO 5,6 37. Zeta Corporation reported positive net earnings for the current year, but its cash balance declined over the year. Which of the following transactions is inconsistent with this scenario?

a) Zeta retired bonds.
b) Zeta paid cash dividends to its stockholders.
c) Zeta's accounts payable balance increased.
d) Zeta bought land for cash.

LO 2 38. Which of the following is NOT considered a cash equivalent if held on December 31, Year 1?

a) A three-month note receivable bought one month before its maturity
b) Money deposited in a 60-day certificate of deposit
c) Commercial paper with a nine-month maturity bought when it was issued on September 1, Year 1
d) Money held in the company's petty cash box

LO 3 39. Which of the following statements is FALSE?

a) Cash flows from operating activities includes cash collections from customers and interest payments to bond holders.
b) Dividends declared but not yet paid should be reported as part of cash flows from financing activities.
c) Equipment acquired in exchange for the issue of a note payable should be reported in a separate schedule rather than directly on the statement of cash flows.
d) A loss on the sale of land is added back to net income to find cash flows from operating activities since the cash flows from the transaction is reported in cash flows from investing activities.

LO 5 40. During Year 2, the accounts payable balance of Player Corporation increased. Which of the following statements is true?

a) Player Corporation's purchases were higher than the cash it paid to its creditors.
b) The increase in accounts payable can be ignored when preparing a statement of cash flow using the direct method.
c) The increase in accounts payable indicates that inventory balances must also have increased during Year 2.
d) An increase in accounts payable could result in net income being higher than cash flows from operations.

LO 6 41. Which of the following is added to net income to find cash flows from operation sunder the indirect method of reporting cash flows from operations?

a) Increases in accounts receivable
b) Decreases in accounts payable
c) Gains on retirement of bonds
d) Losses on sale of long-term assets

LO 5 42. If a company uses the indirect method of reporting cash flows from operations, it must separately and additionally report which of the following?

a) Cash received from customers and cash paid to suppliers
b) Cash received from the sale of fixed assets and cash paid for investments
c) Cash paid for purchases of inventory and cash received from customers
d) Income taxes paid and interest paid

LO 6 43. A company has net income of $2,000,000 and cash flows from operations of $1,000,000 for the year ended December 31, 1997. All purchases and sales were on credit. Which of the following would not be consistent with these facts?

a) The company's cash receipts from customers were less than total sales during the year.
b) The company's inventory increased during the year.
c) The company reduced its prepayments balance during the year.
d) The company's credit sales were less than the cash paid to suppliers.

Use the following information to answer questions 44 and 45:

The following information appears in Ventura Inc.'s financial statements for the year ended December 31, 1997:

Year ended December 31,	**1997**	**1996**
Buildings and equipment		
Original cost	$ 3,500	$ 2,500
Accumulated depreciation	2,000	1,500
Net book value	1,500	1,000

During the year equipment with an original cost of $1,000 and a net book value of $250 was sold. All acquisitions of fixed assets during the year were for cash.

LO 5 44. The cash paid to acquire new buildings and equipment during 1997 was

a) $1,000
b) $2,000
c) $1,250
d) $750

LO 5 45. The depreciation expense for 1997 was

a) $1,250
b) $500
c) $750
d) $1,500

Answer each of the following problems:

LO 5,6 46. The financial statements for Zeta Corporation are presented below.

Zeta Corporation Income Statement
For Year Ended December 31

$ in millions	1997	1996
Revenue	$25,000	$22,600
Cost of sales	(23,650)	(21,210)
Gross profit	$1,350	$1,390
Selling, general and administrative (including depreciation)	(1,148)	(1,248)
Operating Income	202	142
Interest expense	(22)	(30)
Earnings before income taxes	180	112
Income tax expense	(30)	(26)
Net earnings	150	86
Common dividends	(60)	(55)
To retained earnings	90	31
Retained earnings January 1	250	219
Retained earnings December 31	$ 340	$ 250

Zeta Corporation Balance Sheet
On December 31

$ millions		1997		1996		1995
Cash		$ 250		$ 350		$400
Accounts receivable		600		500		300
Inventory		1,300		1,000		800
Prepaid insurance		0		50		269
Total current assets		2,150		1,900		1,769
Buildings and Equipment	2,000		1,900		1,800	
Accumulated depreciation	(1,700)		(1,450)		(1,350)	
		300		450		450
Land		1,660		1,200		1,000
Total long-term assets		1,960		1,650		1,450
Total assets		$4,110		$3,550		$3,219
Accounts payable		800		500		400
Notes payable		750		500		300
Total current liabilities		1,550		1,000		700
Bonds payable		220		300		300
Total liabilities		1,770		1,300		1,000
Common stock, 50 cents par value		2,000		2,000		2,000
Retained earnings		340		250		219
Stockholders' equity		2,340		2,250		2,219
Total liabilities and stockholders' equity		$4,110		$3,550		$3,219

Required

Prepare the statement of cash flows for Zeta for the years ended December 31, 1997, and December 31, 1996, using both the direct and indirect methods for reporting cash flows from operating activities.

LO 7 47. Refer to the information in Problem 46.

Required

Complete the following statement of cash flows worksheet for the year ended December 31, 1997.

	Balances			Cash inflows and outflows		
Accounts	**Dec. 31, 1997**	**Jan. 1, 1996**	**Changes**	**Operating**	**Investing**	**Financing**
Cash						
Accounts receivable						
Inventory						
Prepaid insurance						
Buildings & equipment						
Accumulated depreciation						
Land						
Accounts payable						
Notes payable						
Bonds payable						
Outstanding stock						
Retained earnings						
Totals						

Critical Thinking Problem

LO 4 48. Exhibit 1 presents the consolidated statements of cash flow for the Compaq Computer Corporation for the years ended December 31, 1996, 1995, and 1994.

CONSOLIDATED STATEMENT OF CASH FLO WS

Year ended December 31, In millions	**1996**	**1995**	**1994**
Cash flows from operating activities:			
Cash received from customers	$17,939	$13,910	$9,986
Cash paid to suppliers and employees	-13,639	-12,437	-9,778
Interest and dividends received	110	53	22
Interest paid	-91	-100	-65
Income taxes paid	-911	-543	-319
Net cash provided by (used in) operating activities	3,408	883	-154
Cash flows from investing activities:			
Purchases of property, plant and equipment, net	-342	-391	-357
Purchases of short-term investments	-1,401		
Proceeds from short-term investments	328		
Acquisition of businesses, net of cash acquired	-22	-318	
Other, net	-26	6	-51
Net cash used in investing activities	-1,463	-703	-408
Cash flows from financing activities:			
Issuance of common stock pursuant to stock option plans	112	79	100
Tax benefit associated with stock options	91	60	53
Issuance of long-term debt			300
Net cash provided by financing activities	203	139	453
Effect of exchange rate changes on cash	27	-45	-47
Net increase (decrease) in cash and cash equivalents	2,175	274	-156
Cash and cash equivalents at beginning of year	745	471	627
Cash and cash equivalents at end of year	$2,920	$745	$471
Reconciliation of net income to net cash provided by (used in) operating activities:			
Net income	$1,313	$789	$867
Depreciation and amortization	285	214	169
Provision for bad debts	155	43	36
Purchased in-process technology		241	
Deferred income taxes	-371	-17	-184
Loss on disposal of assets	5	2	2
Exchange rate effect	14	33	46
Increase in accounts receivable	-210	-863	-926
Decrease (increase) in inventories	1,004	-135	-882
Decrease (increase) in other current assets	5	-41	-55
Increase in accounts payable	586	479	248
Increase (decrease) in income taxes payable	131	-61	173
Increase in other current liabilities	491	199	352
Net cash provided by (used in) operating activities	$3,408	$883	($154)

Required

1. Does Compaq use the direct or indirect method to present its cash flows from operations?

2. What is the main cause of the change in cash flows from operations over the three years?

3. Did Compaq raise additional capital during the three years?

4. What were Compaq's main investing activities during the three years?

5. Has income increased over the three years as much as cash flows from operations?

Solutions

Fill in the Blanks

1. investing
2. operating
3. financing
4. direct
5. $40,000
6. cash equivalents
7. $4,000
8. $12,000
9. - $5,000
10. - $11,000
11. added to
12. added to
13. added to
14. $44,000
15. $29,000

True/False

		COMMENT/EXPLANATION
16.	False	Under the indirect method, depreciation expense is added back to net income because it is a noncash expense. Increasing depreciation charges in any year decreases reported net income but has no impact on cash flows.
17.	False	Cash flow statements should report changes in cash and cash equivalents.
18.	False	Stock splits have no cash flow implications and therefore do not appear in the cash flow statement.
19.	True	
20.	False	The note receivable would be a cash equivalent since it can be readily converted into a known amount of cash and has a maturity of three months or less.
21.	False	An increase in salaries payable indicates that less cash was paid during the period than was earned. Therefore, cash paid for salaries was less than salaries expense.
22.	False	An increase in inventory indicates that goods sold or used during the period are less than goods purchased.
23.	True	
24.	True	
25.	False	No cash flow takes place on conversion.
26.	False	A 30-day T-Bill is a cash equivalent.
27.	True	
28.	True	
29.	True	
30.	False	The indirect method finds cash flows from operations by making adjustments to net income.

Multiple Choice

31. b
32. d
33. b
34. c
35. a
36. d
37. c
38. c
39. b
40. a
41. d
42. d
43. c
44. b
45. a

Problem 46

Zeta Corporation Statement of Cash Flows - Indirect Method
For Year Ended December 31

$ in millions	1997	1996
Cash flows from operating activities		
Net income	$ 150	$ 86
Increase in accounts receivable	(100)	(200)
Increase in inventory	(300)	(200)
Decrease in prepayments	50	219
Increase in accounts payable	300	100
Increase in notes payable	250	200
Depreciation	250	100
Cash flows from operating activities	$ 600	$ 305
Cash flows from investing activities		
Purchase of land	(460)	(200)
Purchase of buildings and equipment	(100)	(100)
Cash flows from investing activities	$ (560)	$ (300)
Cash flows from financing activities		
Redemption of bonds	(80)	-
Dividend payment	(60)	(55)
Cash flows from financing activities	$ (140)	$ (55)
Net cash flow	(100)	(50)
Opening cash balance	350	400
Closing cash balance	$250	$350

Zeta Corporation Statement of Cash Flow - Direct Method
For Year Ended December 31

$ in millions	1997	1996
Cash flows from operating activities		
Cash receipts from customers	$ 24,900	$ 22,400
Cash from issue of notes payable	250	200
Cash paid to suppliers	(23,650)	(21,310)
Cash paid for selling and administrative expenses *	(848)	(929)
Interest paid	(22)	(30)
Income tax paid	(30)	(26)
Cash flows from operating activities	$ 600	$ 305
Cash flows from investing activities		
Purchase of land	(460)	(200)
Purchase of buildings and equipment	(100)	(100)
Cash flows from investing activities	$ (560)	$ (300)
Cash flows from financing activities		
Redemption of bonds	(80)	-
Dividend payment	(60)	(55)
Cash flows from financing activities	$ (140)	$ (55)
Net cash flow	(100)	(50)
Opening cash balance	350	400
Closing cash balance	$250	$350

Selling and administrative expenses include depreciation and a component of prepaid insurance. To find the cash flow associated with these expenses, it is necessary to exclude depreciation and adjust for the change in the prepaid balance. Thus for the year ended December 31, 1997, the cash flows from selling and administrative expenses is ($1,098 + $250 - $50) = $848.

Problem 47

	Balances			Cash inflows and outflows		
Accounts	**Dec. 31, 1997**	**Jan. 1, 1996**	**Changes (see below)**	**Operating**	**Investing**	**Financing**
Cash	250	350	(100)			
Accounts receivable	600	500	[1] 100	[1] (100)		
Inventory	1,300	1,000	[2] 300	[2] (300)		
Prepaid insurance	0	50	[3] (50)	[3] 50		
Buildings & equipment	2,000	1,900	[4] 100		[4] (100)	
Accumulated depreciation	1,700	1,450	[5] (250)	[5] 250		
Land	1,660	1,200	[6] 460		[6] (460)	
Accounts payable	800	500	[7] (300)	[7] 300		
Notes payable	750	500	[8] (250)	[8] 250		
Bonds payable	220	300	[9] 80			[9] (80)
Outstanding stock	2,000	2,000				
Retained earnings	340	250	[10] 60 [11] (150)			[10] (60) [11] 150
Totals			**0**	**600**	**560**	**140**

Comments

1. & 2. Increases in accounts receivable and inventory appear as decreases in operating cash flows.

3. A decrease in prepaid insurance appears as an increase in operating cash flows.

4. $100 was spent on buildings and appears as an outflow of cash for investing activities.

5. Depreciation for the year must be added back to operating cash flows since it is a noncash expense.

6. $460 was spent on land and appears as a cash outflow for investing activities.

7. & 8. The increased balances in accounts and notes payable appear as increases in operating cash flows.

9. Bonds are redeemed for $80 that appears as a cash outflow for financing activities.

10. Cash dividends are deducted in the financing column.

11. Net income of $150 appears as a cash inflow in the cash flows from operations column.

Critical Thinking Problem 48

1. Compaq uses the direct method to present its cash flows from operations. Note however that it also provides a reconciliation of net income to cash flows from operations.

2. The main cause of the change in cash flows from operations over the three years is the increase in cash received from customers. Clearly, Compaq's sales have increased significantly over the last year, and cash has been received for these sales, resulting in large cash inflows.

3. Apart from issuing long-term debt in 1994, Compaq raised almost no financing during the three years, suggesting that any expansion was from internally generated funds.

4. Compaq's main investing activities during the three years appeared to be the purchase of short-term securities in 1996. This probably indicates that the additional cash flows from operations have been invested to obtain short-term return until Compaq decides how to use the funds in the longer term. It may be planning a major expansion or acquisition and be "parking" the funds until it is ready to use them.

5. Income has not increased over the three years as much as cash flows from operations, although net income has grown healthily, and the company has now been profitable for three consecutive years.

Chapter 15

Financial Statement Analysis

The chapter, dedicated to the analysis of financial statements, represents the culmination of the book. Your objective is to acquire the skills needed to analyze financial statements and to gain an understanding of how these skills can be used to help various types of decision making.

Learning Objectives

LO 1 Explain the various limitations and considerations in financial statement analysis.

LO 2 Use comparative financial statements to analyze a company over time (horizontal analysis).

LO 3 Use common-size financial statements to compare various financial statement items (vertical analysis).

LO 4 Compute and use various ratios to assess liquidity.

LO 5 Compute and use various ratios to assess solvency.

LO 6 Compute and use various ratios to assess profitability.

Key Textbook Exhibit

Exhibit 15-8 provides you with a summary of key financial ratios. Note how different ratios are used to gain insight into different aspects of the business's performance, such as liquidity, solvency, and profitability.

Review of Key Concepts

We use the income statements, balance sheets, and statements of cash flows for Zeta Corporation from Problem 31 in Chapter 14 to illustrate the material in this chapter.

Zeta Corporation Income Statement for Year Ended December 31

$ in millions	1997	1996
Revenue	$25,000	$22,600
Cost of sales	(23,650)	(21,210)
Gross profit	$1,350	$1,390
Selling, general and administrative (including depreciation)	(1,148)	(1,248)
Operating Income	202	142
Interest expense	(22)	(30)
Earnings before income taxes	180	112
Income tax expense	(30)	(26)
Net earnings	150	86
Common dividends	(60)	(55)
To retained earnings	90	31
Retained earnings January 1	250	219
Retained earnings December 31	$ 340	$ 250

Zeta Corporation Balance Sheet on December 31

$ millions		1997		1996		1995
Cash		$ 250		$ 350		$400
Accounts receivable		600		500		300
Inventory		1,300		1,000		800
Prepaid insurance		0		50		269
Total current assets		2,150		1,900		1,769
Buildings and Equipment	2,000		1,900		1,800	
Accumulated depreciation	(1,700)		(1,450)		(1,350)	
		300		450		450
Land		1,660		1,200		1,000
Total long term assets		1,960		1,650		1,450
Total assets		$4,110		$3,550		$3,219
Accounts payable		800		500		400
Notes payable		750		500		300
Total current liabilities		1,550		1,000		700
Bonds payable		220		300		300
Total liabilities		1,770		1,300		1,000
Common stock, 50 cents par value		2,000		2,000		2,000
Retained earnings		340		250		219
Stockholders' equity		2,340		2,250		2,219
Total liabilities and stockholders' equity		$4,110		$3,550		$3,219

Zeta Corporation Statement of Cash Flows - Indirect Method for Year Ended December 31

$ in millions	1997	1996
Cash flows from operating activities		
Net income	$ 150	$ 86
Increase in accounts receivable	(100)	(200)
Increase in inventory	(300)	(200)
Decrease in prepayments	50	219
Increase in accounts payable	300	100
Increase in notes payable	250	200
Depreciation	250	100
Cash flows from operating activities	$ 600	$ 305
Cash flows from investing activities		
Purchase of land	(460)	(200)
Purchase of buildings and equipment	(100)	(100)
Cash flows from investing activities	$ (560)	$ (300)
Cash flows from financing activities		
Redemption of bonds	(80)	-
Dividend payment	(60)	(55)
Cash flows from financing activities	$ (140)	$ (55)
Net cash flow	(100)	(50)
Opening cash balance	350	400
Closing cash balance	$250	$350

Note: Zeta Corporation's marginal tax rate is 40%. On December 31, 1997, its stock price was 75 cents and on December 31, 1996, it was 57 cents.

LO 1 In analyzing financial statements, attention must be given to the assumptions on which the statements are based. In particular, the accounting principles used (for example, the depreciation method and inventory cost flow assumption) can have a significant impact on financial ratios.

- Analysis of a set of financial statements should include comparisons both with statements from previous periods and with statements from similar companies in the same industry. Comparisons with previous periods allow us to identify trends and patterns in the company's performance. Comparisons with companies in the same industry provide insights into how the industry is performing. For example, if an entire industry is in decline, it may be that an apparently poor performance by the company is better than that of other companies in the industry.
- Inflation can have a significant impact on the validity of the information provided in financial statements. For example, land that was bought decades ago is reported at historic cost even though it is unlikely to bear any relationship to the current market value of the land. In analyzing companies, it is important to recognize this type of limitation of historic cost.

LO 2 **Horizontal analysis** involves analyzing the company over time. The following table presents the horizontal analysis of Zeta Corporation over years 1996 and 1997.

Zeta Corporation Income Statement
Horizontal Analysis for Year Ended December 31

$ in millions	1997	1996	Increase or Decrease $	%
Revenue	$25,000	$22,600	$2,400	11%
Cost of sales	(23,650)	(21,210)	(2,440)	12%
Gross profit	$1,350	$1,390	(40)	- 3%
Selling, general and administrative (including depreciation)	(1,148)	(1,248)	100	- 8%
Operating Income	202	142	60	42%
Interest expense	(22)	(30)	8	- 27%
Earnings before income taxes	180	112	68	61%
Income tax expense	(30)	(26)	(4)	15%
Net earnings	150	86	64	74%
Common dividends	(60)	(55)	(5)	9%
To retained earnings	90	31	$ 59	190%
Retained earnings January 1	250	219		
Retained earnings December 31	$ 340	$ 250		

Zeta Corporation Balance Sheet
Horizontal Analysis on December 31

$ millions		1997		1996	Increase or Decrease $	%
Cash		$ 250		$ 350	(100)	- 29%
Accounts receivable		600		500	100	20%
Inventory		1,300		1,000	300	30%
Prepaid insurance		0		50	(50)	- 100%
Total current assets		2,150		1,900	250	13%
Buildings and Equipment	2,000		1,900		100	5%
Accumulated depreciation	(1,700)		(1,450)		(250)	17%
		300		450	(150)	- 33%
Land		1,660		1,200	460	38%
Total long term assets		1,960		1,650	310	19%
Total assets		$4,110		$3,550	$560	16%
Accounts payable		800		500	300	60%
Notes payable		750		500	250	50%
Total current liabilities		1,550		1,000	550	55%
Bonds payable		220		300	(80)	- 27%
Total liabilities		1,770		1,300	470	36%
Common stock, 50 cents par value		2,000		2,000	0	0%
Retained earnings		340		250	90	36%
Stockholders' equity		2,340		2,250	90	4%
Total liabilities and stockholders' equity		$4,110		$3,550	$560	16%

- **Calculation:** For each item in the balance sheet and income statement, the change from the earlier period to the later period is found; this change is then expressed as a percentage of the earlier figure. For example, for revenue, the increase from 1996 to 1997 is found from $25,000 - $22,600 = $2,400, and the percentage change is found by dividing $2,400 by 1996 revenue, $2,400/$22,600 = 11%.
- **Discussion:** The horizontal analysis of the income statement reveals that Zeta Corporation's net earnings over the year have increased by 74%. This is explained by both an increase in operating income (up 42%) and a decrease in interest expense (down 27%). The operating income has increased because of the decrease in selling, administrative, and general expenses. Gross profit has in fact decreased because cost of sales increased more than revenue, but the decrease in the selling and general expenses more than compensates. When we look at the balance sheet, we see that this improvement in profitability has been accompanied by a decrease in cash, though both inventory and accounts receivable have increased. Zeta's assets have increased in total, but plant and machinery has decreased while the company has increased its land holdings. Short-term liabilities have increased substantially, but the company has redeemed some of its long term debt. Stockholders' equity has increased by a modest 4%, even though net income increased by 74%.

LO 3 Companies of different sizes can be difficult to compare. For example, Little Green dwarfs most other computer manufacturers, and comparing profits or losses of several billion dollars with that of a few hundred thousand dollars is difficult, unless the profit is related to other financial variables. Vertical analysis, through **common-size statements,** is used as a way of factoring out size as a variable in the financial analysis. It is useful both for different companies and for the same company over different time periods. The following table presents the common-size statements for Zeta. Note that in the following table, rounding may cause totals to differ from the sum of the individual percentages.

Zeta Corporation Income Statement
Vertical Analysis for Year Ended December 31

	1997		1996	
	$	%	$	%
Revenue	$25,000	100%	$22,600	100%
Cost of sales	(23,650)	- 95%	(21,210)	- 94%
Gross profit	1,350	5%	1,390	6%
Selling, general, and administrative	(1,148)	- 5%	(1,248)	- 6%
Operating Income	202	1%	142	1%
Interest expense	(22)	0%	(30)	0%
Earnings before income taxes	180	1%	112	1%
Income tax expense	(30)	0%	(26)	0%
Net earnings	$150	1%	$86	1%

Zeta Corporation Balance Sheet
Vertical Analysis on December 31

	1997			1996		
	$	$	%	$	$	%
Cash		$ 250	6%		$ 350	10%
Accounts receivable		600	15%		500	14%
Inventory		1,300	32%		1,000	28%
Prepaid insurance		0	0%		50	1%
Total current assets		2,150	52%		1,900	53%
Buildings and Equipment	$ 2,000		49%	$ 1,900		54%
Accumulated depreciation	(1,700)		- 41%	(1,450)		- 41%
		300	8%		450	13%
Land		1,660	40%		1,200	34%
Total long term assets		1,960	48%		1,650	47%
Total assets		$4,110	100%		$3,550	100%
Accounts payable		$800	19%		$500	14%
Notes payable		750	18%		500	14%
Total current liabilities		1,550	38%		1,000	28%
Bonds payable		220	5%		300	8%
Total liabilities		1,770	43%		1,300	37%
Common stock, 50 cents par value		2,000	49%		2,000	56%
Retained earnings		340	8%		250	7%
Total stockholders' equity		2,340	57%		2,250	63%
Total liabilities and stockholders' equity		$4,110	100%		$3,550	100%

Each item in the balance sheet is calculated as a percentage of total assets, which of course is equal to total liabilities plus stockholders' equity. For example, cash in the balance sheet for December 31, 1997 is $250/$4110 = 6%. Similarly, each item in the income statement is expressed as a percentage of net sales; cost of sales in 1996 is equal to $762/$960 = 68%.

The vertical analysis of the income statement reveals two key ratios that relate the profit the company made to the level of its sales: the gross profit ratio (equal to the gross profit as a percentage of net sales) and the profit margin ratio (equal to net income to net sales). For Zeta, the gross profit ratio decreased and the profit margin ratio stayed the same because the selling and general expenses reduced significantly. Note how large the net sales figure is relative to the operating income. In this situation, items below operating income in the income statement tend to be swamped by the large denominator, making interpretation difficult. In the balance sheets, cash as a percent of total assets has decreased substantially, though overall the total current assets percentage has only dropped slightly. The land percentage has increased and the plant and machinery percentage has decreased, resulting in a small net increase in the long term assets percentage. The total liabilities percentage is higher, resulting from a reduction in long term liabilities and an increase in short-term liabilities. Though the company appears profitable, it has become more reliant on short-term debt than it was previously and its cash reserves are lower. In addition, its inventory and accounts receivable have increased. Together, these would indicate that the company may face problems in meeting its short-term liabilities in future, a possibility we examine further in LO 5 below.

LO 4 **Liquidity** refers to a company's ability to meet its short-term obligations. Many profitable companies have failed because of a lack of liquidity, and liquidity is therefore a critical measure when assessing financial performance. Table 15-1 summarizes the key ratios used to assess liquidity and provides the detailed calculations for Zeta's 1997 statements and the ratios for both 1996 and 1997. In assessing a company's liquidity, it is critical to gain insight into the company's ability both to meet short-term liabilities and to generate short-term cash inflows.

- The **current ratio, the acid-test ratio**, and **working capital** all relate short-term assets to short-term liabilities. The current ratio is a measure of the cover for short-term liabilities provided by short-term assets. The acid-test ratio is a stricter test of the company's short liquidity since it excludes both inventory and prepayments, which are not as readily convertible to cash as other short-term assets. Working capital is simply the difference between current assets and current liabilities. Although Zeta's working capital has increased in absolute terms over the year, both the current ratio and the acid-test ratio have deteriorated.
- **Cash flows from operations to current liabilities** ratio provides a measure of how the flows of cash over a period relate to the average short-term claims on that cash. For Zeta, this ratio has improved over the year. The turnover ratios for both accounts receivable and inventory provide insight into how well these two short-term assets are being managed.
- The **accounts receivable turnover ratio** gives the average number of times that accounts were turned over (or collected) during the year. This ratio can also be used to find the **number of days' sales in receivables**, or the average number of days that accounts remain outstanding. For Zeta, there has been a slight drop in both ratios, indicating that collections from customers have slowed slightly.
- The **inventory turnover ratio** gives the number of times the inventory was replaced during the year, and **the number of days' sales in inventory ratio** provides the number of days on average that goods spent in inventory. These ratios have again declined slightly for Zeta.
- The **cash-to-cash operating cycle** gives the number of days on average it takes between goods being bought and the cash being received. Zeta had an increase in this cycle of about four days. Overall, Zeta's short-term liquidity has deteriorated, with the most significant deterioration being in the coverage of short-term liabilities.

LO 5 **Solvency** refers to a company's ability to remain in business in the long term. Solvency is determined mainly by the ability of a company to service its debts and pay for its investments. Measures of solvency are therefore based on the relationship between long term debt and equity, and on the ability to cover financing costs and investment. Table 15-2 summarizes the key ratios used to assess solvency and provides the detailed calculations for Zeta's 1997 statements and the ratios for both 1996 and 1997.

- A critical measure of a company's solvency is its **debt-to-equity** ratio. This ratio measures the extent to which the company is reliant on debt to finance its activities, or its **capital structure**. Since debt is less risky than equity and the required return on debt is lower than that required on equity, and since interest is tax deductible, debt provides the company with a relatively cheap source of financing. Very high levels of debt can threaten the company's existence, since failure to meet capital and interest payments can result in the debt holders liquidating the company to ensure repayment of what they are owed. The debt-to-equity ratio provides a measure of the company's reliance on debt. Zeta's ratio has increased over the year, indicating that Zeta is becoming more reliant on debt. Whether or not this is likely to cause problems in turn depends on how easily the company can meet its interest payments.
- The **times interest earned ratio** indicates the company's ability to meet its current year's interest payments out of current year's earnings. Because Zeta's earnings increased and its interest expense decreased over the year, the times interest earned ratio increased, indicating that Zeta's ability to meet its interest payments had improved.

- Since net income and cash flows from operations often differ substantially, the times interest earned ratio does not necessarily measure the company's ability to meet the cash obligations associated with debt, but the **debt service coverage ratio** does. For Zeta, this ratio has decreased over the period largely as a result of the redemption of debt in 1997. In order to survive, companies must invest.
- The majority of investment by companies is funded internally and the **cash flows from operations to capital expenditure ratio** provides a measure of the company's ability to fund its capital expenditure from internally generated funds. Though Zeta's ratio has increased over the year, it is still unable to generate internally all the cash it needs for investment.

LO 6 Ultimately, the company's ability to survive depends how effectively the resources of the company are used. **Profitability** measures indicate the return that is earned on the resources of the company as a whole and on the investment of various groups. Table 15-3 summarizes the key ratios used to assess profitability and provides the detailed calculations for Zeta's 1997 statements and the ratios for both 1996 and 1997. We have already discussed both the gross profit ratio and the profit margin ratio. We now consider the rate of return ratios, which measure the relationship between income earned and investment made.

The **return on assets** ratio is the income earned on all assets used by the company. In the numerator of the ratio, the return to the equity holders (net income) is added to the return to debt holders (interest expense). However, since net income is measured after tax, interest expense is also measured after tax. Zeta's return on assets has increased in 1997. Return on assets can be broken down into **return on sales** and **asset turnover**.

$$\text{Return on assets} = \frac{\text{Net income} + \text{Interest expense, net of tax}}{\text{Average total assets}}$$

$$= \frac{\text{Net income} + \text{Interest expense, net of tax}}{\text{Net sales}} \times \frac{\text{Net sales}}{\text{Average total assets}}$$

Return on assets	=	Return on sales	x	Asset turnover

We can see that Zeta's return on sales has increased over the year, but its assets turnover has decreased slightly. We conclude that the increased return on assets is due to a higher return on sales. A further group of profitability ratios consider the various components of returns to stockholders.

- **Return on stockholders' equity** is the rate of return paid on the average funds provided by common stockholders. For Zeta, this has increased substantially over the year. **Earnings per share** is the earnings after interest and taxes attributable to each share of common stock. Again for Zeta, this has increased over the year.
- The **dividend payout ratio** measures the proportion of earnings per share that are paid out as dividends. For Zeta, this ratio has decreased, indicating that a higher proportion of Zeta's earnings have been retained than in the previous year. Two further ratios are of importance when assessing the return to common stockholders.
- **The price-earnings ratio** compares the current market price with current earnings per share. This ratio is often regarded as an indication of the stock market's confidence in the company, but it must be interpreted with caution since factors such as choice of accounting method and the firm's discount rate can also impact the price-earnings ratio. It would appear that in Zeta's case, in spite of higher earnings, the market is not as confident in the company as it was.
- A further ratio that is related to the company's market price is the **dividend yield**, which expresses dividend per share as a percentage of market price per share. Dividend yield must again be interpreted with caution since the dividend is only one component of

the return that stockholders receive, the other being the change in the stock's market price. For Zeta, the dividend yield has decreased over the period.

Table 15-1 Liquidity analysis

Measure/Ratio	Formula	Calculation	1997	1996
Working capital	Current assets - Current liabilities	2150 - 1550	600	100
Current ratio	Current assets / Current liabilities	2150 / 1550	1.39	1.9
Acid-test ratio (quick ratio)	Cash + Marketable securities + Short-term receivables / Current liabilities	850 / 1550	0.55	0.85
Cash flows from operations to current liabilities ratio	Net cash from operations / Average current liabilities	600 / 0.5 x (1550 + 1000)	0.47	0.36
Accounts receivable turnover ratio	Net credit sales / Average accounts receivable	2500 / 0.5 x (600 + 500)	45.5 times	56.5 times
Number of days' sales in receivables ratio	Number of days in period / Accounts receivable turnover	360 / 45.5	7.9 days	6.4 days
Inventory turnover ratio	Cost of goods sold / Average inventory	23650 / 0.5 x (1300 + 1000)	20.6 times	23.6 times
Number of days' sales in inventory ratio	Number of days in period / Inventory turnover	360 / 20.6	17.5 days	15.3 days
Cash to cash operating cycle ratio	Number days' sales in inventory + Number days' sales in receivables	7.9 + 17.5	25.4 days	21.7 days

Table 15-2 Solvency analysis

Measure/Ratio	Formula	Calculation	1997	1996
Debt-to-equity ratio	Total liabilities / Total stockholders' equity	1770 / 2340	0.75	0.58
Times interest earned ratio	Net Income + Interest expense + Income tax expense / Interest expense	150 + 22 + 30 / 22	9.18	4.73
Debt service coverage ratio	Cash flows from operations, before interest and tax / Interest and principal payments	600 + 22 + 30 / 22 + 80	6.39	12.03
Cash flows from operations to capital expenditure ratio	Cash flows from operations-Total dividends paid / Cash paid for acquisitions	600 - 60 / 560	0.96	0.83

Table 15-3 Profitability analysis

Measure/Ratio	Formula	Calculation	1997	1996
Gross profit ratio	Gross profit / Net sales	1350 / 25000	5.4%	6.2%
Profit margin ratio	Net income / Net sales	150 / 25000	0.6%	0.4%
Return on assets	Net income + Interest expense, net of tax / Average total assets	150 + 20 x (1 - 0.4) / 0.5 x (4110 + 3550)	4.2%	3,1%
Return on sales	Net income + Interest expense, net of tax / Net sales	150 + 20 x (1 - 0.4) / 25000	0.6%	0.4%
Asset turnover ratio	Net sales / Average total assets	25000 / 0.5 x (4110 + 3550)	6.53	6.58
Return on stockholders' equity	Net income - Preferred dividends / Average common stockholders' equity	150 / 0.5 x (2340 + 2250)	6.53%	3.7%
Earnings per share	Net income - Preferred dividends / Weighted average no. of common shares outstanding	150 / 4000	3.75 cents	2.1 cents
Price-earnings ratio	Current market price / Earnings per share	75 cents / 3.75 cents	20 times	27 times
Dividend payout ratio	Common dividends per share / Earnings per share	1.5 cents / 3.75 cents	0.4	0.6
Dividend yield ratio	Common dividends per share / Market price per share	1.5 cents / 75 cents	2.0%	2.4%

Review of Key Terms

Accounts receivable turnover ratio	A measure of the number of times accounts receivable are collected in a period.
Acid-test or quick ratio	A stricter test of liquidity than the current ratio that excludes inventory and prepayments from the numerator.
Asset turnover ratio	The relationship between net sales and total assets.
Cash flows from operations to capital expenditures ratio	A measure of the ability of a company to finance long term asset acquisitions from cash from operations.
Cash flows from operations to current liabilities ratio	A measure of the ability to pay current debts from operating cash flows.
Cash-to-cash operating cycle	The length of time from the sale of inventory to the collection of any receivable from the sale.
Current ratio	The ratio of current assets to current liabilities.
Debt service coverage ratio	A statement of cash flows measure of the ability of a company to meet its interest and principal payments.
Debt-to-equity ratio	The ratio of total liabilities to total stockholders' equity.
Dividend payout ratio	The percentage of earnings paid out as dividends.
Dividend yield ratio	The relationship between dividends and market price of a company's stock.
Earnings per share	A company's bottom line stated on a per-share basis.
Gross profit ratio	Gross profit to net sales.
Horizontal analysis	A comparison of financial statement items over a period of time.
Inventory turnover ratio	A measure of the number of times inventory is sold during a period.
Leverage	The use of borrowed funds and amounts contributed by preferred stockholders to earn an overall return higher than the cost of these funds.
Liquidity	The nearness to cash of the assets and liabilities.
Number of days' sales in inventory	A measure of how long it takes to sell inventory.
Number of days' sales in receivables	A measure of the average age of accounts receivable.
Price-earnings ratio	The relationship between a company's performance in the income statement compared with its performance in the stock market.
Profit margin ratio	Net income to net sales.
Profitability	How well management is using company resources to earn a return on the funds invested by the various groups.
Return on assets	A measure of a company's success in earning a return for all providers of capital.
Return on sales	A variation of the profit margin ratio; it measures earnings before payments to creditors.
Return on stockholders' equity	A measure of a company's success in earning a return for the common stockholders.

Solvency	The ability of a company to remain in business over the long term.
Times interest earned ratio	An income statement measure of the ability of a company to meet its interest payments.
Vertical analysis	A comparison of various financial statement items within a single period with the use of common-size statements.
Working capital	Current assets minus current liabilities.

Practice Test
Questions and Problems

Complete each of the following statements:

LO 6 1. The net income attributable to each share of common stock is known as the ____________________.

Use the following information to answer questions 2 through 6:

Beezo Corporation Selected financial information	**Year ended Dec. 31, Year 2**	**Year ended Dec. 31, Year 1**
Net income	$ 300,000	$ 200,000
Interest expense	50,000	40,000
Total liabilities	1,150,000	950,000
Total stockholders' equity	1,300,000	1,000,000
Net sales	1,000,000	800,000

Beezo's marginal tax rate is 40%.

LO 5 2. Beezo's interest expense net of tax for Year 2 is ____________________.

LO 5 3. Beezo's average assets over Year 2 is ____________________.

LO 5 4. Beezo's return on sales for Year 2 is ____________________.

LO 5 5. Beezo's asset turnover for Year 2 is ____________________.

LO 5 6. Beezo's return on assets for Year 2 is ____________________.

LO 5 7. The ratio that indicates a company's ability to meet current year's interest payments out of current year's earnings is ____________________.

LO 4 8. For a retailer or wholesaler, the average length of time between the purchase of merchandise for sale and the eventual collection of cash from the sale is called the ____________________.

LO 5 9. A company can reduce its ____________________ ratio by retiring debt and issuing additional stock.

LO 4 10. ____________________ turnover can be improved by adopting more stringent credit policies for customers.

LO 3 11. ____________________ is a comparison of various financial statement items within a single period with the use of common-size statements.

LO 4 12. ____________________ is a measure of the ability of a company to finance long term asset acquisitions from cash from operations.

LO 4 13. ____________________ is a measure of the ability to pay current debts from operating cash flows.

LO 5 14. The ability of a company to remain in business over the long term is called ____________________.

LO 6 15. ____________________ indicates how well management is using company resources to earn a return on the funds invested by the various groups.

Indicate whether each of the following statements is true or false:

LO 2 16. Horizontal analysis allows significant changes across time to be identified.

LO 1 17. Changes in the accounting principles of a company can be ignored when performance is being analyzed over time.

LO 3 18. Inflation can result in performance appearing better than it actually is.

LO 4 19. Common size statements are most useful if the companies being compared are of similar size.

LO 4 20. The quick assets ratio and the current ratio both indicate ability to stay in business in the long term.

LO 4 21. Turnover ratios indicate the level of activity in a particular area, the higher the ratio, the higher the level of activity.

LO 4 22. If the current ratio increases over a period, then working capital also increases.

LO 5 23. Return on assets can be analyzed into return on sales and asset turnover.

LO 5 24. Even though debt is a cheaper form of financing than equity, a company that has high levels of debt may be jeopardizing its ability to stay in business in the long term.

LO 3 25. Vertical analysis involves relating balances in the balance sheet to their related income statement item.

LO 5 26. When a company issues stock for cash, its debt-to-equity ratio decreases.

LO 4 27. When a company issues stock for cash, its quick ratio increases.

LO 6 28. When a company issues debt for cash, its gross profit increases.

LO 4 29. When a company has a stock split, its current ratio is unaffected.

LO 6 30. When a company pays interest on its bonds, its profit margin ratio decreases.

For each of the following questions, circle the alternative that best answers the question:

LO 4 31. Which of the following ratios is most likely to be specified in a debt covenant requiring adequate liquidity to be maintained?
a) Debt-to-equity ratio
b) Quick ratio
c) Asset turnover ratio
d) Earnings per share

LO 4,5 32. Which of the following ratios is immediately affected by a stock repurchase?
a) Dividend payout ratio
b) Debt-to-equity ratio
c) Gross profit ratio
d) Inventory turnover ratio

LO 6 33. Corporation A and Company B have price-earnings ratios of 18 and 35 respectively. Which of the following cannot be concluded from the companies having different price-earnings ratios?
a) A's stock price is lower than B's and its earnings are higher.
b) B's stock price is expected to grow faster than A's, though their earnings are currently identical.
c) A and B's stock prices are identical, but B has low earnings in the current year because of an extraordinary loss.
d) A is a better bargain than B since both companies' earnings are identical but A's stock price is cheaper.

LO 2 34. Which of the following types of analysis is most useful in comparing the accounts of two companies of very different sizes?
a) Horizontal analysis
b) Vertical analysis
c) Comparisons with industry norms
d) Comparisons with data for the economy as a whole

LO 3 35. Which of the following calculations would be carried out in a vertical analysis?
a) Accounts receivable is calculated as a percentage of total assets.
b) The difference over two years between the net book value of fixed assets is calculated as a percentage of the first year's fixed assets book value.
c) Current assets are expressed as a percentage of current liabilities.
d) Net credit sales are expressed as a percentage of average accounts receivable.

Use the following summary information from Beta Company's financial statements for its first and second years of operations to answer questions 36 through 40.

Beta Company ($000's)	**Year ended Dec. 31, Year 2**	**Year ended Dec. 31, Year 1**
Sales	$1,400	$1,000
Cost of sales	1,200	800
Net income	50	40
Current assets	800	650
Current liabilities	700	500
Inventories	500	400
Cash and marketable securities	100	75

LO 4,6 36. Which of the following statements is FALSE?
a) Although sales increased, both the gross profit ratio and the profit margin ratio declined during Year 2.
b) Sales, gross margin, and net income either were unchanged or increased in Year 2.
c) Working capital increased in Year 2.
d) Inventories were a smaller percentage of current assets in Year 1 than in Year 2.

LO 4 37. The current ratio for Year 2 is
a) 1.143
b) 0.625
c) 0.143
d) 0.714

LO 4 38. The inventory turnover ratio in Year 2 is
a) 2.4
b) 2.67
c) 2.8
d) 3.11

LO 5 39. The company announces a stock dividend. The effect on the debt-to-equity ratio is
a) an increase.
b) a decrease.
c) no change.

LO 4 40. Beta Company increased the credit period allowed to customers. The increase in the credit period would
a) increase working capital.
b) decrease accounts receivable turnover.
c) increase cost of sales.
d) increase debt-to-equity ratio.

LO 5 41. Alpha and Beta are identical companies except that Alpha's debt-to-equity ratio is 4:1, and Beta's debt-to-equity ratio is 1:1. Which of the following statements is true?
a) Alpha's return on stockholders' equity can be expected to be lower than Beta's.
b) Alpha's is less risky than Beta.
c) Alpha's inventory turnover can be expected to be higher than Beta's.
d) Alpha's times interest earned ratio will be expected to be lower than Beta's.

LO 5 42. Jalama Jugs Inc. have a debt-to-equity ratio of 3:1 on December 31, 1997, and a debt-to-equity ratio of 2:1 on December 31, 1996. Which of the following transactions, taken alone, could result in that change in the debt-to-equity ratio?

a) Jalama repaid bonds during 1997.
b) Jalama paid a large cash dividend during 1997.
c) Jalama issued common stock during 1997.
d) Jalama paid interest on bonds during 1997.

LO 4 43. Jalama Jugs Inc. have a quick ratio of 1:1 on December 31, 1997, and a quick ratio of 0.5:1 on December 31, 1996. Which of the following, taken alone, could result in that change in the quick ratio?

a) Jalama's cash flows from operations is positive.
b) Jalama buys plant and equipment for cash.
c) Jalama's accounts payable decreases.
d) Jalama's accounts receivable increases.

LO 6 44. For the year to March 31, 1998, Field Flowers Corporation has a return on assets of 8% and a return on sales of 2%. Field's asset turnover is

a) 16 times.
b) 8 times.
c) 0.25 times.
d) 4 times.

LO 6 45. For the years ended December 31, 1997 and 1996, Solvang Danish Corporation has gross profit margins of 15% and 10%, and profit margin ratios of 3% and 5% respectively. Total revenues in each year were identical. Which of the following is consistent with this scenario?

a) Cost of sales was higher in 1997 than in 1996, and selling, general, and administrative costs were lower in 1997 than in 1996.
b) Cost of sales was lower in 1997 than in 1996, and selling, general, and administrative costs were higher in 1997 than in 1996.
c) Cost of sales was higher in 1997 than in 1996, and selling, general, and administrative costs were identical in 1997 and in 1996.
d) Cost of sales was identical in 1997 than in 1996, and selling, general, and administrative costs were higher in 1997 and in 1996.

Answer each of the following problems:

LO 2,3 46. The income statement of Little Green Inc., a computer manufacturer, for the three years 1995 through 1997 is given below.

Little Green Inc.
Statement of earnings

$ in millions Year ended	December 31, 1997	December 31, 1996	December 31, 1995
Revenue	$ 64,523	$ 64,766	$ 68,931
Cost of sales	35,069	32,073	30,715
Gross profit	29,454	32,693	38,216
Operating expenses			
Selling, general, and administrative	- 19,526	- 21,375	- 20,709
Research, development, and engineering	- 6,522	- 6,644	- 6,554
Restructuring charges	- 11,645	- 3,735	-0-
	- 37,693	- 31,754	- 27,263
Operating income	- 8,239	939	10,953
Other income, principally interest	573	602	495
Interest expense	- 1,360	- 1,423	- 1,324
Earnings before income taxes	- 9,026	118	10,124
Provision for income taxes	2,161	- 716	- 4,157
Net earnings before changes in accounting principles	- 6,865	- 598	- 5,967
Effect of changes in accounting principles	1,900	- 2,263	-0-
Net earnings	$ - 4,965	$ - 2,861	$ 5,967

Required

1. Prepare a horizontal analysis of Little Green for the three years.

2. Prepare a vertical analysis of Little Green for the three years.

3. **On the basis of your analysis, comment on Little Green's profitability for the three years.**

4. When Little Green announced its results for 1997, the stock price of Little Green increased. Can you think of an explanation of why such a massive loss should result in an increase in stock price?

LO 4,5 47. For each of the transactions listed below, indicate the immediate effect on each of the following: debt-to-equity ratio, current ratio, and profit margin. Use + to indicate an increase, - to indicate a decrease, ? to indicate an indeterminate effect, and 0 to indicate no effect. Assume an initial current ratio of more than 1-to-1.

		Debt-to-equity ratio	**Current ratio**	**Profit margin ratio**
1.	Cash is acquired through issue of additional common stock.			
2.	Federal income tax due for the previous year is paid.			
3.	A fixed asset is sold for cash at less than book value.			
4.	Merchandise is sold on credit at a loss.			
5.	Payment is made to trade creditors for previous purchases.			
6	A cash dividend is declared and paid.			
7.	Short-term notes receivable are sold at a discount.			
8.	A profitable firm increases its fixed assets depreciation allowance account.			
9.	Trading securities are sold below the fair value shown in the balance sheet.			
10.	Ten-year notes are issued to pay off accounts payable.			
11.	A wholly depreciated asset is retired.			
12.	Accounts receivable are collected.			
13.	A stock dividend is declared and paid.			
14.	Equipment is purchased with short-term notes.			
15.	35% of the common stock of another firm is acquired by the issue of additional common stock and accounted for by the equity method.			

Critical Thinking Problem

LO 4,5 48. The Goleta Fruit Company was established on January 1, Year 1, and the following information is available for its first year of operations:

Net income	$60,000
Accounts payable	$30,000
Short-term notes payable	$70,000
Return on sales	20%
Gross margin	60%
Quick ratio	100%
Receivables turnover	10
Inventory turnover	6

All sales were on credit. Accounts payable and short-term notes payable are the only current liabilities at year-end. Cash and cash equivalents, inventory and accounts receivable are the only current assets at year-end.

Required

Find the following for Year 1.

1. Sales revenue

2. Gross margin

3. Cost of sales

4. Year-end inventory

5. Purchases

6. Cash paid to creditors

7. Year-end receivables

8. Cash received from customers

9. Year-end cash balance

10. Year-end current ratio

Solutions

Fill in the Blanks

1. earnings per share
2. $30,000
3. $2,200,000
4. 33%
5. 0.4545
6. 15%
7. times interest earned ratio
8. cash-to-cash operating cycle
9. debt-to-equity
10. receivables
11. vertical analysis
12. cash flows from operations to capital expenditure ratio
13. cash flows from operations to current liabilities
14. solvency
15. profitability

True/False

		COMMENT/EXPLANATION
16.	True	
17.	False	Changes in accounting principles can have a significant impact on both the income statement and the balance sheet. These changes should be considered when analyzing a period in which a change in accounting principle took place.
18.	True	
19.	False	Common-size statements allow companies of different sizes to be meaningfully compared since each income statement figure is expressed as a percentage of sales and each balance sheet figure is expressed as a percentage of total assets.
20.	False	Both the quick assets ratio and the current ratio are measures of liquidity, which indicates the ability of the company to meet short-term obligations.
21.	True	
22.	True	If the current ratio increased over a period, then current assets increased more than current liabilities. Working capital, which is the difference between current assets and current liabilities, therefore must also have increased over the period.
23.	True	
24.	True	
25.	False	In a vertical analysis, each income statement figure is expressed as a percentage of sales and each balance sheet figure is expressed as a percentage of total assets.
26.	True	
27.	True	
28.	False	Issuing debt has no immediate impact on profitability.
29.	True	
30.	True	

Multiple Choice

31. b
32. b
33. d
34. b
35. a
36. c
37. a
38. b
39. c
40. b
41. c
42. a
43. a
44. d
45. b

Problem 46

1. **Horizontal analysis**

% Change from previous year

Year ended	**Dec. 31, 1997**	**Dec. 31, 1996**
Revenue	-0.38%	-6.04%
Cost of sales	9.34%	4.42%
Gross profit	-9.91%	-14.45%
Operating expenses		
Selling, general and administrative	-8.65%	3.22%
Research, development and engineering	-1.84%	1.37%
Restructuring charges	211.78%	∞
Operating income	-977.42%	-91.43%
Other income, principally interest	-4.82%	21.62%
Interest expense	-4.43%	7.48%
Earnings before income taxes	-7749.15%	-98.83%
Provision for income taxes	401.82%	-82.78%
Net earnings before changes in accounting principles	-1047.99%	-89.98%
Effect of changes in accounting principles	-183.96%	∞
Net earnings	-73.54%	-147.75%

2. **Vertical analysis**

Year ended	**Dec. 31, 1997**	**Dec. 31, 1996**	**Dec. 31, 1995**
Revenue	100%	100%	100%
Cost of sales	54.35%	49.52%	44.56%
Gross profit	45.65%	50.48%	55.44%
Operating expenses			
Selling, general and administrative	-30.26%	-33%	-30.04%
Research, development and engineering	-10.11%	-10.26%	-9.51%
Restructuring charges	-18.05%	-5.77%	0
	-58.42%	-49.03%	-39.55%
Operating income	-12.77%	1.45%	15.89%
Other income, principally interest	0.89%	0.93%	0.72%
Interest expense	-2.11%	-2.2%	-1.92%
Earnings before income taxes	-13.99%	0.18%	14.69%
Provision for income taxes	3.35%	-1.11%	-6.03%
Net earnings before changes in accounting principles	-10.64%	-0.92%	8.66%
Effect of changes in accounting principles	2.94%	-3.49%	0
Net earnings	-7.69%	-4.42%	8.66%

3. Little Green's results over the three years are dominated by the massive restructuring charges for 1997 and 1996. These charges include the costs of both divesting Little Green of unprofitable divisions and downsizing staff numbers. From the vertical analysis, we can see that the gross profit margin declined over the three years but that selling and research and development costs stayed relatively stable. From the horizontal analysis we can see that revenues declined and that costs rose, resulting in the drop in gross margins observed above. Overall, however, the restructuring charges are the dominant feature of these three years' results.

4. Stock prices reflect expectations about the future. The fact that the stock price rose on the announcement of 1997's results suggests that expectations about the company improved. One possible explanation is that the large restructuring charges were a signal to investors that Little Green's management was addressing some of the problems that the company had been experiencing over a number of years. Although in the short term the large restructuring costs led to losses, in the long run they would result in a more streamlined, efficient, and profitable company.

Problem 47

		Debt-to-equity ratio	Current ratio	Profit margin ratio
1.	Cash is acquired through issue of additional common stock.	-	+	0
2.	Federal income tax due for the previous year is paid.	-	+	0
3.	A fixed asset is sold for less than book value.	+	+	-
4.	Merchandise is sold on credit at a loss.	+	-	-
5.	Payment is made to trade creditors for previous purchases.	-	+	0
6	A cash dividend is declared and paid.	+	-	0
7.	Short-term notes receivable are sold at a discount.	+	-	-
8.	A profitable firm increases its fixed assets depreciation allowance account.	+	0	-
9.	Trading securities are sold below the fair value shown in the balance sheet.	+	-	-
10.	Ten-year notes are issued to pay off accounts payable.	0	+	0
11.	A wholly depreciated asset is retired.	0	0	0
12.	Accounts receivable are collected.	0	0	0
13.	A stock dividend is declared and paid.	0	0	0
14.	Equipment is purchased with short-term notes.	+	-	0
15.	35% of the common stock of another firm is acquired by the issue of additional common stock and accounted for by the equity method.	-	0	0

Critical Thinking Problem 48

1. Return on sales $= \dfrac{\text{Net income}}{\text{Sales}}$

$$20\% = \frac{\$60{,}000}{\text{Sales}}$$

$$\text{Sales} = \frac{\$60{,}000}{20\%}$$

$$\text{Sales} = \$300{,}000$$

2. Gross margin = 60% x Sales

= $180,000

3. Cost of sales = Sales - Cost of sales

= $120,000

4. Inventory turnover = $\dfrac{\text{Cost of sales}}{\text{Average inventory}}$

Average inventory = $\dfrac{\text{Cost of sales}}{\text{Inventory turnover}}$

Average inventory = $\dfrac{\$120{,}000}{6}$

= $20,000

= 0.5 x (Opening inventory + Closing inventory)

and Opening inventory = $0

so Closing inventory = $40,000

5.

Inventory			
Jan. 1	0	120,000	Cost of sales
Purchases	**160,000**	40,000	Dec. 31

6.

Accounts payable			
Cash to creditors	**130,000**	0	Jan. 1
Dec. 31	30,000	160,000	Purchases

7. Receivables turnover = $\dfrac{\text{Sales}}{\text{Average accounts receivable}}$

Average accounts receivable = 30,000

Ending accounts receivable = 60,000

8.

Accounts receivable			
Jan. 1	0	**240,000**	**Cash received from customers**
Sales	300,000	60,000	Dec. 31

9. Quick ratio = $\dfrac{\text{Cash}}{\text{Current liabilities}}$

Cash = 100% x (30,000 + 70,000)

= 100,000

10. Current ratio

$$= \frac{\text{Current assets}}{\text{Current liabilities}}$$

$$= \frac{240{,}000 + 40{,}000 + 60{,}000}{100{,}000}$$

$$= 3.4$$